Please remember that this is a library book,
and that it belongs only temporarily to each
person who uses it. Be considerate. Do
not write in this, or any, library book.

The Young Adolescent

Peter Blos

The Young Adolescent
CLINICAL STUDIES

THE FREE PRESS, NEW YORK

COLLIER-MACMILLAN LTD., LONDON

For M. G. B.

The Free Press
A Division of The Macmillan Company
866 Third Avenue, New York, New York 10022

Collier-Macmillan Canada Ltd., Toronto, Ontario

Library of Congress Catalog Card Number: 73–125597

printing number
1   2   3   4   5   6   7   8   9   10

PREFACE

The writing of this book was made possible, to begin with, by conditions and influences that have by now encompassed a lifetime of clinical work. This clinical practice started out in the field of child analysis; soon after, it reached out into the adult years and then, gradually, narrowed down to the adolescent period.

In retrospect, I like to think of this progressive specialization as a determined approach—as it were—to the two shores of a river at the same time, tracking my way from the vast hinterlands of both childhood and adulthood to the connecting link between those two shores—namely, adolescence. Having arrived at the bridge that

v

spans this river, I then set up camp in the middle of its crowded thoroughfare, observing the endless traffic moving back and forth on it—now rushing ahead, then stopping and waiting; now retreating, then changing direction altogether.

As observer and recorder of adolescence, as well as theorizer about it, my indebtedness extends to so many of my psychoanalytic colleagues that I cannot possibly list their names. This I have done with great care in my primarily theoretical book *On Adolescence* (1962), to which the present clinical monograph is meant to serve as a companion volume.

There are, however, a few individuals whose distinctive contributions have made the completion of this book a reality. The writing of this monograph extended over a number of years, and the fact that I did not falter in my labors is due, in large measure, to those who supported and encouraged my enterprise during those years. My wife, Merta Blos, A.C.S.W., has participated critically, empathically and creatively in the project from its inception. Her enthusiasm and her clear grasp of my intentions have carried me through the discouragements and doubts that the preparation of this kind of book has in store for its author. It was her keen perceptiveness and her good judgment concerning the quality and authenticity of its thought as well as of its expression that shaped—through many long working summers—the preliminary drafts, before the final manuscript stood up well to both our scrutiny.

My gratitude goes to Dr. Andrée Royon, psychoanalytic colleague and friend, who rekindled my interest in the project, some years ago, after reading the first draft of "Susan"; later, she subjected the finished manuscript to a critical appraisal. Her thoughtful comments are here acknowledged with the same appreciation as is her professional endorsement of the monograph as a useful clinical document.

Further, I am indebted to Mrs. Sheldon Bennett for encouraging me to use, to the fullest extent needed, the endless time it takes to put clinical data into readable form. It thus became possible to demonstrate, by way of clinical example, those theoretical propositions that, at one and the same time, render the behavior of the young adolescent boy and girl intelligible, render more effective the child therapist for this age, and open up new avenues for developmental research.

Peter Blos

New Year's Day 1970
Holderness, N.H.

CONTENTS

INTRODUCTION

In order to assure this study its proper place in the adolescent research that I have pursued for many years, I have to recount the story of its origin. From my work with adolescents in psychoanalysis and psychotherapy, there has accrued a body of observations that have coalesced into a theory of adolescent development. The many puzzlements that confront the student of adolescence have made me search, over the years, for concepts or principles around which clinical observations can be organized. Only a theoretical frame of reference promised to bring order into the clinical material, to serve as a guide in therapy and to provide a rationale for the assessment of normal and abnormal development.

A substantial body of psychoanalytic studies on adolescence was, of course, available to me when I was making my own clinical observations. I am indebted to the many writers who have published their findings in this field; their specific contributions have been acknowledged in my earlier book, *On Adolescence* (1962). I have found it necessary to expand, modify and specify some of the theoretical formulations that had already been advanced by others. In this endeavor I have held firmly to two guidelines—namely, clinical observation and the developmental point of view. My own analytic work with adolescents had already demonstrated to me a sequential order of psychological development, which I have described as the six phases of adolescence (Blos, 1962). That developmental schema was in need of clinical description and evidence for its support. This I set out to furnish in this monograph, with reference to the initial stage of adolescence.

I should now like to account for what prompted me to focus my adolescent research on the young adolescent. In speaking of the young adolescent, I am referring to the age of 10+ to 14±. This time span must make allowance for a chronological yet unequal latitude in relation to boy and girl in general and to the individual's tempo and style of maturation and development in particular. Any reference to chronological age has to be complemented by an assessment of the developmental age.

A review of the vast literature on adolescence reveals, at first glance, that an only inconspicuous corner is assigned to the young adolescent. The focus of research has been instead on the spectacular and dramatic stages of Adolescence Proper and Late Adolescence. Yet clinical observation leaves no doubt that deviant adolescent development has its onset, if not its roots, in the initial stage of adolescence. It has been my experience that all adolescent disturbances reflect the existence of a developmental impasse at the early stage of adolescence.

I have gained the conviction from my analytic work with older adolescents that their deviancy, immaturity or emotional disturbance is always and significantly attached to developmental failures at the initial stage of adolescence. In other words, the phase-specific conflicts of the young adolescent loom large behind the turbulence of subsequent stages of adolescence. The urgency of those problems that the late adolescent brings to the clinician, tends to distract the expert's attention from the crucial developmental failures that had already made their imprint at the initial stage of adolescence. It follows that a thorough study of that stage is of value, not only to the student of adolescent development, but equally to the clinician who is working with adolescents of any age (Blos, 1954, 1967, 1970). The specific reasons why entry into adolescence constitutes a normative crisis that decisively affects all later development will be presented by way of case material.

The young adolescent's development is so enormously complex that any shortcut to a developmental schema of that stage might well seem, to many, to be a more desirable contribution than such a labyrinthine tracing of its course as has been pursued in this monograph. The case material offers ample evidence of this complexity; it will probably, for that very reason, discourage one reader, while hopefully arousing curiosity and fascination in another. There is no question that, with respect to the initial stage of adolescence, we find ourselves at this point in a psychological territory that still contains many unexplored and uncharted stretches and patches. These I have set out to penetrate, fully realizing the enormity of the task.

It seemed no longer sufficient to draw on clinical vignettes in order to illustrate certain theoretical propositions. Now these formulations had to be demonstrated *in vivo,* with deliberate and explicit concreteness; this in turn had to be pursued along a time continuum and to encompass the various, yet simultaneous developmental processes that account, in their totality, for the personality functioning and psychic restructuring of initial adolescence. Specifically, it is the place and effect of the initial stage of adolescence in relation to the entire adolescent process, that I have set out to investigate and clarify in this study.

The peak of adolescence (Adolescence Proper), along with the descending pathways that lead slowly into adulthood (Late Adolescence), remain fairly readily accessible to adult recall, in the detail of experiences, even though much of the anguish or the elation that accompanied these events has succumbed to certain idiosyncratic elaborations of memory. The inevitable narcissistic injuries of adolescence are in effect wiped out by idealizations, which then become enshrined in a special sanctuary of the mind. Not so with the memories that pertain to the initial stage of adolescence, because some of the most crucial emotional experiences of this stage are altogether lost to the introspective mind of the adult. For the most part, they are not preserved in any form that is available to adult consciousness, but have instead fallen into the dark recesses of the mind. The case studies will show how the apprehensions and fears that the young adolescent generally experiences along the regressive pathways of this stage are, soon enough, bleached away—if all goes well—by the glare of his victories.

As a result, the young adolescent tends to be looked upon as either a miniature adolescent or an overgrown child. Since he is in passage from childhood to adolescence, the young adolescent belongs at one and the same time to both stages, without any longer being in the one nor yet being in the other. What appears as an in-between stage is in fact a developmental phase that is set off both from what was before and from what comes after, by discrete yet pervasive characteristics of mental functioning. This developmental phase needs to be defined and delineated along the lines of those developmental sequences that constitute, in their totality, the orderly psychological progression from infancy to adulthood.

In this connection, I must point out that, in my earlier writings (Blos, 1962), I attributed too large a role in adolescent conflict formation to libidinal strivings and relegated the aggressive drive to an almost exclusively defensive function. This I have subsequently corrected (Blos, 1965). Thus, my theoretical model of adolescence converges more closely with the dual instinct theory.

Clinical work had convinced me that puberty intensifies the aggressive and the libidinal drive, in equal measure. The former, in its unattenuated and primitive form, can be observed with ease during adolescence. This kind of aggression is the result of defusion of the instincts— in other words, of libido and aggression. This defusion occurs as a concomitant of adolescent regression (Blos, 1967). Aggression that is employed for defensive purposes, however, is qualitatively different, in that, in order to take on such function, it had first to be modified by and adapted to the interests of the ego.

Research in the growth and physiology of adolescence has to be conducted, obviously, along gender lines; it is hardly imaginable that anyone would attempt to do otherwise. In developmental and psychological research, however, this differentiation is often blurred by our speaking about the adolescent "in general." It seems to me that the democratic ideal of "All Men are Created Equal" has here spilled over from political philosophy into developmental psychology. Lecturing on this subject has taught me that a developmental theory of the young adolescent that is founded on the separate paths of psychosexual development of boy and girl, seems to many listeners to be tantamount to advocating inequality between the sexes or to attributing superiority to one sex over the other.

It is not surprising that the study of Late Adolescence has caught everybody's interest and imagination. At this stage, it is the problem of personality consolidation that stands in the forefront, while the problems of regressive object relations and of sexual identity have receded into the background. I might say facetiously that one risks one's popularity and credibility by attempting to move the differences in the psychological development of boy and girl into the forefront of public attention. Yet it is hardly questionable that masculine or feminine identity formation constitutes one of the major psychological assignments of adolence, and that that assignment can be fulfilled only via totally different pathways.

Needless to say, my adolescent research has constantly endeavored to elucidate the psychological development of boy and girl, as it accompanies their respective pubertal maturation. In the present study, I have continued to make this distinction; in fact, the organization of this monograph is founded on it, so that it is divided into two parts, one of which traces the development of the young adolescent boy, the other that of the girl. For the sake of clarity and order, I have formulated the specific developmental challenges, conflicts, tasks and resolutions of male and female adolescence, as it moves from the latency period to adolescence proper.

In order to accomplish this task, I had to take several steps. First, I had to lay before the reader certain specimen situations, drawn from therapy sessions. To facilitate their comprehension, I employed the theoretical formulations I had proposed in my earlier writings. Thus, clinical evidence has been brought to bear on these theoretical constructs as one way of testing their validity. In other words, therapeutic interventions—their effects or their effectiveness—have been called upon as the ultimate witnesses to testify as to the significant and meaningful relevance between clinical facts and theoretical propositions.

If one undertakes such an awesome task, one is well advised to approach it with intellectual humility and with bridled zeal. I know of no better statement for inducing this state of mind than the passage Freud wrote in outlining "A Difficulty in Psycho-Analysis." "For the mind," he says in this essay, "is not a simple thing; on the contrary, it is a hierarchy of superordinated and subordinated agencies, a labyrinth of impulses striving independently of one another toward action, corresponding with the multiplicity of instincts and of relations with the external world, many of which are antagonistic to one another and incompatible."

Since development from infancy through middle childhood exerts an influence on the second decade of life, I found it invaluable for my comprehension of adolescence to have analyzed pre-latency and latency children. In addition to my private analytic practice, I had worked for many years as both consultant and supervisor in a child guidance clinic. This experience brought me into contact with the sort of clinical material that the child analyst is rarely in a position to study at close sight. The clinical setting gave me the opportunity to bring to bear my experience as child analyst on the treatment of children and adolescents.

The psychotherapy of the cases I shall report was conducted by psychiatric social workers. I have no doubt that the treatment recorded in this monograph will reveal the extraordinary usefulness of the child analyst in a child guidance clinic. The expertise of the child analyst enables him to give to the child therapist a dimension of insight that might otherwise remain altogether outside his grasp. The developmental studies reported here were carried out in the setting of the Madelaine Borg Child Guidance Institute of the Jewish Board of Guardians in New York City.

Let me briefly describe how this research came into being. My theoretical study of adolescence (1962) required me to render clinical substance to the concepts and formulations that I had posited there. Clinical studies were now in order, so as to weld together practice, theory and clinical evidence. A number of adolescent cases, including some latency children who would grow into their adolescence during the course of therapy, were being treated in psychotherapy at the clinic in weekly sessions by psychiatric social workers who were supervised by me. Each supervisory conference covered two or three consecutive therapy sessions, which were recorded in detail with, as much as possible, verbatim recall of what either child or therapist said. No notes were taken during the sessions. This process-recording was complemented by an ongoing synopsis of the supervisory sessions, which was kept by therapist and supervisor for later use. The project was carried on for six years.

"Susan" and "Ben" were the cases I selected for presentation, after I had decided to restrict the present study to the initial stage of male and female adolescence. Both Susan and Ben come from so-called intact families; neither one of them is an only child. The families of both children maintain, with extreme effort but often without success, a minimal level of economic independence. The ages of the two cases call for some explanation. The years during which Ben was studied extend from 12 to 15; those of Susan, from 8 to 13. These are not exactly the age one usually associates with the young adolescent. Here I would remind the reader of the by now generally accepted fact that adolescent development does not necessarily run parallel with either pubertal maturation or chronological age.

Before I proceed, the terms "development" and "maturation" have to be clarified as to their meaning in this study. Maturation refers to the unfolding of inborn potentialities—such as, for example, speech, locomotion, memory, growth, puberty, etc. These processes have their species-bound timing and are subject to the epigenetic principle. They are regarded as autonomous, by contrast with developmental sequences, which are brought into motion, elaborated and maintained, through the interaction between the organism and its environment.

Developmental sequences also have their optimal timing; in fact, their synchronicity with biological maturation is a prerequisite for normal development. Infancy and early childhood have always demonstrated this principle with the greatest clarity. For the delight of the reader, I shall quote the enchanting lines by A. A. Milne who, in poetic language, paid tribute to the orderly sequence of developmental stages:

> *When I was One,*
> *I had just begun.*
> *When I was Two,*
> *I was nearly new.*
> *When I was Three,*
> *I was hardly Me.*
> *When I was Four,*
> *I was not much more.*
> *When I was Five,*
> *I was just alive.*
> *But now I am Six, I'm as clever as clever.*
> *So I think I'll be Six for ever and ever.*

I must forgo my wish to write a counterpart poem about the developmental stages of the young adolescent; instead I return to the sober language of my profession.

It must be stated at this point that the latitude of the synchronicity that permits maturation and development to progress within the boundaries of normality is limited. Therefore, a point of critical disparity is reached when phase-specific development and pubertal maturation become too distant in time from each other. At that point, deviant personality formation sets in. It is my opinion that adolescent development can take its normal course only within a certain chronological distance from the biological process of puberty. To speak of an "eternal adolescent" is to employ a *contradictio in adjectu*. Colloquially, we refer to the intertwined processes of maturation and development as "growing up."

While I adhere strictly to the definitions noted above with regard to "maturation" and "development," the reader will notice my less rigid use of the adjectives "immature," "mature" and "maturational", as well as of the verb "to mature." In so doing I may be referring, for instance, to the consolidation of an autonomous ego function, its ripening, or its progression to a higher level of integration or to a more mature state in its natural history. The specific connotation I have in mind each time will always become obvious from the context.

An ego function—speech, for example—is the result of the maturation of an *Anlage* that nevertheless requires environmental stimulation for its articulation and differentiation, as well as for its use as a vehicle of communication. It is within the social envelope that speech reaches the status of an independent or autonomous ego function. At that point, the expression "it develops" is to be replaced by "it matures." I concede that this reflects a lack of verbal precision, but hope to prevent any misunderstanding by anticipating it.

Physiological maturation, which is first evidenced by hormonal metabolism, precedes the bodily manifestations of puberty that everyone is able to observe. It is an acknowledged and documented fact that the onset of pubescence within the present generation has shifted to an earlier age. The significant consequence of this change in maturational timing is not under discussion within the context of this presentation, which sets out to investigate a given individual's psychic restructuring within a specific biological and environmental setting.* At any rate, pre-

* The statistical fact of earlier pubescence has to be complemented by clinical research before its effect on individual

pubertal hormonal changes raise the level of drive tension; such intensification becomes apparent both in behavior and in mental content. These phenomena alert us to the fact that the first advances in preadolescent psychic restructuring are under way. The infirmity and tentativeness of these processes imbues the preadolescent as much with the desire to go ahead into the unknown, as with a fear of losing familiar ground. A lasting compromise between these two feelings leads to an impasse of development, to which I have referred as a fixation on the phase of preadolescence or of early adolescence, respectively.

Like any other childhood fixation, this one bears in equal measure the marks of a compelling preference for certain kinds of tension regulation—a preference that is manifested in specific drive and ego accommodations. The biological event of puberty is accountable for the ascendancy of new drive directions, in terms of object and aim. As with fixations on pregenital phases of development, the initial stage of adolescence presents new potential fixation points along the road to genitality. A fixation of drive and ego, along the sequential steps of adolescent development, is destined to forestall normal progression to adult personality formation. The sequelae of such a catastrophic impediment to the unfolding and integration of the adolescent process are best demonstrated by way of clinical studies.

The objectives of this study are sevenfold: (1) to investigate the transition from latency to adolescence; (2) to abstract from the case material those developmental occurrences that are typical of the initial stage of male and female adolescence; (3) to trace the resolution of an

---

development can be understood and properly assessed. The shift in maturational timing has given rise to much speculative thought, even though clinical observations and psychodynamic conclusions, with reference to individual development, are not yet fully at our disposal.

emotional illness within the ongoing developmental process of adolescence; (4) to differentiate between the pathognomic manifestations of an emotional illness and the phase-specific, transient upheavals of preadolescence and early adolescence; (5) to gauge the influence of the environment as either a growth-promoting or a growth-impeding variable, within the context of the neurotic fixities of a more or less pathognomic valence; (6) to ascertain the effects of deviant developmental propensities, as these are carried forward from the individual past into adolescence; and (7) to determine the extent to which the adolescent process is in and of itself corrective, potentiating the neutralization or transformation of infantile emotional liabilities.

The multifaceted description of an individual, as he passes through developmental sequences, requires its own form and method. Ideally, the material should be so organized as to encompass the clinical, the therapeutic, the developmental-maturational and the theoretical aspects within a panoramic yet detailed scope. In order to approximate this goal, I have chosen a form of presentation that calls for some explanation.

It seems reasonable to say that a case description that remains entirely specific, systematic and chronological tends to obscure the psychological complexities, by virtue of the fact that inadequate attention is of necessity paid to the many interconnections that penetrate and affect all layers of the mind. On the other hand, a persistent pursuit of these same complexities would tend to obscure the clarity of the various influences, from within and from without, as well as the developmental sequences that I have set out to demonstrate. In order not to lose out on either end, I have employed a shift of focus from one to the other.

The reader should therefore expect the case material to be interspersed with discussions of theory and of therapeutic technique. The consideration of developmental aspects finds its logical place within this alternation of focus. Thoughts that have a bearing on any issue under discussion will appear, throughout, as marginal comments. It is its didactic intent, aiming at the training of the child therapist, that lends this form of presentation its broad base. In this way, the thoughts and contemplations that guided and accompanied treatment will be made explicit. By the same token, the soundness of the study itself is laid open to objective scrutiny.

A skeptical, or at least a cautious attitude must prevail whenever developmental research is made part of a treatment process; indeed, the question must constantly be asked whether certain therapeutic interventions might not have slanted the developmental study in favor of *a priori* assumptions. As far as this research aims at the validation, modification or refutation of a theory of adolescent development (Blos, 1962), the approach to the case material, it must be obvious, was of necessity biased. For this very reason, I have regarded it as imperative that I state explicitly those assumptions that were operative in treatment, so that they can be evaluated in the light of their positive or negative influence on theory building, as well as on the development of the boy or girl under study.

Treatment has always been carried forward in a mood of investigative and explorative curiosity. The scientific attitude strives to correlate, test and validate observations in order, ultimately, to abstract from them principles that transcend the individual case. The cumulative and discursive presentation of both the clinical data and the theoretical issues should make it easy for the reader to pay close attention to all the details of the clinical material as they appear, within varying context, as well as to appreciate their significance in terms of personality formation, maturational processes, therapeutic technique and the assessment of both normal and abnormal development.

PART I Susan

The Initial Stage of Female Adolescence

CHAPTER 1

THE CLINICAL PICTURE

The treatment of Susan's emotional disturbance coincides with the transition (from childhood to puberty) or, in psychological terms, from latency to adolescence (pre-adolescence and early adolescence). The reason for using a dual terminology lies in the fact that "puberty" denotes the *physiological* and *morphological* changes that accompany sexual maturation, while the term "adolescence" encompasses the sum total of those *psychological* changes that are attributable, directly or indirectly, to the onset of puberty.

I have emphasized repeatedly (Blos, 1962, 1967) the importance of the latency period as a preparatory phase for the entry into adolescence and, consequently, for the adolescent process as a whole. In order to study this particular developmental problem with reference to the formation of psychic structure, it seemed advisable to select for study a case that was still in the latency period. In that way, it will be possible to demonstrate clinically the transition from middle childhood into puberty and to bring into sharp relief the specific psychic tasks and emotional conflicts that are typical for the young adolescent female.

The case of Susan constitutes, of course, a unique constellation of life circumstances, externally and internally; this sets it off from all other cases of the same age. Each case, however, if properly understood within a coherent theoretical framework of personality development, permits inferences to be drawn and generalizations to be abstracted. These prove to be valid in terms of phase-specific characteristics and developmental patterns, as well as their typical sequential order. Deviant development only highlights these various aspects; clinical investigation demonstrates, *ad oculos*, what otherwise remain shadowy constructs. Regardless of the clinical uniqueness of a given case, theoretical formulations emerge that will assist the therapist in ordering his observations along developmental lines and will thus test the usefulness of theory building for clinical work.

Susan entered treatment when she was 8 years old; she terminated at the age of 13, seven months after menarche. During these five years she was seen in psychotherapy in weekly sessions; there was a total of 162 interviews. When first encountered, Susan was an appealing, normally developed girl. She was responsive, curious and observant. She possessed—at least in the interview situation—an extraordinary facility for verbal expression and social competence, both of which contrasted sharply with her childish, indeed infantile, behavior at home and her social inarticulateness in school and neighborhood. She was eager to be helped with her many problems, of which she was well aware. At the top of her list of particulars stood the fact that, while she is the oldest in her class, her work is poor. The combination of excessive daydreaming and incessant talking makes her a problem child in the classroom. She has trouble with reading (identified by the school as strephosymbolia), but it is the spelling mistakes that annoy her the most. She forgets, periodically, how to spell the most simple word, such as, for example, "very". Her grasp of arithmetic operations is, at times, woefully below grade level. But it is chiefly Susan's unpredictability, her inconsistency and unevenness of performance, that have turned the teachers against her. They know that Susan is a bright and capable girl, yet they cannot help noticing that her work swings almost daily, between "excellent" and "sloppy". Second on her own list of problems stands her social failure, her lack of friends: she considers herself to be an outsider and an onlooker.

The mother complains that at home Susan is an angry, dissatisfied and anxious child. She is still a slow and dreamy eater. In fact, she can be seized by absent-mindedness whatever she is doing—whether this be dressing, homework or setting the table. Susan's absent-mindedness is the cause for endless bickering between mother and daughter. When the quarrel is over, Susan becomes fearful of the consequences, although she is not able to say what these might be. To be good or to be bad —these are the ever present alternatives of her self-conscious existence. While she loves her father, she provokes him until he inflicts physical punishment on her. It is obvious to everybody—last but not least to Susan—that she envies and resents her brother, who is three and a half years younger than she is.

To complete the clinical picture, I shall indicate some

of Susan's many symptoms, not all of which were known at the beginning of therapy. Susan is an enuretic child; lately, the mother has observed, on a few occasions, what might be called an involuntary token-soiling (staining) during school time. She suffers from frightening dreams, which occasionally assume the nature of nightmares. She has difficulty in falling asleep and is afraid of the dark. She grinds her teeth in her sleep. On one or two occasions she has "pulled her hair." However, no bald spot is visible and it is not clear whether what the mother reported is a nervous habit or an ominous pathognomic sign. She bites her nails. When she is angry with her mother, she complains of a headache; when she is jealous of her little brother, she feels sick to her stomach. She dresses neatly and is given to compulsive cleanliness. While she lies habitually, she rarely refuses to admit it when questioned. Persistent and uncontrollable masturbation turn out to be the major reason why Susan's mother has decided to seek help for her daughter. Susan has always been an exceptionally healthy child, with no illness of any significance, no accidents and no bodily blemishes. She is left handed.

An assessment of this case, let alone a diagnostic designation, would have to take into account, among the many determinants involved, the life history of the child, including the family history, as well as the course of symptom formation or symptom transformation, starting at the beginning of Susan's life and bringing it up to the present. The way in which this case is presented here deviates from the customary pattern. I shall introduce the child's constitutional givens and her life experiences, past and present, as cogent information flowing from the therapeutic process. The final and conclusive assessment of the case has to be held in abeyance until the time of treatment termination. By that time the symptoms will be, hopefully, more thoroughly understood in their genetic and dynamic aspects than was possible at the initial evaluation. The treatment process itself will enable us to gauge the reversibility of deviant development, as well as the child's adaptive potential. By the same token, we will thus be able to gauge the degree of irreversible development damage, as well as those particular constitutional inadequacies that have been keeping her psychic differentiation within circumscribed bounds.

At this point in the initial assessment, we could say that the clinical picture points to an established—that is, structured—multi-symptomatic illness of a predominantly psychoneurotic nature. Some features, such as the attempted hair pulling and the token soiling on the part of an eight-year-old girl, caution against unreserved therapeutic optimism. On the other hand, the psychoneurotic components, the patient's therapeutic readiness and introspective capacity, along with the family's determined support of treatment—all these factors speak persuasively in favor of taking Susan into therapy.

CHAPTER **2**

FROM LATENCY TO ADOLESCENCE

It is well established that certain conflictual configurations of early childhood are re-experienced and re-organized during adolescence. At that time they make their appearance either as transient deviancies or as organized symptoms. Certain persistent pathognomic signs can often be recognized more clearly at this stage than during the earlier years, because they have by this time become condensed into symptoms or character traits, or into idiosyncratic or syndromic entities, each of which, in its own way, tells the history of an emotional illness *in nuce*.

It would, however, be misleading if the roots of

adolescent psychopathology were to be sought solely in the reactivation of childhood conflict or trauma. Departure from normal development can be due, in equal measure, to inadequacies of existing psychic structure. Fragilities and deficiencies of this kind become apparent of course, only when inordinate stress is brought to bear on the psychic organism. In other words, the strength of the adolescent ego is relative. Puberty constitutes a period of intensified stress and, as a consequence, it readily exposes certain inadequacies of psychic structure that were previously, for all practical purposes, either non-existent or seemingly irrelevant.

We are concerned, then, with the treatment of an adolescent who has both conflictual and structural problems. It is common knowledge that instinctual tensions rise in the wake of pubertal maturation. The intensification of libidinal and aggressive drives, already observable at prepuberty, can lead, on the one hand, to a reinstatement of prelatency forms of drive gratification and of defenses or else, on the other hand, it can become a challenge to move on to higher levels of differentiation.

Adolescent development progresses, normally, via the detour of regression. The phases of preadolescence and early adolescence are characterized by regression to pre-oedipal and pregenital levels, while adolescence proper has the positive oedipus complex at the center of its regressive modification. The psychological consequences of pubescent drive pressures are determined by the level of ego differentiation and of autonomy attained during the latency period. Among these consequences, the most significant one is reflected in the ego's distancing from the id. This forward move in ego autonomy results in the expansion and firm reliability of such ego functions as cognition, memory, anticipation, tension tolerance, self-awareness, and the ability to make a distinction between reality and fantasy (reality testing), or between action and thought.

Whenever these facilities remain critically undeveloped, we speak of an incomplete or abortive latency. Many adolescent disturbances are due to such developmental deficiencies. What we then observe is a continuation of deviant latency accommodations. It is in vain that we search for a transition into adolescence: what we find is an intensified revival of infantile forms of drive discharge and, indeed, a camouflaged perseverance at this immature stage of emotional development. This is tantamount to a foreclosure of adolescence.

The transition into adolescence can be effected only if drive tensions lead to conflict formation and resolution. This presupposes a capacity for internalization, as opposed to prolonged dependency on environmental adjustments to the child's needs. We can conceptualize this developmental impasse at prepuberty as a regression in the service of drive gratification. That is to say, the infantile modality of drive gratification remains an aim in itself and it does not come into conflict with, nor is it challenged by, the adaptive requirements for the psychosexual stage of adolescence.

By contrast, in its normal course, puberty activates regression in the service of progressive development (Blos, 1962). This, however, is possible only if the ego has already acquired that degree of autonomy and stability that protects it against fragmentation or dissolution during the process of regression. Under such conditions, the ego is incapable of regressing to the undifferentiated stage of object relations (merger), as the result of its firm, albeit tenuous, anchorage at the level of differentiated self- and object-representations. I have elsewhere described this process at greater length (Blos, 1962, 1967); there I have noted that it is only the capacity for limited and controlled regression that can promote the adolescent process. This capacity rests on a relatively adequate ego development during the latency period.

Resolution of the instinctual conflicts, such as is

typical for adolescence, presupposes that structural changes had been attained before puberty. Only then can conflicts be elaborated and also tolerated; only then can drive tensions be opposed, modified and internally qualified by ego, superego and ego-ideal influences, which lead to psychic differentiation and emotional maturity.

The more-or-less orderly course of development during latency is thrown into disarray with the child's entry into adolescence. This is due to the fact that the resurgence of infantile drive positions take precedence, temporarily, over the mastery of current reality and over the adaptive responsiveness to every-day life. The result is a state of personality disequilibrium, which is an obligatory corollary of certain stages in development. It remains a constant differential query what, in the manifest state of personality dysfunction at adolescence, is to be attributed to developmental processes and, therefore, not to be regarded as pathognomic, and what constitutes a truly pathological impasse that will impede or, indeed, forestall progression. We shall return to this problem when the case of Susan renders these considerations of urgent and practical concern.

It is a common clinical observation that in many an adolescent, and particularly in the young adolescent who is in need of treatment, the consolidation of the latency period has not been achieved. On the other hand, we also see young adolescents who have overachieved at this stage. The defensive forcefulness of rushing into latency has, in such children, so completely estranged the ego from the drives that the resultant ego competency bears the signs of a compulsive quasi-resolution of prelatency conflicts. That is to say, the child has acquired a latency rigidity that resembles a reactive character formation.

By the same token, the personality has lost the ability to adapt to altered maturational conditions, such as puberty. In that case, a premature closure of developmental fluidity, both regressive and progressive, has preempted the preconditions for subsequent ego differentiation. The unyielding enmity of the ego to the instinctual life becomes apparent in the inflexibility of the ego's patterned responses to anxiety arousal. We can, therefore, speak of a premature characterological consolidation; if this is sufficiently severe, it precludes progressive development (Blos, 1968).

By contrast, whenever insufficient ego autonomy is the result of the latency years, we observe a protracted dependency on object relations. Usually, this is due to incomplete internalization—that is, to identification—which gives the psychic organization of this type of adolescent a decidedly infantile quality. This quality can either be apparent in the child's behavior or it can be totally hidden in symptom formation. Should it find expression in all kinds of infantile gratification and dependency, and should these override or outwit the educational and socializing efforts of the environment, then therapy in adolescence faces a particularly vexing problem. In fact, this condition might, for some time or even entirely, defeat psychotherapy, because the conflict between self-interests and environmental demands is successfully avoided by sham sublimations and by an indiscriminate recourse to camouflaged instinct gratifications.

In such cases, the conflict remains an external one, raging between child and environment, with the child expecting, even demanding, that the environment change, since there is no other measure available to him by which he can control his anxiety. This condition precludes the internalization of conflict; in such cases, the therapist is expected to do what the environment had failed to accomplish. Both the child's dissatisfaction with the environment and his demandingness upon it together provide the expression of an anachronistic and therefore abortive effort to reconstitute the infantile situation in accordance with his level of maturation. It remains the task of therapy to bring these trends into the therapeutic situation. If all goes well, this will gradually lead to internalization and to conflict formation. Continuous conflict elaboration remains a precondition for treatment; if it does not already exist, it has to be brought into being during the preparatory phase of treatment.

Whenever the essential attainments of the latency period are conspicuously absent, psychotherapy sets out methodically to make up for that development deficit. This aspect of treatment plays a particularly prominent role in the treatment of the prepuberty child—which does not mean that a pedagogical attitude dominates the therapeutic process. It only emphasizes the fact that treatment, at any given age, uses as its frame of reference the developmental stage that corresponds to the age of the child in treatment. We know that the loosening of fixations mobilizes a forward movement of libido and aggression. During the course of that movement, the residues of the pathogenetic conflict reach the age-adequate level, at which the conflict has to assert itself anew. The ensuing condition, then, provides the opportunity to reach the pathogenetic core, first in relation to the present developmental impasse and then in relation to the historical determinants.

The internalization of conflict creates, by its very nature, representational equivalents of those forces that were, once, directed outward and, furthermore, of those forces that have since been emanating from the environment, such as punishment, condemnation, gratification, seduction, etc. The interaction of these two forces, antagonistic or complementary as they might be, appears in the form of fantasies, dreams, thoughts, and associative linkages, in relation to sensory stimuli, cognitive processes, or inner promptings. How these internal interactions change in quality and quantity, from one level of development to the other—as, for example, from latency to adolescence—will be illustrated by way of the case of Susan.

Each developmental phase makes its characteristic contribution to the progressive unfolding of the personality. The one that is typical for the latency period is represented by repression and sublimation and, generally, by ego expansion. Cumulatively, this leads to the maintenance of psychological homeostasis by way of inner controls that are partially, but not totally independent of outside support. The child still requires a sense of belonging, acceptance and security within the social envelope of the family. Achievements of this nature are contained in and interwoven with the progression from object relations to identifications as regulators of behavior. The ego acquires independence and autonomy through internalization, revealing in the process the uniqueness of object relations, as these have become part of the child's self or of his self-representation. Here, we find the internal microcosm, with its reflections of abandoned or partly abandoned object relations, including their positive and negative, their realistic and imaginary components. As long as the child continues to blame persons in the outer world, especially the mother, for his sufferings, and to demand that she, or the world at large, change in order to spare him frustration, anxiety, rage and depression, from his life, there remains little else for the therapist to do, but to draw the flood of accusations, rage and demands upon himself and to bring about, through the transference, an advance to higher levels of psychic functioning. In order to ensure that his valued helper will remain within reach, the child resorts to all sorts of accommodations, dictated at first by fear of the loss of love and, eventually, by the desire to grow up or, hopefully, by the wish to get well, whatever the cost. The rudiments of the therapeutic alliance are to be found in this constellation, which reflects the adaptive use of dependency needs.

The internalization of conflict renders infantile needs amenable to psychological transformation. That is to say, these needs are no longer channeled into direct drive expressions, but appear instead in the form of drive derivatives. It is the intervention of the ego that makes this transformation possible. When adolescence introduces new complications into the emotional life of the child, then the defects in ego autonomy—especially in the ego's synthesizing capacity—become apparent. Viewed within the therapeutic process, these complications are not detrimental to treatment; on the contrary, they become the carriers of treatment, provided the therapeutic alliance remains unassailable. Nevertheless, even under such favorable conditions, the relative strength of the ego must always be gauged carefully as to its adequacy vis-à-vis any upsurge of primitive drives.

If the free expression of drives is indiscriminately permitted or even encouraged by the therapist, the child, as we shall see in Susan's case, will repress dangerous, object-destructive urges and flee from an imagined seductive encounter. We seldom know, until much later, what special meaning the therapist's permissiveness or his yielding to infantile wishes has had for the child or, what special meaning the child is attaching to therapy itself. This knowledge, so indispensable for the conduct of therapy, is not easy to come by. Susan revealed it at one point by pleadingly yet cryptically saying to the therapist: "Please do not turn me into a boy." This was exactly what she thought the therapist might do or rather what she secretly wished would happen. If any of Susan's infantile wishes, which had survived in full force, could have been granted, it would have been, of course, the transformation of gender. What she expected from therapy was precisely the liberation from this complex that had, as we shall see, affected every facet of her life.

In the treatment of a child who is standing on the threshold of puberty, the pathogenetic elements of the deviant development have to be worked through twice, on two levels of development. The first concerns itself with the infantile conflict and the related defenses, and the second with the same strivings, as they assert themselves anew in relation to pubertal maturation or to adolescent sexuality. It remains a limitation of child therapy that the pathogenetic nucleus can be removed or neutralized only up to the level of emotional development that corresponds normatively with the age of the child.* While this achievement cannot be overestimated because it does provide future development with a far more favorable potential, nevertheless one cannot predict whether or not adolescence might, at some point, be thrown off its normal course by the very same trends that had caused the original illness. These trends can be recognized in persistent drive proclivities and in unyielding, rigid—i.e., infantile—superego and ego characteristics.

The foregoing discussion of the specific importance that I attribute to the latency period as necessary preparation for adolescence, has been comprehensive; yet it has also been general, without any reference to the case of Susan. What has been said so far might well reflect what a therapist would have to keep in mind in undertaking the treatment of a child of Susan's age. We shall now see how these generalizations and concepts, as stated in the abstract, appear in the clinical situation, rendering observed behavior meaningful and consequently therapeutically productive. Treatment was carried out by a woman therapist.**

When Susan entered the office at the age of eight, the first thing she noticed was the jars of fingerpaint.

* See: "Ben," Chapter 7.
** It gives me great pleasure to acknowledge the superb work done by Florence Lieberman, D.S.W. Her skill in conducting the treatment, her cooperation in supervision and her faithful recording—all these assets made my study of Susan not only possible, but extremely rewarding.

She was immediately attracted to these colorful jars; yet anxiety made her keep at a "safe" distance from them. The temptation to mess and smear was, initially, resisted by this meticulously clean and proper girl. With unhalting reservation, she compromised and used a paint brush. Unintentionally—she emphasized this—a drop of paint fell on her hand and then on the table. This drop caused an enormous fright reaction, as well as a frantic effort to undo the crime of dirtying herself, and, indirectly, the therapist. By cleaning and scrubbing, she sought to dispel anxiety and guilt.

The temptation to smear—or, to be more exact, to throw open the floodgates to actions, fantasies and emotions that were related to anal impulses—precipitated massive anxiety. She controlled her anxiety by frantic expiation and repair or, in other words, by the well-known defenses of denial and turning-into-the-opposite. Fleetingly, the therapist would make a mental note. What was it that had interfered with the normal progression from reaction formation to ego autonomy? The degree of object involvement, of fear of the therapist, was remarkable. Did indulgence in drive gratification still mean loss of love or punishment by rejection?

Susan could bear frustration, suppressed anger and renunciation only if she received a compensatory gratification, symbolic in nature. She asked the therapist for a gift: she wanted to be given a paintbrush for her birthday, so as to have her own to take home, without having to share it with other children. The therapist registered the thought that Susan's "birthday wish" might compensate her for having been cheated at birth by the mother who had not given her a penis, as she had to Susan's brother (those "other children"). Of course, no such interpretation was given at the time; it had to remain a mere guess, stored away for possible future use.

The strength of Susan's defenses at the beginning of therapy made it obvious that she in no way possessed the

capacity to absorb such an insight. It is not, after all,
sufficient for the therapist to be right in his deductions;
what makes them useful is only the patient's ability to
utilize them integratively. The interpretation of symbols
is usually a better guide for the therapist, who is in search
of genetic and dynamic clues, than it is for the patient,
who is in search of relief from anxiety. In Susan's case,
it seemed more desirable to let her develop the theme of
grievance, rage and reparation at her own good time.

How true this supposition was became evident much
later, when Susan herself put it into words. At the
present moment she could only report that the gift of the
paintbrush "didn't do any good," because "my father
broke it" and "my mother gave it away." Both these
statements were untrue, but they did contain her "truth"
in the matter. The same thing might be said about her
statement that she was never able to use the paintbrush
at home because "my mother never lets me paint." It was
in such "lies" as these that Susan couched her private
"truth," before she was able to utter it in a language that
needed no deciphering. At this stage of treatment, the
"truth" is communicable only in metaphor, symbol, and
circumlocution. Susan's "truth" was, naturally, considered
a lie by her parents and by the environment at large.

After about five months of treatment, Susan
abandoned her insistence on neatness and cleanliness;
she had tested the therapist sufficiently to risk a show of
her objectionable self. First gingerly and then with complete abandon, she gave free rein to anal impulses that
had prematurely fallen under repression. Susan plunged
into the fingerpaint jars, relishing the texture of the
"squashy, gooey" substance, the delicious "peppermint
smell" and the dirty color that resulted from her smearing together all the colors of the rainbow. She drifted
into a veritable orgy of tactile sensuousness.

Soon, however, the excitement evoked by this "messing," in conjunction with associated fantasies, both con-

scious and unconscious, rendered the activity of smearing unpleasant. The regression to anal modes of drive expression was sternly criticized by prohibiting and controlling influences in the child's own mind. This led to sudden bouts of nausea and "weak knees." Susan expressed the fear that she might put her dirty hands into her mouth, or touch the therapist's face with them. She was striving to effect a compromise between her private inclinations and the requirements of decorum, which her social awareness demanded. In this fashion Susan's infantile strivings were rendered invisible, having disappeared under the magic hood of sophistication.

When anxiety put an end to the smearing, words took over, these being even more distant than action had been from the arousal of anal impulses. She called the therapist a "skunk" and a "stinker," relishing the sound and the daring of these words, and she branded the brown jacket of the therapist as being a "disgustingly dirty color." Each of these verbal attacks was followed immediately by a state of fright: she would suddenly grow pale and impassive, or else she would resort to scrubbing and cleaning blackboard, floor and walls in the office. When these maneuvers were found to be incommensurate with the intensity of her anxiety, Susan would declare that she would not return for therapy ever again. Making the ultimate sacrifice, she said: "You can tell the man who comes before me and the boy who comes after me that they can have more time." These threats were pleading expressions of self-effacement and resignation; they were never meant as intentions or decisions to be carried into action. She was talking to herself, not to the world, hoping that the therapist would understand.

At one point, Susan renounced her pleasure in smearing with absolute finality. One day she arrived for her session carrying a roll of shelfpaper, determined to tidy up the room. Perhaps she could paint the shelves to look clean and shiny. In school, she explained, she was the one who kept the blackboard washed—adding, contemptuously, that other children were "so afraid of getting dirty." In her pursuit of cleanliness and order, the splashes and spots she acquired in the process were amply vindicated by the virtuous goal of her action. Even her contemptuous sneers at the other children, who were less dedicated than she was to "beauty", seemed thus justified; her earlier haughtiness had now become her well deserved mark of moral superiority.

We must pause here a moment, to consider the nature of this change in behavior and attitude. The question arises whether such a change heralds a turning away from infantile positions for good, or simply reflects a reinstatement of the defensive organization, which continues to keep the symptom complex intact and immutable. The practical implications for therapy lie in the decision to see in this change either a progression in development that had better be left unchallenged or a resistance to treatment, a defensive maneuver that has to be brought to a halt. The interpretation of defenses would seemingly be the intervention of choice. Whether this is correct cannot be answered in an either-or fashion, because the issue does not lie in the alternative of defensive *versus* adaptive, but in how much of each is involved in the total phenomenon of change that is making its appearance before our eyes. Only a differential assessment can serve here as a guide in therapy.

Susan's recourse to defensive mastery of anxiety contains two elements. One of these reflects her urgent striving for ego expansion, as a prerequisite for regressing to those primitive drive positions, with their ensuing conflicts, that had never been lifted above their original level. The other element reflects a trend to withdraw into the safety of her defensive organization—namely, into the symptoms of her emotional illness. The therapist's approach to Susan's changed behavior is a guarded one.

To start with, he assesses the partial gains in ego expansion, their genuineness and their stability. In Susan's case, the school problem had declined to the point of disappearance, without ever having been dealt with in particular.

We know that ego growth has to be given time to consolidate, before drive fixations and the related defenses can be approached anew. Usually, the young patient gives the signal when this point has been reached. In fact, one can rely on this, if the therapeutic alliance remains intact after episodic storms. Had Susan allied herself with the therapist's ego by identification? If so, then she was experiencing her symptoms as ego-dystonic. Thus both child and therapist joined forces in bringing development into motion once again, by loosening it from its pathogenetic moorings.

Susan stated that "from now on [she] would only work and not play any more." Indeed, her school work had improved and nothing was any longer heard about her reading difficulty. She insisted that the fingerpaint jars be thrown away, and she insisted, with equal zeal, that her mother take her to the public library to get books and, coincidentally, to meet a boy there whom she called a "lady-killer" and whom she "adored." This simultaneous wave of repression and forward surge into adolescence closed the door to expressions of the anal modality. Ego expansion and the concomitant, yet tenuous, advance in drive development combined at one point to bring the repressed, in a derivative form, to the psychological surface—or, phenomenologically speaking, onto the level of behavior and conscious thought. About one year had to elapse before this could occur.

The first period in Susan's therapy was accompanied by increased bedwetting. The nightmares had disappeared completely, and now only "bad dreams" occurred; infrequently, these awoke her. She belabored her mother with the obsessive wish to be given a dog.

Streams of tears, before she went to sleep, were directed against the mother's unfairness in denying her this one and only wish. As an argument in persuading her mother, she exclaimed: "But I know a boy who has *eleven* dogs." This exaggeration—a "lie" but her "truth" —should at last drive home the inordinate injustice that she, as a girl, had to suffer. When the wish for a dog remained unfulfilled, she asked the therapist for a gift before a long interruption of her regular visits as the result of the therapist's impending vacation. What she wanted was a hammer or a screwdriver.

To provide such symbolic substitutes for her unconscious wishes was, of course, no answer to Susan's problem. It was at the core of her illness that she expected a reward for renouncing anal impulses—sadistic ones, in particular—in the form of a phallic gift. There was no other way to wipe out the sense of injustice and unfairness that had become entrenched, when her mother gave birth to a boy, at a time when Susan was three and a half years old. Special circumstances, to be recounted later, compounded Susan's wish to be a boy. What should be emphasized here is the disappearance of the anal material, until its reappearance years later, after an unsuccessful flight into girlishness, or rather into heterosexual playacting and heterosexual preoccupation in fantasy.

Susan can be seen at this stage in the transition from latency to adolescence; she is standing at the threshold of preadolescence. The pubertal drive increase initiates a progressive push toward a genital organization, but the fixations on infantile modalities (oral, anal, phallic) had left their mark on the drive quality of her preadolescence. The reappearance of Susan's infantile instinctual organization, which had fallen out of sight for some time, under the influence of her latency ego alterations, was heralded by Susan's hinting at her problem of anal masturbation. This set the stage for a thorough investigation of her sexual confusion, or to be exact, of her bisexual identity. The distortions of the body image, which were due in part to anal fixation, could not possibly have been rectified with definitiveness at the time of their first appearance during the protracted latency period, when she was 8-10 years old. They therefore had to be dealt with a second time when a few years later, anality asserted itself again, but now with a genital focus, under the influence of pubertal maturation.

The essential developments, as outlined above, will now be summarized. A wave of repression threw Susan's infantile strivings into a temporary eclipse; this was followed by an improvement in school and a disappearance of the nightmares. On the other hand, the bedwetting became worse; lying and the compulsive search for restitution remained unabated in their force. Such is the price that has to be paid for recapturing the lost momentum of development. Each partial insight facilitates a partial advance in ego and drive development. While the processes of integration and consolidation are at work, the pathogenetic determinants become elusive; often they disappear altogether from therapy. This stage taxes therapeutic tact and patience to the utmost, because repression and integration make their appearance in the deceptive form of a standstill. This is too often and too hastily called "resistance," and dealt with accordingly. With the restructuring of the defenses, however, the road is being paved for a reappearance of the pathogenetic determinants, which will make possible a more detailed and less frenzied investigation of the genesis of the illness. Whenever a new insight has been gained, we can be sure that the doors to further reconstructive and interpretive work will once again be thrown open.

CHAPTER 3

PREADOLESCENT REGRESSION

The onset of puberty sets in motion a process of psychic restructuring. To understand this reorganization in its full complexity and extent, one has to trace its sequential pattern, as that can be discerned during the course of development and maturation.

Clinical experience has taught us that each successive developmental stage resurrects the residues of unassimilated or unintegrated experiences, which had neither been transformed into stable psychic structures (character traits, adaptive accommodations, defensive organization), nor effected drive modifications in harmony with the changing physical and social status of the growing child. These residues are, usually, the result of "too much" or "too little," with regard to phase-specific experience or accommodations, past and present. One can say, in the most general terms, that each developmental stage faces anew, and in various degrees, the disorganizing influence of drive and ego fixations, and each stage attempts once again to unify and harmonize these discordant and anachronistic strivings of ego and id. This is the task and challenge of each developmental phase.

In other words, the aim of each phase-specific task lies precisely in the attainment of an increasing psychic differentiation and of an ego synthesis of ever greater complexity and higher order. In its strivings toward this end, each developmental phase finds a new persistent impediment or obstacle in its path. A progressively more competent body and mind make a ceaseless effort either to accommodate infantile strivings and compensate for defective structure, as in symptom formation, or by some other means to render the deterrents to progressive drive and ego development innocuous, as in sublimation, in character formation, in splitting of the ego—to name only the most prominent ones.

It is not surprising to see the prepuberty child using to his advantage the ego equipment that he has acquired during the latency period, in order to cope with the imminent task of adolescence. Drive and ego components that had previously failed to play any role in the forward movement of psychological development, make their appearance once again. They are easily identifiable as residue phenomena, due to the fixation and trauma, and now cast into the form of prepubertal reactions. That is to say, these residues take on the form and content of the prepuberty drive constellation, in an effort to remain in consonance with the phase-appropriate level of development. We can recognize these infantile residues in the emphatic turn to a genital orientation and to its concomitant imagery, thought and behavior, as displayed by the prepubertal girl.

Infantile—and this includes preverbal—memories attach themselves to genital modalities and thereby become communicable, as the case of Susan will demonstrate. Of course, the preadolescent regressive and progressive strivings become subject to ego, ego ideal and superego influences; the ensuing conflicts give rise to a kaleidoscopic employment of defenses. Certain defenses will become permanent attributes of character, while others will prove to be *ad hoc* formations, dropping away in time, without leaving any perceptible traces. Still others, as we know from our young patients, belong to a pathological defensive system that we can rarely penetrate completely at the stage of preadolescence.*

The increase of drive intensity that accompanies pubertal maturation makes itself felt before any physical signs, such as secondary sex characteristics, come into evidence. This shift in the balance between ego and id has a profound effect on cathectic processes. As a consequence of the drive increase, memory traces or fantasies that are related to infantile experiences, wishes and affects become re-cathected. They make their appearance in consciousness after an elaborate transposition of the infantile nature of the drives has "elevated" them onto a more ego-syntonic—i.e., genital—modality. The defensive aspect that is implicit in this transposition is obvious. Nevertheless, irrespective of the defensive aspect, one must not overlook the implicit striving toward mastery, or rather toward adaptive accommodations, within the total process of growth. The fact remains however that an increase in drive energy is typical for prepuberty and that, as a consequence, the latency balance between ego and id is upset. A regressive movement, alternating with a defensive holding position, constitutes the characteristics or phase-specific development of pre-

* See: "Ben," Chapter 17.

adolescence. A forward movement of the libido serves as a signal that a new balance has been reached between ego and id, and that adaptive accommodations to the relevant stage of physical maturation are in progress.

The above comments on preadolescent drive and ego organization are of a general nature; they apply with equal relevancy to boy and girl. We have, however, reached the point when the accepted similarity between male and female preadolescent psychosexual, and to some extent ego development has come to an end. More specific characteristics, as they pertain to each sex, are now in order (Blos, 1958, 1962). The boy's preadolescent regression is more massive than the girl's; it is action-oriented and concretistic. In the first onrush of pubescence, the boy turns away, with derision and contempt, from the opposite sex. The girl, by contrast, pushes heterosexual wishes or fantasies into the foreground, while regressive tendencies assert themselves, peripherally and secretively.

The girl's regressive escapades always remain counterbalanced by her turn to the other sex. She rarely loses herself as completely in regressive behavior as the boy does. In fact, girls at this age are known to be better students than boys, and their capacity for introspection is superior to that of the boys. Of course, what the girl at this stage has acquired is not genuine femininity; it is aggression and possessiveness that dominate her relationship to the other sex. These infantile modes of object relation barely hide the narcissistic aspect of her yearnings—namely, the need to find a sense of completion in object possession. Again, the case of Susan will be used to illustrate this point.

I have found that the emotional vulnerability of the preadolescent girl is twofold. One aspect of this consists in the regressive pull to the preoedipal mother, thereby re-instituting the ambivalence of early object relations. The other aspect lies in the bisexual identity that is typical for this stage and is eloquently demonstrated in the "tomboy." The girl's fixation on the preadolescent phase always has one of these complexes—or, indeed both—at the center. Of course, these conflicts or themes do not originate in the preadolescent phase. When I speak of preadolescent fixation, I am referring to the perpetuation of the phase-specific—i.e., preadolescent— model of coming to terms with persistent infantile needs and ego immaturities at the level of pubertal drive expression.

The most striking example of this is to be found in the delinquent girl, whose heterosexual acting-out behavior represents her defense against regression to the preoedipal mother (Blos, 1957, 1969). She displaces the regressive pull onto the opposite sex, where her infantile contact hunger finds substitute gratification. Infantile fixations tend to lead preadolescent development into a deviant path. As the result of pubertal maturation, the genital is destined to become the erotogenetic zone through which infantile needs for security and bodily closeness continue to be actualized. The involvement of the genital at puberty and the execution of the heterosexual act does not by any means indicate that either emotional maturity or genitality has been attained.

From the beginning of her adolescence, the girl is far more preoccupied with the vicissitudes of object relations than the boy; his energies are directed outward, toward the control of and dominance over the physical environment.

In order to complete the picture of normal female preadolescence, we must now define the developmental task of this phase. That task is, of course, implicit in the conflict that has been described: it consists in successful resistance to the regressive pull toward the preoedipal mother and, further, in renunciation of pregenital drive gratifications. It will become apparent, in the case of Susan, how changes in drive organization and in psychic structure affected and shaped her social behavior, as well as her various social roles, such as being a pupil, a friend, a scout, a camper, etc.

The expectations and the normative influences of the environment are not only a stimulus to growth; they also channel and define the elemental and formless forces of the drives, as these emerge with each successive stage of development. Conversely, the ego acquires ("learns") the *modi* of mastery that prevail in the environment. Compromise formations between the private and public world are thus developed for the sake of social survival. The active formalization and stringent socialization that the environment imposes are indispensable for the growing child. They avert the danger of random, idiosyncratic externalizations which the environment rejects. Positive, as well as corrective and punitive responses of the environment are necessary not only for the advance of individual development, but also in order to protect developmental achievements from being weakened or lost.

We shall now return to the case of Susan and follow her entry into preadolescence. On the psychological level, we may expect to witness the appearance of drive and ego manifestations that will throw light on the mental life of preadolescence, as it has been discussed above. A consolidation of the latency period had been achieved belatedly, with the result that Susan's school performance and social behavior had improved considerably. The nightmares had disappeared in direct consequence of the regressive play during therapy and the transference interpretations in relation to it. The therapist had become both Susan's antagonist and protagonist, against whom she directed her destructive urges and toward whom she turned as omnipotent helper and protector.

After the orgiastic messing and the wallowing in fingerpaint had gradually subsided, Susan made more purposeful use of verbal expressions. A few relapses of smearing occurred, but these were not accompanied by uncontrollable excitation, nor by the same panic and terror of guilt as had been in evidence earlier. The relapses remained within the capacity of her ego to control attendant anxiety. For the most part, she now painted with a brush and with poster paint, more often using crayons for her drawings or else turning to the exacting and restraining outlines of a coloring book. A trend toward social conformity and organized group participation showed itself, not only in school but also in her social life. She found delight in her Scout uniform, which made her look "just like all the other girls."

During the period following the decline of her anal regression, Susan showed an expanding interest in many different things, such as birds, plants, books, Scout knowledge, schoolwork, photography and swimming. While she was thus actively extending her participation in constructive activities, she was also concentrating in her therapy, with singleminded determination, on the obstacles that stood in the way of her becoming "a big girl." These obstacles were to be found in the fixation on a trauma that had given her emotional development a pathological turn. Susan's neurotic illness cannot be understood without the knowledge of certain crucial circumstances of her life. Such data appear, in each case, as a unique set of variables. Our interest here is primarily focused on the question of how a given childhood trauma asserts itself in relation to the phase-specific conflict, task and resolution of preadolescence.

Before we turn to this topic, I want to emphasize that trauma, as here conceived, does not constitute a single pathogenetic occurrence in the life of an unfortunate child. Quite the contrary, I assume that trauma is a universal human condition during infancy and early childhood, and leaves, even under the most favorable circumstances, a permanent residue (Blos, 1962, 1968). How childhood trauma, in conjunction with affects, thoughts and fantasies influences the entry into adolescence will now be demonstrated by means of Susan's early history and her preadolescent personality formation.

CHAPTER 4

THE EFFECT OF TRAUMA ON PREADOLESCENT DRIVE ORGANIZATION

When Susan was five, her mother had a psychotic episode of a depressive nature and was suddenly hospitalized. Without knowing why her mother had been taken to the hospital, the child was sent to relatives halfway across the country. She vaguely knew her destination because it had a name, but she had no comprehension of where it was or why she was going there. After she had settled in her aunt's house, nobody ever mentioned the mother; there were never any letters or phone calls from her.

While the father did continue to keep in touch with the child, his evasiveness only served to increase Susan's sense of uncertainty and mystification.

She took the puzzling silence as a cue not to ask questions about the unspeakable event that had removed her mother from her life. The explanation that "mother had an operation" sounded to her more like a subterfuge than the truth. She tried for a long time, but in vain, to figure things out for herself, and she remembers the persistent thought: "Other children's mothers did not stay that long in the hospital for an operation—certainly not a whole year." Susan was also separated from her little brother when she was sent off to her relatives; he was then two years old. Why had *he* not been sent far away? She knew that he was instead taken in by the grandparents in her home town. Not only did he thus remain near mother and father—close enough to arouse Susan's jealousy and envy—but he was also allowed to return home three months earlier. This added insult to injury.

The year in exile was called by Susan "the Wisconsin year." It was a time, in Susan's recollection, that was filled with delights and wonderful experiences and adventures. Wisconsin was a world where children were happy, where she could exchange the dull life of the city for the wide open spaces through which horses roamed, where she could ride on a beloved, beautiful stallion, where she had been received at the station, upon arrival, in a horse-drawn carriage and taken to a big house with many, many rooms. It was wonder over wonder. The denial of her loneliness was so complete that she thought of the happy days in Wisconsin whenever she felt unhappy, lost and afraid at the present time.

She knew, and eventually she admitted that her wonderful memories were make-believe stories and lies. In fact, she wanted explicitly to be helped with her irresistible urge to make up the stories that she had to relate to people as facts. Susan knew—and once said so quite plainly—that her lying and her bedwetting were but two sides of the same coin: both had started in Wisconsin; they were both symptoms of denial and reversal of affect. Memories eventually emerged that spoke of her fears of being lost and of drowning. These frightful memories existed side by side with the make-believe recollection of having lived in paradise.

Two such typical memories from the Wisconsin year may describe her state of mind. Without any sign of affect, she spoke of the first day in nursery school, when her aunt forgot to pick her up and she had to walk out into the street alone. Not knowing where to find her aunt's house in the still unfamiliar surroundings, she wandered about until a policeman took her to a police station. On her way there, she suddenly saw her aunt passing by in a car. The aunt later stopped at the police station to pick up the child, and Susan told her that she was two hours late. Upon questioning, Susan said: "Oh, no, I was not afraid."

She also had other memories, related to water and to floods. She was glad that she lived in a room high above the ground; that being so, a flood would not be able to wash her away. Not until the end of treatment did Susan acknowledge the anxiety that the sound of rushing water always aroused in her. Of course, by then she knew what the object of her terror was—namely, the fear of losing in the flushing toilet that body part that was most treasured by her: the illusory phallus. What else could it have been that bestowed on her brother the privilege of remaining near the parents? The aggressive and retaliatory affect of her bedwetting was projected and added its share to the terror of rushing waters. At this point, I can only hint at the problem and must ask the reader for the patience to allow the "water theme" to unfold itself, through the successive steps that led Susan to insight into this problem.

The "Wisconsin year"—or, in other words, the abandonment trauma—had effected a split in the ego: symptom formation succeeded in binding the unmanageable aggression. Simultaneously, a fantasy repertoire was built up; it was assisted by a facility—perhaps one should call it a gift—for make-believe of extraordinary realness, and became an ever-ready refuge from any kind of unpleasure. This aftermath of trauma endowed Susan's preadolescence with developmental liabilities that endangered her passage through adolescence. The danger consisted in her carrying forward into adolescence the split in the ego. It was this split, as we have seen, that had channeled a major part of her aggression into symptom formation and made her fantasy life the source of comfort and security. Both avenues had rendered Susan increasingly inaccessible to reality demands.

Basically, the two aspects of her accommodation to anxiety—longing and retaliation or, simply, love and hate—reflect a severe ambivalence conflict of long standing, in relation to the mother. The danger, then, can be defined in its ultimate form as a lasting inability to form stable—i.e. post-ambivalent—object relations. This, in itself, would bring about a miscarriage of the adolescent process.

Now that a relevant fragment of Susan's history has been reported, we shall return to the treatment situation. The material that took the center of the stage, after the smearing and messing had more or less dropped out of sight, was a most specific one: it revolved around one word—namely, "F-u-c-k", written by Susan in this fashion on the blackboard. She also painted it; she said it; she sang it. She begged for permission to use the word in the session and, subsequently, she obtained permission from her mother to say the word aloud when she was alone in the apartment. "Fuck" represented a conglomeration or condensation of pregenital and genital drives, wishes and fantasies, as well as of such affective states as provocation, rage, anger, pleasure and fear. The linkage of sexual fantasies and aggressive affects gave Susan's "fuck-period" the vastness and unspecific nature that is characteristic of preadolescent regression.

In treatment, the various components of the regressive panorama were sorted out and identified in relation to defenses, wishes, fantasies, actual experiences and perceptions. This process depended heavily on the therapist's ability to understand Susan's pronouncements within the context of her experience, her fantasy, her present reality and her life history. To comprehend this kind of talking, the therapist has to be familiar with syncretic thought and with the mechanism of condensation. Otherwise, one easily becomes ensnared in the literalness of words and syntax.

Saying the word "fuck" was accompanied by a feeling, on Susan's part, of daring, excitement and sensual pleasure. The word was also used to provoke the therapist, to tease, shock and insult him. These various meanings became clear as separate aspects of the global word. Susan herself thought that the word referred to a boy and a girl, both undressed, the boy rubbing his penis against the girl who, as a consequence, had a bowel movement. Anal activity figured prominently in her conception of sexual relations: the female production of stool represented the counterpart of penile erection. There was no reference to anal birth in the clinical data. This is typical for female preadolescence, when female procreativity is overshadowed by the problem of bisexuality. However, some details of her infantile sexual theory had become evident.

Pursuing the "word of many meanings" with an extraordinary perspicacity, as was characteristic of Susan, she one day announced that "fuck means that a girl wants a penis." Since she had never seen one, or so she said, she did not know what it was she wanted. Her ignorance once having been challenged, Susan quite readily abandoned this obvious subterfuge, which she had con-

trived to hide her doubts about her own genital-anal
compound. "Fuck" became, finally, an object that, she
said, was under her bed. This place turned out to be her
favorite hideout for masturbation. When she dolefully
admitted that "my fuck doesn't feel big", it became clear
that, in masturbating, she was searching for her penis.
Masturbation under the bed was accompanied by a sing-
song and a sense of anticipation, which Susan put into
these words: "I think something will happen; I don't
know what, and it never does."

The search for a body part that was either lost or
could not be found has to be understood within the
broader ramifications of object loss: the loss of the
mother. It was this loss that threatened the child with
depressing, helpless rage when she was sent into "exile"
—which had indeed happened during her phallic phase.
The Wisconsin experience would not, of course, have
been as critical and devastating as it turned out to be, if
a precondition to the fear of loss had not been laid down
in the early mother-child relationship. What deserves our
attention at this point is the preadolescent girl's body image formation—or rather its defectiveness in Susan's case
—in which the defectiveness of early object relations is
recognizable.

We are able to observe, close at hand, the influence of
early object relations on the formation of the self and on
the body representation in particular. In child therapy,
drawing and painting frequently become the graphic reflections of the self-representation. Susan drew and
painted horses, always male, as she never failed to assert; they had become her comforting companions in fantasy life at the time when she had been separated from
home. "Fuck is something animals do," she explained;
but why, then, were there only males in her world of
horses? In defiance and anger—directed, alternately,
against therapist or mother—Susan made up a song to
the lyric "fuck, shit, damn, hell." This song was kept as

much a secret as were her sexual fantasies of an infantile—i.e., regressed—nature.

All during this period, Susan was dressed in colorful, prim and neat clothes. Her scout uniform was kept, without fail, in exemplary condition. Outwardly, Susan appeared like any other ten-year-old girl of propriety and decorum. The more she revealed to the therapist of her secret life, the less was her behavior and appearance in public affected by it. It was during the so called "fuck period," for example, that Susan's behavior and performance in school improved. She received quite satisfactory grades in conduct and achievement. Her secret and florid fantasy life had found a trustworthy repository in the therapeutic situation. It was here that they belonged, because it was here that she "learned" how to make sense out of them and how to grow up. Susan would have been the last one to believe that any real gains had been made simply because she did well in school and as a scout. She knew that her "secret life" remained the source of constant anxiety and the root of her troubles.

We shall now scrutinize the clinical material in terms of the developmental characteristics of female preadolescence. This material is so totally steeped in the unique life history and the unique personality of a given child that the transposition of the clinical record into theoretical formulations is no easy task. To begin with, there has to be evidence and purpose in the process. The first, of course, is provided by the record. The second is contained in the expectation that theoretical concepts that have been derived from clinical data will ultimately enhance the efficacy of child and adolescent therapy. It remains for the reader to test and judge both.

Susan's "fuck period", in terms of drive regression, constituted a revival of the search for the early, preoedipal mother. This regressive pull was accompanied by anxiety, which alerted the ego to the emergence of dependency wishes and passive strivings. Ambivalence conflicts flared up in the flight from regression to symbiotic partnership; a regression as far back as to the merger of self and object, however, did not take place. This resistivity to total regression was considered to be an indicator of the girl's essential health; or, to put it differently, it was regarded as proof of a neurotic disturbance, rather than of a borderline condition. In the light of the hereditary history and of certain symptoms, such as encompresis, hair pulling (doubtful), and somatization, a borderline condition was naturally thought of.

Instead of regression to passive dependency in her search for completeness, however, Susan experienced the disturbing feelings and thoughts of "I don't like my mother." "Such a thought is bad," Susan said with remorse and guilt. Her move toward emotional disengagement from the preoedipal mother became apparent in a newly acquired self-assertion, a "bossiness" at home that contrasted sharply with the previous provocative demandingness and obstinate extortion of love or punishment. Furthermore, her newly acquired independence became apparent in the physical freedom of her moving about through the neighborhood, and in her more active social participation within her peer group.

The emerging fear of the early—i.e., preoedipal—mother should particularly interest us here, because that fear reveals the ambivalence that is so characteristic of early object relations. The preadolescent girl experiences, in her search for new object relations, an intensification of the primary emotional tie, and this leads her, of necessity, to the early mother. Of course, the "early mother" (preoedipal) and the "present mother" (postoedipal) are not identical, except in the sameness of person. In speaking of the regressive pull to the early mother, we refer to the object representation of the early mother. Here is to be found the mental trace in which the early mother survives in the mind of the child, independently of the various roles that every mother is destined to play in relation to the child, over the years of his growth.

It is self-evident that the mother-child relationship was negatively affected in Susan's childhood by the prolonged separation, or the exile trauma, at the age of five; it had thereby become cast into a particular, virulent and persistent form. It is the form that this loss took—or, rather, the mental representation in which it became embedded—that attracts our attention and arouses our curiosity.

The global word "fuck" contained aspects of excitement, disappointment, hopelessness and sadness—all of which were related to her sense of physical incompleteness, of bodily impoverishment and, generally, of a sustained fear of abandonment and loss. We assume that the abandonment, the deprivation of an essential object tie, became deflected onto the body, in terms of a body-part loss. Of course, masturbation itself had intervened, independently, as a provider of comfort (tension reduction) at times of grieving and sadness. Her masturbatory search for the lost penis, however, left her dejected, angry and frightened. Superego anxiety always interfered with the measure of gratification she obtained from auto-erotic activity.

It was not difficult to discover behind Susan's solitary and secret sexual play a search for completeness that can in essence be acquired only through primary, stable object relations. These lead, eventually and gradually, into identification with the mother. The original loss is the loss of the nipple; its availability or possession represents *pars pro toto*—that primordial oneness from which all psychic differentiation takes its start. Here lies the genetic rock-bottom from which are derived the subsequent pathological reactions to loss.

The nipple or the breast, in the broad sense referred to here, encompasses the total mothering and feeding experience, including the many concurrent sensory stimuli, whether these be gratifying or distressing in quality. It is true that the experience of primary loss is not retrieved, in the psychotherapy of the preadolescent girl, at the level of affective repetition or conscious realization. Both, however, become recognizable in their derivative forms at this phase—for example, in the exacerbation of eating problems, or in a general greediness and demandingness, bordering on ruthless extortion.

None of these manifestations was noticeable in Susan's case. We know from the history that, when she was little, Susan needed to be close to her mother in the loneliness of the night. After her return from exile, she used to scream for her mother and demand that she be taken into bed with her. Only the mother's presence could dispel the terror of her nightmares. She told the therapist at the beginning of treatment that she screams every night, but that her mother does not hear her any more, as she used to when she was little. This account is another example of Susan's "lies," which we have termed her "truth." Obviously, the story of her screaming without being answered refers to the time when the child was separated from the mother. She remembered the anxiety attacks that she experienced when the mother had become unreachable and seemed lost forever.

It must not be forgotten that little Susan and her mother had been unusually close, and that the "unreasonable love" the mother had felt for the child contributed to Susan's extraordinary relatedness. It belongs to the paradox of the human condition that the source from which Susan derived the strength that carried her, successfully, through therapy constituted at the same time the source from which her neurotic vulnerability issued. Be that as it may, it had become clear from the course of treatment that the "bad mother" who disappears remained, unduly long, an object representation that stood side by side with that of the "good mother" who comforts and loves.

Both prolonged ambivalence and incomplete object constancy precluded whole-object identification; or to put it another way, both laid the foundation for an ambivalent sense of self and for an ambiguous body image. As a consequence of this split, then, no stable sexual identification could take form. Clinically, this became manifest in Susan's fluctuating aspirations to be a boy or a girl, to wear dresses or "ugly girl pants." The "bad mother" was depicted by Susan, in a picture painted in black, as a "mean witch who eats children." The picture had many green spots along the margin; "these," Susan explained, "are the tears of the crying children, who are very frightened." Susan now spoke of the time when her mother had been "awful, because she left her child alone and went to the hospital."

The nightmares that Susan reported early in treatment began to throw light on the kind of anxiety she had failed to master, either by her defenses or by her symptoms. Her dreams reflected a pervasive sense of abandonment and loneliness. The anxiety she experienced in dream or nightmare repeated the trauma of object loss, of depressive helplessness, of hostile rage, and of the retaliatory attack by the lost love object. In the latter, we recognize the projection of the child's destructive rage, which turns the love object into a monster.

In one of her dreams (which she illustrated by painting it), a little girl is enclosed in a big bubble. She has a pony tail, and she is down in the bubble, terribly frightened and crying. A gorilla with large teeth and hands, a scary looking beast, is keeping the little girl locked up in the bubble. Susan knew, of course, that the little girl is herself when little. In association to the dream, Susan referred to the therapy room as a schoolroom ("because I love school"), and to the therapist as her teacher, whom she has all to herself with no other children around. Therapy for Susan became a liberation from the bubble and an overcoming of the anaclitic depression that she had tried to master by denial ("nothing will happen to my mother"), by reversal ("I am the happiest child in Wisconsin"), and by bisexual identity ("If I am a boy, my mother will keep me close to her"). While the therapist emphasized those aspects of the dream that reflected the pathogenetic experience (trauma), the mother's psychotic illness was never ignored in its disturbing effect on the child.

Susan's fixation at the level of preoedipal object relation had become evident through her dreams, fantasies and transference replications. She vigorously resisted the return to infantile passivity; instead, she took on the active, bossy role of the boy, or more apparently of the father. This is a typical defensive maneuver of the preadolescent girl, at the time when the regressive pull of this phase arouses unmanageable anxiety. She then identifies transiently with the male role (the tomboy), and turns to the father, in flight from the mother whose engulfment of her into a state of primary passivity she thereby averts. The oedipal theme stands, often dramatically, in the forefront of the clinical material, and an oedipal interpretation seems to fit the occasion. It has been my experience that an interpretation of the oedipal conflict only gives support to the girl's defensive maneuver, by allowing the problem of the unresolved tie to the preoedipal mother to recede into oblivion. I have referred to this constellation as "the oedipal defense of the preadolescent girl"; the case of Susan illustrates this contention.

The defensive maneuver that protected Susan against regression to the early mother also strengthened her identification with the father: "Father and I are alike; we are one, and we do the same things." What appears now as oedipal hostility to the mother is, in fact, her negative attitude toward the active and controlling, the frustrating and withholding preoedipal mother; what seems to be a positive oedipal turn to the father represents a narcissistic identification with him on the phallic level. No doubt, oedipality does have a place in the picture, but in a larval state only; it is the defensive aspect that plays the dominant role.

Susan now thinks that she is father's favorite child, because father and she are alike; they have the same interests, the same "things," while "my mother and my brother have none of them." "Only father and I can draw and only father and I like horses." "We are equestrians." The identification with the father, as well as her interest in boys, belong to the realm of narcissistic object relations, in which an assumed sameness of body and mind gives the emotional attachment its essential quality. These very attributes and likenesses, which are part and parcel of the negative oedipus complex, or her oedipal identification with the father, lead back indirectly to the infantile attachment to the mother.

She appropriates by her masculine identification the places that father and brother occupied when she was "in exile," while they were both enjoying the bodily closeness to and possession of the mother. She now lives, in short, by proxy. The closeness to the father shows the characteristics of the dyadic partnership that is typical of preoedipal object relations. The far-reaching dangers to the girl's psychosexual development that are inherent in her defensive use of the oedipal constellation lie in the perpetuation of her preoedipal object relations and their transfer, during adolescence, onto her final heterosexual accommodations.

In cases of female delinquency, we observe, in stark clarity, the girl's constant search for a heterosexual partner to gratify her infantile need for body contact and object possession, without her actually being able to form relationships of personal intimacy and emotional mutuality. In addition, her heterosexual "cuddling" (pseudo-heterosexuality), without genital excitation, serves as a defense against regression to the preoedipal mother and therefore against homosexuality. I mention these matters here only in passing, in order to hint at the far reaching clinical consequences of the concept I have introduced earlier (Blos, 1957, 1969). None of these solutions had any place within the orbit of Susan's psychological propensities.

The history of the early mother-child relationship must now be recounted, with special attention to the mother's fantasies about her child and their particular role in mothering. It remains a fateful circumstance surrounding the infant that each mother, in the normative crises of pregnancy and birth, envelops the infant with fantasies, both conscious and unconscious. These fantasies are rather persistent in nature; they, indeed, reach a second high point after their first flourish during babyhood, when the child is approaching or entering puberty. The regressive closeness to the mother that is re-established during preadolescence resensitizes the girl's perceptiveness of the mother's fantasies about her. This "tuned-inness" activates in the young adolescent girl an emotional distancing from the mother, as a protection of her own autonomy.

Fantasies about the baby, universal as they are, can take on inordinate proportions if they are not checked and corrected by the actual baby, both its physical reality and its temperamental qualities. Otherwise, they cast the baby into a fantasy mold, with the result that interactional patterns become confused and confusing. The baby, being helpless and dependent, can only protest, in an effort to contradict the mismatched partnership, by way of somatic breakdowns and developmental irregularities. Maternal fantasies are, for example, to be found in relation to the sex of the child, to her own sense of body incompleteness, to competitive strivings within a past sibling situation, to narcissistic gratifications, and to many more factors. All together, or any one of them taken separately, they can reach a point at which the child's cues are critically misread in relation to feeding, holding, cuddling, sleeping, etc.

It is not a matter of conjecture when we attribute importance to some of the aforementioned conditions as affecting the early mother-child relationship in Susan's case. Susan's mother had reported a vivid recollection of how the wish for a baby had been induced by the death of her own mother. Becoming pregnant had aided her in her efforts to cope with an extremely painful mourning process: the wished-for baby had to be a girl, and to be named after the maternal grandmother. Repeatedly, the mother described her feelings for the child in these terms: "I loved her beyond all reason." The replacement role that was being assigned to the child imbued the relationship with a highly idiosyncratic flavor, and dulled the mother's ability to read the infant's cues and to respond appropriately to the ebb and flow of the baby's needs. The mother described herself as being "a bug for balanced meals, sleep and cleanliness."

Susan was precocious in her self-feeding, renouncing the bottle early. She "trained herself" at the age of six months—or so the mother reported, no doubt by exaggerating. The self-training of the child was the mother's most "thrilling experience." The mother, enuretic herself until the age of 20, would not take a chance with delayed toilet training, but saw to it that everything came under control at the earliest possible time. Susan was dry before she walked, at the age of 15 months. While she was, according to the mother, "a late walker," she was on the other hand an "early talker." The mother recalls with delight that Susan was able to "carry on a conversation at the age of nine months." Such memory falsifications throw light on the wishful side of child-rearing, in the same measure as they throw doubt on the accuracy of historical reporting. It is of interest to note that the mother vividly recalls her own childhood wish to be a boy. Ever since her menarche, she "hates everybody"—including herself, one might add—during her menses.

Considering the mother's use of the child for the replication and the repair of her own past and, further-more, as a restitutional object in the completion of her acute mourning, it would seem reasonable to assume that the mother's emotional availability was, at best, fluctuating and inconsistent. What provided the greatest pleasure for the mother was Susan's precocious ego development, her mastery of bowel and bladder, and her early talking. It was a blow to the mother's pride when a relapse of wetting occurred at the age of two. Susan was retrained during the following year, and remained dry until noc-turnal wetting became established as a symptom at the age of five, when she lived "in exile."

The role of aggression must be emphasized in Susan's precocious ego development. The child lived up to the mother's expectations as well as she could, suppressing her aggressive drive in relation to the normal range of timely oral and anal experiences. While the early deter-minants of Susan's drive modifications are not known in detail, the exigencies—whatever they were—resulted in an exceedingly early and rigid reaction formation that was subsequently maintained by a punitive superego. Object relations aimed, first of all, at pleasing and giving pleasure. Naughtiness was used, at an early age, to pro-voke punishment—namely, being spanked. This need was revived in treatment, where she expected punishment for having been a bad girl, soiling her pants, smearing with finger paint or using dirty words. Signs of fixation at the oral, and especially at the anal-sadistic level, appear in abundance in the record.

The precursors of the major trauma, at the age of five, each contributed its share in turn to the elaboration of the climactic experience—namely, the mother's unexplainable illness and the child's abrupt removal from her familiar environment. This occurred, as has been noted, at a time when Susan was in the phallic phase. We were able to observe, in part from the history and in part from the clinical record, how the cumulative conflicts of previous instinctual phases, including their adaptive and defensive settlements, found their definitive articulation in phallic terms. We were prepared to find in Susan's "boy complex" the condensation of conflictual and structural disturbances, ranging from the stage of infancy and early childhood to the phallic-oedipal period. We shall now turn our attention to the consolidation of the neurotic trends—namely, to the formation of the childhood neurosis. This neurotic structuralization took place at a time when Susan had reached a complete impasse in her progressive development. The neurotic accommodation took place in response to an intolerable and overwhelming situation that had been thrust on her by unfortunate circumstances.

CHAPTER **5**

DOUBLE GENDER IDENTITY: ITS BEHAVIORAL AND ATTITUDINAL EQUIVALENTS

Early in treatment, in the tenth session, Susan related a fantasy about a king and queen asleep in the spire of their castle. She told the story in a whisper, so that the king and the queen would not wake up. The story was simply that the royal couple possessed precious jewels which Susan would have liked to see; she was afraid, however, that they might wake up and punish her for her curiosity. They were a mean king and queen; they stole money from little girls' pocketbooks. While painting the scene in the castle, Susan suddenly turns to the therapist and says: "You better don't turn me into a boy—you better just don't."

The story is a typical primal scene fantasy, with the parents elevated to royal status. Envy and peeping thinly disguise the child's sexual curiosity. What is striking in the story is the accusation that the royal couple steals money from little girls' pocketbooks. In their meanness, they deprive the little girl of her valuable possession. We can only surmise at this stage of the treatment that this is related to her not being a boy. Our supposition, however, becomes strengthened by Susan's abrupt warning, when she says: "don't turn me into a boy."

The changeability of gender is on her mind. She wants to be a girl who possesses the privileges and the physical equipment of a boy. Wishes and fears of this kind had gained such force that they kept her awake at night, because she was afraid she might wake up from sleep to find herself a boy. A dream will illustrate her belief that genders are not mutually exclusive, but can co-exist in one person: she dreamed of a girl in boy's clothing, remarking that she looked pretty as a boy, although she had looked ugly as a girl. In fact, she added pointedly, "The girl who was dressed as a boy looked better than the boy himself."

Her belief in the changeability and interchangeability of gender was firmly imbedded in her thinking; it provided evidence of the role that magic played in her grasp of reality. When she implored the therapist not to turn her into a boy, she had herself projected these magical powers, and was now pleading that they should not be used. In doing so, she struck a double theme that continued to reverberate through the years of treatment; it can be seen in the wish to be a boy and in the concurrent hope to become a girl—but a *real* one, all the way and forever. Becoming a real boy or a real girl—these were, for Susan, the two alternative ways of growing up.

It would be too narrow a view to conceive of Susan's preoccupation with gender as the sole promoter of such fantasies. They must rather be seen as the most recent in a series of fantasies, the specific content of which changes with the prevailing libidinal phase through which the child is passing. In each instance, drive, defense and adaptation are interwoven. In the precious jewels, we recognize the sum total of desirable pleasures and powers that parents can dispense from the store of their inexhaustible riches; in the selfish and punitive royal couple at sleep, we recognize the exclusion of the child from the parental bedroom or bed. Both of these represent, on a primitive level, the child's loneliness and yearning for the mother. Considering Susan's precocious ego and superego development, it is not surprising that night fears appeared early and that an anxious flight to mother's bed had become a nightly routine at that time.

The early enforcement of self-control aroused anaclitic yearnings, as well as hostile and retaliatory impulses. Fear and guilt brought them both to a halt, resulting in an inhibition of object-directed aggression. Libidinal tension found relief in autoerotic gratification, and in the creation of a fantasy world all her own. The proliferation of these fantasies promoted a heightened concentration on her inner life. While these fantasies abounded in the direct expression of her desire to be a boy, it also became clear that Susan's ego-syntonic self-image was female: what she expected was that therapy would help her to become a complete girl.

Susan sensed, if only dimly, that her bisexual identity was but an expression of her unresolved ambivalence toward the mother and of her all-consuming envy of the baby brother. His infantile privileges had aroused her infantile greed. When she was finally sent away, at the height of the phallic-oedipal stage, the absence of the penis and her frantic search for it replaced the absence of the parent and the incomprehensible disappearance of the mother. Autoerotic restitution-fantasies were embedded in her compulsive masturbation—genital and anal—and temporarily assuaged the child's sense of loss and abandonment. As derivatives of this disturbance in psychosexual development, traits and attitudes emerged that were anchored in this impasse. They could be detected in her ceaseless demandingness, her simultaneous contempt toward and envy of children, her ingratiating assertiveness to strangers, and her social as well as intellectual inhibitions. Every effort at self-assertion or success was followed by a sense of disappointment, hopelessness and guilt. The symptoms proper gradually became elucidated via drive derivatives, defenses and fantasies.

Soon after Susan entered treatment, prepuberty intensified the instinctual pressures and moved her preadolescent sexual fantasies into the foreground. Their pregenital nature, in terms of both content and behavioral expression, has been discussed earlier; this pregenital modality also pertains to her "boy complex." The fact that she was born on December 24th made her say: "Only Jesus and I are born on Christmas, and therefore I am special. I'll get anything I want, my mother told me." Such self-assuring remarks alternated with a sense of defeat and a stubborn pretense of being a boy or, at least, similar to a boy. When she had her hair cut, she felt elated, because now she looked more like a boy; this was also true when she exchanged skirts for pants. On the other hand, she suddenly turned pale when she reflected on the difference between boys and girls. She just could not think where the difference lay, except in the fact that boys wear pants; but, she mused, girls wear pants too.

This comparison between herself and others, between boys and girls and their respective competencies and expectations, filled Susan's daily thoughts. She was un-

able to write down any words on the blackboard in the
office without being sure that her spelling of them was
correct; exposing her ignorance was exceedingly humili-
ating to her, and had to be avoided at any cost. She
complained that the pieces of chalk that the therapist put
at her disposal in the office were far too small. Immediately, her fantasy would take over and she would tell
about an enormous piece of chalk—"about two feet long"
—that was kept in the basement of her school. Small
pieces, scraped off from this giant stick of chalk, were
given to the children; it was no wonder that her writing
was not very good. The secret store of treasures was
always kept by adults for themselves and out of reach of
children.

The typical sexual (genital) fantasies of the preadolescent girl make their appearance in pregenital modalities, as Susan's case illustrates abundantly. For example,
she told a story of a boy, called "Fuckerfaster," who had
lost his little red wagon. At last, he spotted the girl who
had found it. The tale then goes on to tell that the boy
persuaded the girl to take off her clothes, so "he could get
into his little red wagon." Intercourse was intimated, yet
her conception of it remained obscure; therefore, no interpretation was given that would fix it in an enlightened
factualness. Thereupon, Susan wallowed in brown paint,
calling it "BM." She talked of the different ways in which
boys and girls urinate. Holding up her brown hands—she
called them "BM gloves"—she announced, both threaten-
ingly and pleadingly at the same time, that she preferred
to come to the sessions in pants rather than in dresses.
Her hope was that permission would be granted and,
thus, her anal attack would be averted.

With an effortless transition, Susan was able to turn
from pregenital drive expression to poetic and childlike
stories, which she made up with the greatest of ease.
Personal references in these tales always remained transparent, as in the story of the little girl who constantly

fought with her brother and got killed on her way to school. The little girl was buried in a grave she had carefully constructed with building blocks, placing a dart on top of it. When father, mother and baby brother are asleep in the dollhouse, the dead little girl rises from her grave; she then returns as an angel to the sleeping family. At this point, Susan asked the therapist to give her a match, because the doll representing the angel should have a magic wand. Here the story ends; both angel and magic wand were silently deposited in the therapist's desk drawer for safe-keeping.

Gradually, Susan's phallic wishes became concrete and verbalized. At the "fuck stage" of treatment, she had declared, literally and directly, that "fuck means that a girl wants a penis." The mouthing of the word "fuck" produced a high degree of excitement, commingled with a magical, phallic self-experience. When masturbation was discussed with Susan, she described her pulling on her quite sparse pubic hair (she was then 12) and on the clitoris, in order to "make a penis." At this time, she and her girl friend would engage in playing "boy-girl," by putting tennis balls into borrowed brassieres, as well as into the genital area. The equation of breasts and testes appears in this bisexual play (Blos, 1960). With another girl friend, she played "two boys fighting": this was really "a dirty game"; it consisted of hitting each other's breast, stomach and genitals. Eventually, this kind of game changed into telling each other love stories, in which Susan impersonated a cowboy.

Whenever Susan got swept away into a desperate wish to be a boy, she always emphasized her fear of becoming one, and sought to enlist the therapist's help in order to remain a girl. So strong, at such moments, was her belief in the magic of thought that she feared to lose the continuity of her self, through becoming the victim of her irresistible wishes. Premature drive repression, in early childhood, had rendered her particularly vulnerable to the danger that the repressive barriers might weaken and that, consequently, her primitive impulses would break through. This complex enveloped a host of fantasies and affects, which were associated with the search for an unambivalent relationship to the mother, attainable only through the mastery of her retaliatory rage. In order to achieve this, she had to come to terms with her boundless envy and with the destructive impulses directed toward the brother.

An additional element of the boy complex came to light. Susan believed that her mother's mental illness, which had precipitated the sudden separation when she was five, had caused something to go wrong, retroactively, with Susan herself when she was born. Upon being questioned as to what that might have been, she answered that the illness might have affected the baby's clitoris—"that thing that sticks out." Susan thought she looked different from the girls in the summer camp she had attended at the age of ten: she was convinced that *her* clitoris protruded. In looking at herself now, at age twelve, she could "see it quite clearly." She drew a self-portrait in the nude with a minuscule protrusion, a rudimentary penis, appearing below the pubic hair. It should be mentioned that, at this time of therapy, the mother was once again hospitalized, and Susan repeatedly asked whether or not her mother's nervousness could have made a difference in the way her daughter's genital was formed. The illusory deformity, besides being a restitution, was simultaneously a punishment for the retaliatory masturbation she had resorted to, when she felt deserted by her mother.

It is not surprising to find among Susan's repertoire for the maintenance and re-establishment of self-esteem the tendency toward exhibitionism. Again, this impulse was thoroughly inhibited; it appeared only—and well-camouflaged, at that—in her fantasy life. When she was thwarted by the therapist, she would show off in a "permissible" way—namely, by attempting to add enormously big numbers on the blackboard, without of course being able to carry through that effort. At the beginning of treatment, the arithmetic concept of addition and subtraction was not yet clear to the child. Arithmetic was too closely associated with the theme of competition between boy and girl. She had to think too hard and, whenever she had to think very hard, she got a headache.

She now got a headache, in fact, whenever her brother received special parental attention—as, for instance, on his birthday. Ego activity, such as thinking, readily became conflicted, through the intrusion of unsublimated aggressive and competitive strivings. On one occasion, Susan asked the therapist to have her painting put on the bulletin board for everyone to see: this included her use of the provocative and magic word "fuck" as her signature. The exhibitionistic tendency could, furthermore, be recognized in her compulsive lying: for example, she told the children at school that she was born in Paris, or else she made herself enviable and mysterious, by attaching to herself experiences that none of the boys or girls could possibly have had.

In another fantasy, Susan was at a dance festival, wearing lipstick; the boys there tried to see what the girls were wearing under their dresses. All the girls were wearing "short shorts," except Susan, who was wearing no shorts at all. The boys knew this and did not lift up her dress. In the second version of the same story, the girls were the ones who picked up their dresses themselves, so as to let the boys see their "short shorts"— again, all except Susan, because she was not wearing any shorts under her dress. This story was followed by her talking about the kind of bathrooms she likes and those she doesn't like, and recounting that the house in Wisconsin had seven bathrooms, while in her own home there is only one. Bringing the session to a happy end, she made up another story in which she was a person with magical powers, possessing a magic wand for everyone to see.

She could, actually, be carried away by this wish, to the extent of attempting to do magic, as when she decided to arrange the crayons on the office table according to colors with her eyes closed, or to do cut-outs without looking. This kind of defensive maneuver provided the opportunity for an interpretation of "make-believe" (reversal)—namely, of the replacement of a painful incapacity, shortcoming, disappointment, loss or envy, by an assertion of her superiority and uniqueness. Such self-aggrandizing and comforting procedures were closely related to autoerotic practices; they were, in fact, equivalents of phallic masturbation.

Susan's therapy dealt first with fantasies and the associated affects and thoughts in their defensive nature, and, secondly, with her autoerotic activity—namely, masturbation itself. This is a common technique of child therapy. Obviously, the more the fantasies are conscious but secret, the more stubbornly they are likely to be kept from disclosure. Eventually, however, their disguised and censored versions become transparent, and clear statements of the child's secrets and conflicts can then be ventured by the therapist. In Susan's case, her stories and symptomatic acts were nothing but involuntary confessions.

It is true that these help the therapist, for long stretches of time, in his effort to gain insight into the child's inner life, rather than benefiting the patient directly and immediately. The defensive barrier is only strengthened by premature confrontation with warded off complexes. Gradually, however, this phase of therapy leads into the disclosure of the "secret"—in Susan's case, masturbation—and of the fantasies, affects and thoughts that have become intimately and inextricably attached to it. In what way and toward what end the infantile components in Susan's compulsive masturbation affect early adolescent development, and furthermore how and whether a fixation on autoerotic activity generally interferes with progressive adolescent development—these will be the topic of the discussion that follows.

CHAPTER 6

MASTURBATION AND PROGRESSIVE DEVELOPMENT

Recourse to masturbation is common in prepuberty, when the intensity of drive pressure increases. The boy's masturbation is by its very nature (erection) undeniable and therefore focused and conscious; the girl, by contrast, elicits genital excitation by various means (thigh pressure, posture, thoughts and fantasies), without necessarily using the hand. In addition, she can derive pleasure and comfort through prolonged and slight elevation of excitation, without reaching a climax. Often, she remains unaware of her practices and oblivious to their erotic nature (Blos, 1962).

We recognize in prepubertal masturbation the residues of pregenital autoerotic practices, as well as their mental content. Specifically, I am here referring to the pregenital stage, which is marked by poorly differentiated components of urethral and phallic-clitoral erotism. The concomitant global affect of excitation and satiation serves as a primitive regulator of tension, and reflects the somatic regulation and maintenance of emotional homeostasis with only dim and tenuous object involvement. Normally, the ego takes over a large sector of the regulatory function, through its progressive mastery over the drives and over the environment. Mastery presupposes internalization, which is recognizable in secondary identification and in the stable psychic representation of the object world; these internalizations give rise to new forms of stimulation and gratification. They can be detected in the sheer exercise of newly gained physical powers of mastery, as well as in the symbolic use of objects and the endless possibilities of their elaboration. The child's play demonstrates this process most eloquently.

The capacity to tolerate delay and tension enables the ego to seek and find gratification of instinctual demands in consonance with object dependencies (socialization), or over time to deflect them into ego-gratificatory activities, which we call "sublimations." The regulation of self-esteem through ego activities eventually becomes commensurate in importance with activities of the id—namely, directing drive discharge and drive gratification. The ability to tolerate tension is built on "confident expectation"—that is, on the assurance and trust that relief of tension is timed well by the caretaking environment. It is this confidence that fosters and assures the effective regulation of anxiety, and prevents the rise of undue psychological emergencies.

Masturbation is one among the many measures that are used in dealing with critical situations of tension. Object-directed emotions and interests become infantilized, if masturbation is excessively practiced, or is excessively preferred as a gratificatory modality. If masturbation absorbs an undue amount of psychic energy (libido and aggression), then object relations become impoverished, to the detriment of the elaboration of psychic structure. This conclusion is based on the assumption that psychic structure takes shape in proportion to the internalization of object relations. In saying this, I am not ignoring the importance of the internalization of the outside world (reality), but I am emphasizing the role of a *primus inter pares*.

The component instincts (sadism, masochism, exhibitionism and voyeurism) find direct gratification in the fantasies that accompany or precede masturbation. This condition can retard, prevent or weaken the transformation of the component instincts, under the aegis of the ego, through combining with and contributing to those ego modifications that expand its conflict-free sphere of functioning. We are well acquainted with these sublimatory faculties from play, learning, performing, skill development, competition, the capacity to observe, to look, to create and so forth. Whenever the component instincts—unduly long-lived or unduly massive—are bound to masturbation, then ego functions either develop poorly, are easily given up or become contaminated by sexual admixtures. This leaves the respective functions conflicted and unstable, as is amply demonstrated in certain learning disturbances of children, Susan among them.

One further consideration is warranted at this point —namely, the so-called masturbation equivalents. By this we mean that the volitional manipulation of the erotogenic zone for the attainment of pleasure can be replaced by compulsions, traits, attitudes, rituals, impulsions (acting out), that also yield self-regulated tension reduction. These behavioral deviations are often the outstanding symptoms that bring a child or an adolescent to the therapist's attention. The displaced autoerotic impulse underlying these symptoms becomes, in many instances, readily apparent, by way of a more or less inadequate reality testing. The condition can be flagrant and obvious, or it can be hidden and obscure, as in those cases in which the ego is split defensively. Through the defensive splitting of the ego, a secret, unconflicted life in fantasy is maintained; this always possesses a stark sense of realness (non-psychotic), while at the same time the ego is executing, even if perfunctorily, those functions that protect the "double life" from self-awareness as well as from outside detection and interference. The clinical picture of such cases shows symptom formation and spurious adaptation riding in tandem.

We are accustomed to seeing children and adolescents keeping up such double lives until, at the consolidation phase of late adolescence, the cumulative developmental deficit leads to emotional bankruptcy. It has been my experience that a cumulative impediment of this nature can be dealt with successfully during childhood or during the initial stage of adolescence. Indeed, therapeutic interference at these stages can prevent the devastating proliferation of an abnormal personality consolidation. Even though remnants of the pathological trend survive in secret crevices of the personality, renewed therapeutic work during post-adolescence or during adulthood becomes a more promising enterprise, as the result of earlier intervention.

Thus it might finally be possible to pry loose the subversive side of the ego and superego from its collusion with primitive instinct gratification and to enlist its faculties instead for the goal of treatment—namely, ego synthesis. Otherwise, the patient will abuse treatment in order to perpetuate the ego split; even though symptomatic improvement takes place, it only simulates emotional maturation. In such cases, the exigencies that first brought the split of the ego into existence, are revived by the new exigency of therapy, which attempts to undo drive and ego fixations in order to mobilize progressive development and personality differentiation. The treatment problem that is inherent in such a structural configuration as has just been described, will be dealt with in Chapters 8 and 9, both of which are addressed to the question of technique.

Susan only gradually revealed her compulsive masturbation and the fantasies that were attached to it. Much earlier in treatment, she had given endless evidences of masturbation equivalents. The transient habit of pulling on her hair belonged in this category;* the most pervasive one, however, was her compulsive lying. She could not stop herself from making believe that something she had made up was actually true, while at the same time she was quite aware that she was telling a lie, for which she deserved punishment. In fact, she became quite afraid of the dreadful consequences of her lying, yet she was unable to give it up. In telling a "pretend" story, she experienced a mixture of the pleasure of being believed and the fear of "hell-fire"—a mixture that she described as "exciting." She often confessed to the therapist that a story she had told him was a lie. The urge to tell a lie really arose whenever her aggressive impulses against the therapist threatened to break through. She was then overcome by the fear that she would be rejected and not loved any longer.

At times, and only in privacy, she resorted to masturbation under similar circumstances, directing her aggressive impulses, in fantasy, against the frustrating person, usually the mother. She tried, on such occasions, to dis-

* It should be mentioned here that Susan's compulsive hair pulling never produced a bare spot on her scalp, and did not reflect the self-destruction intent that this habit usually possesses in the psychotic child. Susan's pulling on her hair is a displacement from below (pulling on the clitoris; see Chapter 5) to above; it was correctly called by her parents a "bad habit."

cover or produce a penis in herself by searching manipulation. This component of Susan's masturbation had acquired all-consuming proportions. When masturbating, as noted earlier, she always expected "something to happen." It never did. The association, indeed equation, of "fuck-penis" aroused sexual excitement when she was hiding under her bed, saying the magic word "fuck." But at the same time it was a source of disappointment and distress to her; in fact, it increasingly depressed her to realize that her clitoris still remained so little.

Susan was convinced, as became evident from her drawings of a girl's genital anatomy, as well as from her masturbation practices, that a hidden penis existed inside her. Drawing the clitoris, she gave it the shape of a large penis, completely out of proportion to the tactile familiarity she had acquired. The identity of penis and clitoris, if it needed any further proof, was made explicit in the striations she gave to both organs in her drawings. When asked what the horizontal lines on the clitoris referred to, she explained that "these are the wrinkles." She had observed them on the male organ.

Susan's masturbation was phallic. Under the influence of her disappointment, she gave it up and instead delegated to fantasy what manipulation had failed to materialize. She now turned to practices that were less distressing to her than those involving tactile perception: she started to put her teddy bear or her pillow between her legs at night. This gave her a pleasant feeling, which made falling asleep easy.

Susan's most vivid recollection of phallic masturbation was related to the years of five and six, when she was separated from the family. At that time she masturbated so much that she "felt sore in front" and became afraid that she had hurt herself. This fear of permanent damage or irreparable castration only served to increase the need for masturbation in order to check that the familiar sensation could still be reproduced. Masturbation, then, in addition to pleasure gain, also served to confirm the fact that no permanent harm had been done. To summarize: the need for object restitution, the incessant fear of permanent loss and, therefore, of incompleteness; the jealousy of the favored infant brother, taken together with a sustained ambivalence toward the mother—all these gradually turned her masturbation into a compulsive symptom.

We could understand this symptom only when we recognized its genesis in her object relations, which, by virtue of their traumatic disruption, threw object libido back onto the autoerotic level. This path had to be reversed in therapy—which meant that autoerotic gratification had to become replaced, to a large extent, by post-ambivalent object relations. That transition went parallel with symptom resolution. We could readily see how masturbation, over the years, had acquired many different facets. In treatment, they were dealt with separately, and many of them were topically far removed from masturbation, in the narrow sense of the term.

The role of magic was outstanding among the many mental operations connected with masturbation. The masturbation complex contained the trends of obstinacy, stubbornness and negativism; and the affect of retaliatory aggression was omnipresent. But above and beyond these attitudes and affects, the very act itself, in wholesale fashion, swept away traumatic anxiety by establishing that no circumstance in life—and especially not loss of any kind—is permanent and unalterable. The defensive aspect of masturbation was plainly the denial of the finality of any existing condition: everything was retrievable, remediable, reversible. The restitutive aspect of masturbation lay in the magic proof that a girl can become a boy and, just as the infant brother had been, can thereby come to be protected against loss. The adaptive aspect of masturbation is to be detected in the ego split that enabled Susan in exile to function fairly well in her new social environment, with the result that she was liked by adults who found her sweet and lovable. Even her bedwetting was tolerated and looked at by the relatives as the unfortunate weakness of an otherwise adorable child.

Susan's memories from the year of separation are worth considering in the light of the preceding discussion. She held fast to a distinction between those "facts" that appeared in dreams and those that were related to real events. Dreams contained her anxieties, couched in floods and drowning; and since these catastrophes were only imaginary, they could be remembered. However, memories of actual events survived only in a jumble of fabrications; they proved to be screen memories. She clung, for a long time, to the fiction that the period away from home was the happiest time she had ever experienced. According to Susan, life in Wisconsin was a paradise for children. The idyllic story book existence started the day she arrived. It will suffice to remind the reader of the horse-drawn wagon and the sprawling house "with seven johns," the pet horse—a stallion, of course—who loved her and whom she loved. These tales —and there were many of them—represented screen memories, covering conflictual and disturbing emotions.

The maintenance of these screen memories served a double function: on the one hand, they averted anxiety by removing from consciousness those painful affects, thoughts and memories that she was unable to integrate, and, on the other hand, they turned these same thoughts and affects into their opposites. Thus, the mother was vindicated of the unforgivable crime she had committed. The rather easy admission on her part of the fabrications that served as screen memories confirmed that Susan had always been half aware of their unreality. These admissions, during therapy, followed in the wake of dreams and thoughts that had as their content aggressive impulses (beating the mother) or accusations against the mother (the witch who eats children).

The dawning awareness of these object-directed and guilt-laden affects made it possible for Susan to link them, associatively, to masturbation; the therapist, finally, lifted these associative links, through interpretation, to the level of insight. Linkage and insight effected a loosening of the compulsive and stereotyped autoerotic activity. In fact, it was followed, in the third year of treatment, by a regression of that stage of psychosexual development that Susan had proclaimed at the very first, when she entered treatment. I refer to her smearing, messing, and smelling, and their opposites—cleaning, scrubbing and washing. After years of quietude, anal impulses asserted themselves anew.

In line with these trends, masturbation followed along a predetermined, regressive path to the anal fixation point. This regression became manifest in anal masturbation. On one hand, manual investigation and, on the other, fantasy elaboration rendered the area around the buttocks—namely, the anal and perineal territory—the essential and only relevant body part of sexual significance. In her drawings, for example, she transposed the pubic hair to the back. We can assume that it was her disappointment in the smallness of her clitoris that made a decisive contribution to this movement in drive regression. This was made quite explicit by Susan, when she said that "exploring the opening in front only hurts and it is too small anyway."

Such a remark was in contrast, at the time of anal masturbation, to her saying that the difference between a girl and boy is the buttocks: "the boy's behind is smaller than the girl's." At last, she had found a point of comparative superiority. Of course, her stools had been larger than those of the brother, when he was little and she was three years old. In penetrating the anus with her finger she could feel a solid mass, especially when she was constipated. This contrasted sharply with the tactile softness in clitoral masturbation, a sensation that had enticed her into frantically and angrily "pulling it out"; this had left her physically sore and emotionally frightened.

The attraction of boys to girls, she now thought, was exclusively lodged in their interest in seeing the girl's behind. When she drew the picture of a boy in the nude (this was at the time of anatomical exploration and enlightenment), she drew him first from the back. It hardly needs mentioning that, from this view, the difference between boy and girl is negligible; in addition, this region is usually inaccessible to direct observation for both sexes.

Anal masturbation, like all her indulgences in "dirty" pursuits, filled Susan with guilt and fear of punishment. She showed the therapist the middle finger of her right hand, pointing to a wart that had grown on it. In her effort to be prepared for punishment in the form of loss of limb (castration), she had trained her left hand in writing and in the performance of activities she normally executed with her right hand. Since Susan was left-handed, these security measures made no sense beyond the fact that they offered a general reassurance that ambidexterity renders the loss of the fingers of one hand less debilitating.

It had become apparent, during the course of body exploration, that Susan's knowledge of female anatomy was utterly confused. In contrast to her intelligence and to the competence in school that she had acquired by the age of twelve, her grasp of human anatomy and physiology was childish and primitive. Sphincter control, which had been established early and precipitately, had permitted only a shallow sensory acquaintance with the eliminatory body orifices. The training period had left an undue amount of aggression attached to these body zones. Under these conditions, the ego had never extended its autonomy over body functions; instead, control was achieved and maintained by way of fear and guilt. No wonder these controls broke down under the impact of trauma: wetting at two (precipitating event unknown), and then, lastingly, at five, with episodic token soiling in school.

Among the many misconceptions of anatomy, there remained Susan's firm belief that a connection, a "kind of bridge" exists between the rear (anus-rectum) and the front (vulva-clitoris). This misconception referred to the cloacal orifice, in which we recognize the survival of the infantile, universal sexual theory of the female child. Perhaps it was the amalgamation of her urinary symptom with anal elements that rendered it so stubborn and re-sistive to treatment. At any rate, enuresis was finally given up, after masturbation had been pried loose from its anal fixation. Approaching menarche no doubt helped this trend along. Clinical observation, however, gave ample evidence of the influence exerted on symptom resolution by cathectic shifts, by psychosexual progres-sion and, by ego autonomy on symptom resolution. The investment of drive energy in object libido and of neu-tralized drive energy into ego development and ego synthesis, paralleled the decline of compulsive mastur-bation, lying, token soiling and enuresis. Their interre-lationship will be taken up separately, when the process of symptom resolution is discussed.

CHAPTER 7

ENTRY INTO ADOLESCENCE

Treatment while maturation and development are in the formative stages always faces the therapist with a need to make a differential assessment of behavior, fantasy, anxiety and defense. Each phase, along the sequential pattern of the unfolding personality, contains critical and typical drive propensities, anxieties and ego accommodations that often cannot be readily distinguished from pathological formations. This fact is most convincingly demonstrated during adolescence, when seemingly pathognomic conditions prove to be transient states, accompanying psychic restructuring. Having de-

scribed elsewhere the vicissitudes of drive and ego during
the five phases of adolescence (Blos, 1962), I shall here
only re-emphasize this fact, before relating it to Susan's
case.

We are well aware of regression as typical of preadolescence. We must now ask: what determines the
difference between phase-specific and pathognomic regression? In assessing phase-adequacy in preadolescence,
one would first have to review the preceding phase of
latency. In approaching this assessment one would have
to keep certain developmental landmarks in mind. An
attempt to enumerate latency achievements turns our
attention, first and foremost, to ego expansion and to
secondary ego autonomy. Both take their start in and
proceed by way of identificatory processes, which replace
earlier object dependencies. Conversely, self-esteem regulation acquires greater independence of environmental
controls. Social adaptation and social anxiety become
more and more noticeable during this time, when the
child is expanding his mastery over the self and the
object world. Skill and competence, perseverance and
ambition become systematically articulated into normative activities taken up through games, school, hobbies
and chores. It is only if these characteristics of the
latency period are recognizable, that we can expect a
progression to the phase of preadolescence to be feasible.

Pre- and early puberty, by their very nature, affect the
balance between drive and ego. Should ego expansion, ego
resourcefulness and ego autonomy—in short, ego style
and structure—be deficient, unstable and uneven, then
the drive pressure of puberty will override the assertions
of the feeble ego. As a result, the simple and unelaborated
reactivation of infantile drive constellations (infantile
sexuality) becomes manifest. Nothing new or distinctly
adolescent can be discerned in the clinical picture. In
preadolescent children with deficient latency development, we detect enclaves of remarkable childishness, in

the form of persistent dependency needs and intolerance of tension. Social incompetence is frequently screened off by imitative behavior and affectations. Private rituals take form within the sanctuary of the family.

One gets the impression of a lop-sided development, or a developmental lag. This lag becomes more noticeable with the arrival of puberty, when the intensification of prelatency positions throws the immaturity of the child into bold relief. Suddenly, the child's immediate environment expresses alarm, because behavior and attitudes that were once restricted to the family now become transferred to the wider social scene—that is, they become exposed to the public eye. What we observe under such circumstances cannot be regarded as due to regression, however, because no decisive latency advances had succeeded in establishing that forward position from which a retreat can originate.

A disruption of, or a break in each child's latency achievement appears normally with the onset of puberty —that is, at prepuberty. Deterioration of manners, of conformity, of concentration and of cooperation are some of the outstanding signs of preadolescent change. Whenever adequate ego growth has indeed taken place during the latency period, a genuine regression can be observed in preadolescence. Drive regression to pregenitality remains the "great secret" that girls at this stage whisper and giggle about. Everybody who is at all acquainted with the content of these "secrets" is well aware that they pertain to the anal and phallic phases, and find expression in terms of component instincts.

The ego's participation in the regressive movement can be recognized in the revival of such primitive defenses as magical thinking, projection and denial, as well as in the appearance of all kinds of obsessive-compulsive traits, habits and thoughts. Avoidance, observances and rituals are characteristic of preadolescence. Ego regression becomes manifest in the form of early ego attitudes and interests—as, for example, in the exaggerated exercise of control over, or dependency on, the environment. Along with the defensive aspects, the adaptive side of ego repression deserves explicit acknowledgment, since it frequently tends to be ignored by the clinician (Blos, 1967).

It remains the hallmark of preadolescent regression that the ego retains its resiliency. This enables it to revert to its advanced post-latency position in emergency, thus reestablishing with ease its mastery and autonomy. Drive and ego regression to pregenital and preoedipal stages of development constitute the psychological characteristics of young adolescents. They must take this course, before a forward thrust toward genitality can be made, during the phase of adolescence proper.

Pathognomic preadolescent regression implies a return to early fixation points—namely, to positions in drive and ego development that had never been successfully relinquished. If one looks closely enough at such cases, one comes to realize that the fixations in question never ceased to assert themselves all through the latency period—in habit or behavior disorders; in obsessive or compulsive symptoms; in somatic dysfunction; in intellectual inhibitions, or social inadequacies. Often enough, the latency child has side-stepped, without that fact being noticed, the tasks of this period; these omissions become apparent only later. The role of the latency period in the scheme of progressive development—namely, as a precondition for entrance into adolescence—has become evident. Only if the essential attainments of the latency period have been secured can one predict, with a fair degree of certainty, that the initial stage of adolescent development will pursue its own specific drive, ego and superego modifications, without undue impediments.

When Susan entered treatment, there was no doubt that her latency development was hampered by drive fixations at the anal level. Her learning performance was unstable to the point of being completely unreliable. She could forget the spelling of the simplest words; the logical comprehension of facts became fragmented, as soon as infantile or magical thinking interfered; perfection and accuracy had assumed a compulsive quality, eliminating judgment and choice. The course of Susan's treatment made it abundantly clear that her ego functions were burdened with restorative and restitutive concerns, whenever her self-image became debased by a sense of incompleteness or badness.

At such times, she would keep the blackboard in school scrubbed and washed, and would express her contempt of the other children, who cared little for cleanliness and order. She wished for not only one but twenty blackboards to wipe clean, but at the same time she was afraid of writing a word on it that she might misspell. This secret preoccupation with "messing and cleaning" kept her estranged from other children, leaving her rather isolated and without any real friends.

She performed best in "Art"; here she showed imagination and her teachers commented favorably on her unusual "creativity." Susan had an excellent command of words; she was, indeed, articulate beyond her age. This faculty, however, faded away at unexpected moments in therapy; then she would reach for paper, pencil and paint to convey, pictorially, what she was unable to express in words. This was the way in which her anatomical drawings originated. Only when the fantasies and affects that were associated with her drawings and stories came to light, through exploration and interpretation, was recourse to direct and sustained verbalization restored. Her fear of the mortification that would result from the children finding out about the lies she had told them made school a time of precarious guardedness and apprehension; this affected, adversely, her concentration and learning.

Ego functions had remained intricately enmeshed

with drive derivatives. Consequently, her defensive resources were continuously taxed by the effort to present
an adequate appearance in public. It made daily life an
ordeal from which, she hoped, therapy would deliver her.
She valiantly allied herself with the aim of therapy and
rarely faltered in this sustained endeavor. She revealed
in therapy her capacity for a trusting relationship. Her
push toward progressive development proved stronger
than any regressive pull or regressive settlement of her
disturbance.

The first achievement in therapy was a belated consolidation of the latency period, through the liberation of
some ego functions from infantile drive fixations, thereby
granting them autonomous status. Ego autonomy followed in the wake of defense interpretations and of the
gradual uncovering of her "secret life." This change went
parallel with drive regression, which was permitted in
the therapeutic situation, and with the recovery of affects,
anxieties and historical realities that were essentially
related to the mysterious separation from the mother.
The very process of "naming" the forgotten afforded it
verbal representation and thus made it accessible to the
ego. This forward step subjected the traumatic experience to introspection and to thought processes—both of
which drew on suppressed memories in the realm of ego
synthesis—i.e., ego integration. One might say that, in
the process of "naming" what the child feels, fantasizes
or remembers, the realm of the ego is extended into an
area of the mental life that, till then, had existed only
in terms of symptoms, somatization, body image, fantasies, affective states, moods and idiosyncratic symbolism.

In order to summarize and clarify what has been
said so far, a tabulation is now introduced. The symptoms
had been traced and retraced through these seven categories many times during the course of therapy.

1. Symptoms—Enuresis, compulsive masturbation,
learning inhibition, lying.

2. Somatization—Headaches, stomach aches, tired-ness, weak knees.

3. Body image—In Susan's words: "All my parts are wrongly put together."

4. Fantasies—The creation of a make-believe world.

5. Affective states—Envy, anger, rage, followed by anxiety and guilt.

6. Moods—Elated and dysphoric states.

7. Symbolism— The "horse"; the "magic wand"; the "rushing water"; the "little red wagon."

It was the task of therapy to identify these various psychological items, and to raise them to the level of verbalization and thought, before their interrelatedness could be experienced by the child. Then, and only then, could the synthesizing function of the ego encompass the various strands of insight and effect their integration. This process, while repeated many times, was never the same. As we well know, the therapeutic work, which is aimed at the renunciation of primitive drive gratification, is involuntarily resisted by the patient, despite his conscious cooperation and the wish to get well. We are never surprised by the fact that defenses have, suddenly and repeatedly, solidified or shifted during the joint endeavor in therapy. The case of Susan offered a kaleidoscopic array of material, inviting the therapist to view the neurotic conflict, or part aspects of it, from constantly new angles. In the "working through" phase of therapy, this repetitiousness tends to provide the greatest therapeutic leverage.*

A significant observation could be made in Susan's material, after the envy of the brother, the ambivalence toward the mother and the anal fixation had been investigated and traced back to their various "hiding places." Susan now began to exhibit a feminine interest in her looks and her attractiveness (age 12). Her preoccupation with attaining phallic completeness—or, at a

* (See "Susan," Chapter 9).

different level, her striving to recapture her mother's undivided love as a prerequisite for a sense of wholeness —became replaced by a preoccupation with feminine beauty. In this we see the belated identification with the mother. Instead of Susan's possessing her bodily, a likeness to her had now become sufficient. The lipstick she bought secretly became an act of rivalry with the mother, and hinted at an oedipal involvement.

She now wished that her father would not find out that she had grown axillary hair and a "slight fuzz in front" (age 12). This negative statement was, in fact, a conflictual pronouncement. Transiently, the father was playing a collusionary role in her self-concious modesty, by inspecting her bed late at night in order to see whether she was wet. Susan was at that time sleeping in the nude, because she was now using her pajamas instead of the pillow, to put between her legs. She had outgrown the teddy bear. The father had always taken an active interest in Susan's problems and was eager to help her; but when the father's nightly inspections came to the attention of the therapist, it was explained to Susan that she was now too old for her father to watch over her bedwetting. She agreed and the matter was thereupon discussed with the father. He was amenable to the suggestion that he give up inspecting her bed.

Slowly, Susan began to look at herself as a girl. She shared feminine delight in the beautification of her body, not just in neatness and decorum; lipstick and brassiere became her proud possessions. Now her interest in correct anatomy and in the functioning of the female genital came to the fore. She hoped to menstruate at 13, because that was the age her mother had started. At this time —age 12—Susan embarked at home on a project of dividing the room she was sharing with her brother. The drawing of floor plans and measurements filled the sessions. A room divider, in the form of a curtain, was to be put up; her side was to be decorated as a girl's room, while the other side would remain a boy's "messy" habitat. In dividing the room she allotted to the brother the larger portion, because "boys have to move around more than girls do."

The arrangement of the room reflected a change in body image or, to put it the other way round, the spatial and esthetic organization of her room was possible only after her body image had undergone transformation. Instead of keeping her pajamas or her pillow between her legs at night, Susan was now using the pillow to hug it. Her fantasies ran the gamut from hugging mother or hugging a baby, to being herself a boy hugging the mother, or being a girl hugging a boy. In the total configuration of her development, this fantasy game can be termed "typically preadolescent."

She had also acquired a girl friend with whom she talked about love in the cowboy country, or else for short interludes she and her friend were both boys. Her fantasies could now be called romantic rather than infantile. At a party with boys and girls, Susan organized such exciting games as "spin the bottle" or "being in heaven" (kissing); these games lasted just a few minutes, otherwise, she said, they would become "boring." This self-protection against overexcitation represented a newly acquired capacity, which stood in sharp contrast to the secret instinctual gratification of the preceding years and the total drive inhibition in social situations.

It is hardly possible to make an assessment of Susan's developmental status as being either pathological or phase-specific, without reviewing the symptoms that had brought her into therapy. Bedwetting had ceased around the turn from 12 to 13; it did not recur during an illness that kept her in bed for a short time. Previously, illness had always aggravated the bedwetting. Now she had interests that kept her busy during the enforced bedrest. The compulsive quality of her genital masturbation had lessened considerably, and anal masturbation had ceased to play any role within the scope of the autoerotism that normally accompanies the entry into adolescence. She had progressed from the cloacal to the human—i.e., female—conception of her genitalia. The token soiling had not occurred for a long time; in fact, it had been the first symptom to disappear. This took place rather early in treatment, after anal aggression was openly directed against the therapist.

The social inadequacy; the sense of being different from other children; the unstable learning process—none of these deficiencies was any longer in evidence. They had become replaced, in equal measure, by social, personal, and academic strivings. These ambitions led to frustrations and disappointments, whenever her means and resources proved to be incompatible with her aspirations; yet she persevered. She joined the Scouts and became an active and enthusiastic member. She looked for adults, outside the confines of the family, to be her models and guides, while gradually relinquishing her infantile dependency on mother and therapist.

CHAPTER 8

THE MUTUAL INFLUENCE OF
MATURATION AND DEVELOPMENT ON
TRANSFERENCE AND RESISTANCE

Transference develops only if certain conditions permit and favor its formation. The patient has to assign to the therapist the place of a meaningful person in his emotional life, and to invest the new relationship, illusory as it is, in part, with sufficient libido and aggression to be able to experience, in relation to the therapist, those critical emotional constellations of his past that continue to exist as virulent, pathogenetic agents in his mental life. Not only must the therapist become the focus of emotional interest; an urgent need must also exist in the patient, compelling him to involve the therapist in his drive and ego activities, even if only in his imagination.

The pattern and sequence of transference reactions eventually reveal the hidden meaning of symptoms. Through repetitious transference manifestations, linked with memories, fantasies and associative thoughts, the life history of the patient gains in clarity, and the critical periods of development become illuminated; then the reconstruction of the deviant course of development can be undertaken. Transference manifestations reflect a multitude of crucial life experiences; they are of uncertain therapeutic value—except as transient cathartic relief —unless they become the bridge to remembering and to verbal expression and thereby make possible the inference of a personal meaning. Recall and verbalization elevate the pathogenetic experience and its sequelae onto the level of the ego, rendering pathogenesis and symptom accessible to investigation and evaluation.

Transference phenomena, in Susan's case, were apparent throughout the clinical material; the reader has no doubt noticed them. If we take a discriminating look at these phenomena, they are found to reveal characteristics that distinguish them from the transference in child analysis. The frequency of sessions in child analysis (five times weekly) allows a continuity of reliving critical and unintegrated experiences, without granting the defenses any opportunity to consolidate their opposition to the exposure of the pathogenetic background; the weekly, or semi-weekly, intervals between sessions in child psychotherapy, by contrast, do grant defensive operations the opportunity to perform their function. To the extent to which the psychopathology of the child has remained an open system, to that same extent psychotherapy serves as an effective therapeutic tool. Child neurosis, however, being a closed system, requires intervention by child analysis, because the relentless temporal continuity of the analytic process tends to draw into its realm the total scope of pathogenesis.

Transference reactions in psychotherapy are, so to speak, shortlived; they bear the character and purpose of a direct communication. They are statements that the child therapist links up with relevant and often already known life-history material, in order to make them available to the ego in a verbalized, causal and temporal form. It was the "what," the "why" and the "where" that helped Susan to organize her life experiences. This in itself had an integrative and adaptive effect, elevating her psychic functioning onto a higher level. This was, no doubt, made possible by the fact that she related with such eager passion, both positive and negative, to the therapist and rather rapidly established a working alliance of unshakeable endurance.

Without the therapist's tactful participation in this process, transference would hardly have developed with such articulate productivity and therapeutic fruitfulness. The "split-off" psychic content and related affects were, descriptively although not dynamically, unconscious. That is to say, both were inaccessible to the ego and, because of Susan's state of isolation, they remained beyond the child's capacity to deal with them integratively. Painful and disorganizing feelings stood in the way. Here, psychotherapy helped to "put all parts together correctly"— to make use of Susan's comment about her body parts, as being "all put together the wrong way."

The essential difference between transference in child psychotherapy and in child analysis now becomes clear. In child analysis, the transference is the therapeutic instrument that brings unconscious psychic content to the light of day or, in other words, brings it within the realm of the ego. This process requires a sustained transference relationship, such as is facilitated by the frequency of sessions. Sessions at an interval of one week, as in Susan's therapy, preclude sustained transference relationship from developing; this is, as we know, indispensable for the recovery of unconscious pathogenetic psychic content.

There is no doubt that, in Susan's therapy, certain pathological nuclei were not dealt with; on the other hand, her emotional advances and the expansion of her ego resources augured well for a less conflicted and less anxiety-ridden psychic life. In other words, a condition was established for integrative processes to take over. Those pathological nuclei that had been left untouched and dormant now became outweighed, through the intervention of psychotherapy, by the ascendancy of autonomous ego functions. When the debilitating defenses slowly became expendable, psychic energy was made available for the promotion of integrative processes.

During childhood (up to the termination of adolescence), there are inherent limitations on transference, because the child-parent relationship is still in full force. Only that aspect of this relationship finds expression in the transference that is internalized, and has ceased to be an active ingredient of an ongoing relationship to parents or siblings. Phase-specific regression, which sets in at preadolescence, buoys up seemingly abandoned infantile object relations in order to facilitate emotional disengagement from them and to bring about the transformation onto the level of adolescence. Manifestations related to this process cannot be called genuine transference reactions; yet they disclose the distorted infantile connotations that have remained attached to primary object ties, and which threaten to become passed on to the extrafamilial relationships of the adult.

The initial stage of adolescence is a favorable period for a therapeutic correction, because at that period development assists the endeavor. On the other hand, the anxiety that is engendered by the regressive pull tends to raise resistance to a level at which therapeutic work has to be brought to a halt. It has been my experience that it is knowledge of the particular psychic constellation of preadolescence that endows the therapist with that therapeutic tact that might forestall therapeutic discouragement and failure. This is, of course, not always feasible. Transference reactions must be related solely to the therapist and the therapeutic situation; otherwise they do not deserve this designation. It is gratuitous to call any behavior in relation to the therapist "transference reaction" when it is, in fact, nothing but the habitual behavior of the child, displayed everywhere and toward everybody.

It has long been recognized that there are certain emotional constellations that work against the establishment of the transference. The two classical ones—mourning and being in love—obviously leave no psychic energy available to sustain an active interest in the outside world, including the therapist and the therapeutic situation. In adolescence, there exists a typical psychological condition that also works against the formation of transference; it is that condition that now deserves our attention.

Emotional dependencies, in their various forms, are usually less ego-dystonic in childhood than they are in adolescence. We know that dependency needs become regressively re-activated at this stage. Regression to infantile states, both drive and ego regression, is resisted and defended against by the adolescent; in therapy, this appears as transference resistance. This form of resistance becomes a subtle technical problem, because the therapist has to distinguish between the resistance that is essentially phase-adequate and one that aims, often under the guise of sham maturity, at the preservation of a pathological condition.

Despite the fact that the phase-specific transference resistance impedes and perhaps even aborts therapy, however, we cannot ignore its adaptive implications. The adolescent aims at the attainment of ego control over the regressive pull. The resistance is in part a distancing device, which dilutes the intensity of infantile object involvement. The implicit request that is made by the therapist through confrontation, explanation and interpretation—namely, that the young adolescent relinquish the need for or fear of emotional distance—only serves to intensify the defensive maneuver. Whenever the adolescent is permitted to rally his forces first—in other words, to maintain the so-called transference resistance unchallenged—he will, at a time of his choosing, reveal the fear of his helplessness and dependency needs. As one adolescent put it: "Now that I have won a point, I'm willing to listen to what *you* have to say." It remains a matter of timing when, as well as of rationing how much or how little the therapist intervenes, to convey what he, at least, has known and understood for a long time.

It lies in the nature of development that each stage contains its preferential or typical defenses. Each stage establishes the repression of "outgrown" drive gratifications, as well as ego adaptations, until the former have faded away or have been consumed by their transformations. This, however, is not always the case. Whenever pathological components of development are swept away in the flood of normal repression (for example, repression of oedipal conflicts upon entry into the latency period), they reappear, in some form, during the recapitulation process of adolescence. At such times, the therapist relies on the therapeutic alliance to help the child recognize, in these resurrected remnants of past positions, anachronistic formations that tend to abort progressive development. By this very special kind of partnership in the therapeutic endeavor, the patient—child or adolescent—experiences the therapist's concern over the "illness" as reflecting, correctly, his own ego interest or his striving toward health and maturity.

This aspect of therapy was convincingly demonstrated in Susan's case. While she said, on occasion, that she would quit therapy, she never carried this threat into action. It was her way of testing the therapist, of determining how well she understood the resistance as the result of anxiety, in relation to Susan's overwhelming dependency needs and ambivalent closeness. Both of these had already reached a critical point at the time when Susan's regression to anal or phallic drive propensities threatened to force their way into the therapeutic situation. I remind the reader here of her "messing" and "fuck" periods. The threat to leave therapy changed into Susan's establishing—at least temporarily—an emotional distance toward the therapist and, concomitantly toward her own conflicts. By this time, the ego had acquired more effective controls: Susan could now stabilize the therapeutic alliance by the timing of her verbalization, as well as by introducing formal elements of expression, whether these be metaphor or symbol. In this way, her inner life gradually became subject to critical scrutiny and insight, within tolerable limits of anxiety and guilt. A degree of independence was thus maintained, while at the same time the therapist's "helping hand"—i.e., understanding —conveyed through comments and interpretations, could be acknowledged and accepted.

I will now draw a longitudinal profile of transference and resistance in the endeavor to highlight those shifting patterns that are due rather to developmental changes than to the dynamic fluctuations within the therapeutic relationship and its defenses. Of course, both components must be included in the profile, since both carry the therapeutic process forward. It is their combined work that permits newly reached developmental stages to consolidate in a phase-specific organization. However, before superimposing such a profile on the case of Susan, a few theoretical considerations have to be mentioned.

Whenever a new level of personality integration has been reached, remnants of the original pathology reappear; in therapy these remnants are, then, scrutinized anew from an advanced vantage point. Residues of conflict and fixations are thus subjected to repeated investigation—a process that is conceptualized as "working through." Parenthetically and speculatively, one might say that it is not until development has ceased, and inner as well as outer conditions have been stabilized, that one can say with certitude that the pathogenetic nucleus has lost its valence—in other words, has ceased to exist. It is the unattainability of this condition in human life that speaks for the relativity of the therapeutic accomplishment.

Considerations such as these are of far more practical importance than may appear at first glance. This becomes particularly evident when we set out to evaluate the results of treatment, as it is terminated within an ongoing process of development, such as childhood or adolescence. The frequent need for the resumption of treatment at a later age—whether this be adolescence, early adulthood, or parenthood—is a well-known clinical fact. I have found, however, that a positive therapeutic experience in childhood or in adolescence, even if it is fragmentary or incomplete, nevertheless remains an enduring asset. From the many cases I have followed, I look at this asset as the reliable foundation on which therapeutic work can be undertaken anew, with a sense of assurance and confidence.

The question has often been asked whether the sex of the therapist is of crucial importance in the development of transference and resistance. From my experience, the question is to be answered in the negative—with one notable exception. I have found that treatment of the young adolescent girl is beset with difficulties if the treatment is conducted by a man. The erotic, and often crudely sexual stimulation that the girl experiences during the session burdens the treatment situation with emotions that lead either to extreme forms of resistance, to perfunctory cooperation, or to acting out. None of these complications yields easily to technical maneuvers that lie within one's reach; the transfer of such cases to a woman therapist remains the only answer.

My own treatment experiences with the young adolescent girl have convinced me that her treatment had better be placed in the hands of a woman, and I have adhered to this precept for many years. As one consequence, I was deprived, in my adolescent research, of a segment that was in need of study. I counteracted this handicap, imposed on me by my sex, through consultations with experienced women child analysts, and through supervision of women child analysts and child therapists. Such was the case with Susan. The sexual material in this case, so indispensable for an understanding of the symptoms, would never have flowed with the same ease and productivity, had she been treated by a man.

The decision to assign Susan to a woman therapist was based on the assumption that her treatment would carry over into her adolescence. This case was chosen as an opportune one for the investigation of the transition from latency into adolescence, as exemplified by one particular girl. It was expected that the structural and developmental concepts I had formulated with regard to female preadolescence and early adolescence would find a valid testing ground in the clinical situation. Furthermore, the therapeutic process and clinical data in general constitute the royal road to the exposition and verification of theory (Blos, 1962).

If we contemplate the profile of Susan's transference reactions over the years of treatment, there emerges a sequential pattern that will now be traced. Initially, she related to the therapist in well-tested social forms, mobilizing the "security measures" of compliance, friendliness and obedience. She was expected to talk, and so she talked. In order to elicit the therapist's interest in her, she "performed": she painted, recited poetry and spelled words. She threw away those paintings that were "not good", thus not only professing the high standards by which she lived, but also demonstrating her wish to be considered perfect. If she encountered the slightest difficulty in any performance, such as fitting plastic blocks together, she would drop that activity under some clever pretext. She would ask the therapist for suggestions and advice, knowing well that adults like children who appreciate their knowledge of "everything." She carried this "gimmick" to the point of being expressly concerned about the therapist and about what she might wish to do herself and then do with her.

These expedient efforts to make herself appreciated, accepted and loved by the therapist, hardly veiled Susan's aggressive dependency. In fact, this trend favored the formation of a therapeutic relationship that was possessive, demanding, controlling and clinging—in short, ambivalent in nature. The ambivalence conflict was already apparent during the second session, when she asked: "How many years can I come?" Embedded in this simple question are two opposing affects—rejection and dependency. One pertains to her disappointment in the slowness with which urgently needed help was forthcoming ("If that's the best you care to do, I'd better leave you"); the other was a pleading hope not to be found unworthy and dispensable ("I wish you would never leave and I could stay with you forever"). The first session, she maintained, had not "helped much." She had hoped to be relieved of her frightening dreams, without having to talk about them. When she realized that nothing had happened, she blamed the therapist who had not bothered to make her feel better. Instead of retreating from therapy, however, she would now tell the therapist her bad dreams.

First gingerly and then brazenly, Susan stopped being the big girl who had asked questions or given answers in a grown-up fashion, and who had looked with disdain at the office toys as childish things. She now complained, during a furtive attempt at doll house play, that none of her so-called girl friends ever let her be the mother when they played family. She expected restitution from the therapist for these rejections and disappointments. She had observed that a little boy had his session after her, and mounting jealousy made her finally demand some explanation of why she could not have a session that lasted the whole afternoon. When this wish was not granted, she wanted certain play materials restricted to her exclusive use; if this could not be done, then at least the therapist should give her a present (paintbrush, crayons). She wanted concrete proof of love, not words; she wanted relief from anxiety, without any intrusion into her fantasy life; she wanted indemnity and restitution in tangible form.

She perceived the therapist as the omniscient and omnipotent helper and soother who, like any good mother, can bestow a state of bliss and a sense of completeness on the child; the therapist, having been cast in this role, was treated by Susan accordingly. Susan asserted that telling her dreams to the therapist did not help, and added that "thinking" about them gave her a headache. She made it clear that she had kept content isolated from affect, thus obstructing anew the work of treatment and contriving another disappointment in the therapist. Her consuming desire for tangible presents worked against the exploration of her fantasy life; this was not measurably changed until the subject of her wishes and her claims became known to both patient and therapist.

Before this occurred, however, a veritable storm of frustration and disappointment broke loose. There was a regressive eruption of infantile rage and instinctual expressions, which had been defended against until then by reaction formation, denial, repression, projection, and somatization. Foremost among these were the manifestations of anal aggression and anal retaliatory attacks in response to the therapist's refusal to make restitution for the deprivations she had imposed—such as "no presents, no favoritism." The transference here reflects the incomplete integration of bowel training; it carries the repressed affects of the anal phase to the surface. Premature bowel training effected a closure of the anal phase, with only incomplete and unstable autonomy of the anal sphincter. In other words, the anal stage was not left behind as a way-station along the path of psycho-sexual progression, but was instead hurriedly abandoned, as if by someone in flight. Libido and aggression therefore remained attached to this erogenous zone, thus crystallizing a fixation point.

Regression to this stage first became evident in the expression of traits, attitudes and characteristics that are representative of the anal modality. In the treatment sessions, Susan became provocative, obstinate, messy, procrastinating, ambivalent. The therapist was referred to as a "skunk" (the "bad" mother of the anal period). This attitude would rapidly shift toward love and dependency, these latter being evoked by the deterrents of fright and terror, lest she destroy the object she had become dependent on. Such was the magnitude of her fear that she suppressed her hostile impulses and controlled her provocative behavior, at the price of "feeling tired and weak." She grew quiet, pale, unhappy, depressed; yet again and again she escaped from sinking into this morass by projecting magic powers onto the therapist. In an anxious voice she said, pleadingly; "Do not turn me into a boy"; with this sentence, her boy complex was clearly stated.

Being a boy and possessing magical and controlling powers were one and the same thing for Susan. As it turns out, the problem is never as simple as it is stated to be by the girl. One customarily relegates the boy complex of the girl to the psychoanalytic concept of "penis envy"; in so doing one shuts the door to its more profound and lasting origins, which are to be found in the sense of body incompleteness. Susan demonstrated this in depth. An adolescent patient of mine, who was also possessed by an all-consuming boy complex, once stated her problem in this way: "No, I do not want to have a penis; but I don't want anybody else to have one." In the last analysis, it was Susan's exclusive possession of the mother that had persisted unchecked and that eventually precluded her normal passage through the phase of preadolescence.

Susan's boy complex could not be fully comprehended so long as she concealed the issue by reverting to obsessive-compulsive defenses that were ritualistic and magical in nature. Avoidances (not to step on black squares, not to use paints, not to say a dirty word) and compulsions (endless washing of the blackboard, floor and walls in the office) were designed to avert the dangers of punishment or of loss of love. At this time, when her school work was occupying her mind, she would use the session to train her left hand in writing.* This, it was learned later, represented a security measure against masturbation guilt and castration fear. Her defensive efforts culminated in her renunciation of therapy. One day, in a mood of ponderous deliberation she poured all the various paints into one jar, thus depriving others of their use ("No one else can use them now"), and declared that she would not return; she added: "Then, the man before me and the boy after me can have more time." This altruistic surrender repeated Susan's ultimate means of holding in check her retaliatory aggression, and securing the continued love and protection of the preoedipal mother, now personified in the therapist.

Certain historical facts are relevant to the above discussion. The birth of the brother must have aroused inordinate jealousy in a child whose precocious ego de-

* She was left handed but had been trained in school to write with her right hand. Her learning and memory patterns, once changed by therapy, affirmed our first impression that her deficiencies in these areas were not due to "mixed dominance."

velopment had rendered her emotionally over-sensitive to a baby's privileges. The brother's birth coincided with the lingering and uncertain settlement of her anal phase requirements, when she was 3.2 years old. Pregnancy and the expectation of a baby had, of course, started earlier, when she was about two and a half. The distinction between the mother of infancy (preoedipal) and of early childhood (oedipal) on the one hand, and on the other the present mother in the life of child or adolescent, needs to be emphasized here; what the transference brings to light is those stages of object relations that can claim actuality only in relation to the past. The re-experiencing of these infantile states is an essential experience in therapy, because without it the forward movement of stagnant portions of libido and aggression cannot be brought about.

The particular way in which drive fixations influence ego functions can be observed in Susan's fixation on the anal phase, on the cloacal body image and on the sense of physical incompleteness. These conditions became, in time, the anachronistic actualities to which the ego had to accommodate itself. They were assembled in the self-representation, which in turn affected adversely the child's ego functions. Susan displayed this correlation in her poor grasp of the physical world, her reading and spelling difficulty, her arithmetic incompetence and her faulty reality-testing. These defects were never directly made the object of treatment, nor was there any attempt to relieve them by tutorial teaching. They were understood as symptomatic and, therefore, not remediable by education.

In a similar vein of reasoning, Susan's mother was never asked to make up for Susan's deprivations in the past. No request was ever made that the mother attempt to gratify the child's regressive needs, by becoming, in actuality, the preoedipal mother. A greater measure of tolerance in relation to the symptomatic manifestations of regression—such as messing, lying or daring (the purchase of a lipstick)—were, however, elicited from her. This was done without difficulty, since the mother well understood the nature of treatment and, as a result of her own illness, had acquired a sympathetic attitude toward the trials and tribulations of therapy. This attitude enabled her to support the treatment of her daughter with extraordinary forbearance.

Resistances such as those described above developed in the wake of drive regression and within the framework of the transference. The strength and scope of the resistance always attest to the magnitude of the imaginary dangers that lie embedded in the therapeutic situation. The danger in Susan's case can be understood as a regressive pull that would ultimately lead to engulfment by the archaic mother. A potential merger of this kind arouses a feeling of panic via the warning signal of anxiety. Powerful defenses are mobilized that become apparent in the transference resistance. In essence, the danger situation of merger is that of eating the love object or of being eaten by it. On one occasion of such imminent danger, Susan had a nightmare in which there appeared a shark with sharp teeth. Describing that dangerous animal, she said: "The shark was the size of this room." The dangers of oral impulses and of their ambivalence was thus revealed: to incorporate or to be incorporated had once been the alternative. Susan never yielded to the regressive pull by total surrender to either one of these primordial states.

Fear of the therapist subsided when Susan moved forward to the phallic phase, abandoning the wish to find restitution, regressively, in the possession of the mother. We can, however, detect in Susan's conflict in the phallic phase a persistent oral component that had undergone transformation. What appeared as a phallic modality could be traced to earlier drive constellations, such as the unrivaled possession of the mother as the absolute attainment of the sense of completeness. This was expressed, on the phallic level, in the wish and search for the penis, or in the undoing of castration or loss.

It is of interest to note that the critical resurgence of oral wishes and conflicts was postponed until a personality integration had been established that was solid enough to assure a dependable protection against regressive surrender and merger. The forward movement to the phallic phase has been described earlier in this history; I need only indicate here that masturbation and the wish for a penis was conveyed to the therapist in all the details of practice, fantasies and sensations, but only after a prolonged resistance, which turned out to be Susan's preparation for her daring, regressive self-revelation. She plunged into the therapeutic process with the so-called "fuck" period, during which the full scope of her sexual confusion, preoccupation and curiosity became known. When this period reached the point of conflictual anxiety, a new wave of repression fell over her instinctual life.

What followed was another period of vigorous ego expansion. The ego's increasing independence of instinctual drives (secondary ego autonomy) became apparent in relation to the therapist, to work and school, to her hobbies, interests, social activities and peer relations. This change was so noticeable that people in Susan's environ- ment commented on it. Tension tolerance, the acceptance of delay and frustration, ushered in a state of increased control and mastery, accompanied by a heightened emotional distance from the therapist. Prelatency object ties had yielded to identification. Susan was now easier to live with, she was managing more competently the requirements of home, school and social intercourse.

In spite of these improvements, the symptoms of enuresis and lying were still present after three years of treatment. They were tolerated by Susan with an absent- minded equanimity. The painful and disturbing night- mares had vanished, having, so to speak, lost their raison d'être, after the aggressive impulses, primitive and violent, had become conscious by being traced through the vicissitudes of her object relations. The belated consolidation of the latency period was recognizable in her personality when she was 10 and 11 years old. With the visible ascendancy of ego interests, Susan would now engage in doing arithmetic with the therapist. The sexual preoccupations and regressive drive expressions that had both been so prominent in her action, play, fantasy, stories and dreams had receded into the background.

One can justifiably pose the question of whether the symptomatic improvement was due entirely to a wave of pathognomic repression or also contained, above and beyond this, an adaptive aspect that was commensurate with developmental progression and typical of the latency period. A wave of repression is, after all, the normal accompaniment of the latency period, especially at its onset. Both these aspects, the defensive and the adaptive, are of course present in Susan's case. The structural changes that are implicit in latency development enabled Susan, not only to endure but to deal, on a higher level of mental functioning, with the conflictual anxiety that had given rise to her symptoms. Conflict resolutions she was now capable of would have remained out of her reach, if her emotional, infantile strivings had continued to survive in full force behind massive defenses, or if these defenses had crumbled and opened the regressive path to the symbiotic stage of object relations.

We can rightly say that Susan's symptoms protected her against total regression. It was now a matter of time until her ego expansion would eventually enable her to surrender her symptoms. The consolidation of the latency period had to be encouraged, or rather not to be opposed, or interfered with by untimely—i.e., premature—drive interpretations, or by gentle proddings to disclose more of her secrets. The therapist's own impatience, curiosity and ambition can best be bridled by adherence to rules of technique that are based on a dynamic theory of development.

Behavioral improvement had to be seen in the proper proportions—namely, not as a sign of total and lasting conflict resolution but in part as a preparation and precondition for the therapeutic work that was still to be done. Here we encounter a therapeutic principle that aplies to the course of treatment, whenever it proceeds within an ongoing developmental process: an anchorage on an age-adequate level of functioning, even if it is only spurious and partial, is indispensable for the continuance of therapy. This is especially true of the beginning stage of adolescence, when regression is resisted, not only defensively but also adaptively. The stronger the regressive pull, the more urgent is the need for a defensive holding position.

The ego, while keeping the defenses in operation, is at the same time progressing, at least in part, in those areas that are defined by certain requirements of the environment, which are relative to the age of the child. Such partial and tenuous ego expansion is decisively affected by the therapeutic situation, which serves as an ego support and relieves anxiety by way of its protective understanding and regular availability. Of course, if therapy never ceases to be more than that, or if therapy itself represents an insurmountable danger situation, then treatment had better be postponed; otherwise, one runs the risk of therapy becoming degraded to a meaningless and permanent holding position. Another, more fateful and, indeed, fatal alternative presents itself: if drive and ego regression, which have both been enhanced by the stage of puberty, should reach the point of merger— namely, the obliteration of the boundary between self and object—then the degree of personality disintegration becomes identical with that of psychotic illness.

After the summer when Susan spent four weeks in camp (age 10), she involved the therapist in re-enacting her infantile sense of abandonment and her need for the active, nurturing mother. It was true, of course, that the therapist had recommended this separation, and it was surprising to see a girl, age 10, who had never played with dolls, suddenly busy herself with complete abandon in playing "mother and baby." As is typical for children playing with dolls, Susan alternated in the roles of mother and baby, or else she played both of them simultaneously. She nursed the baby with a toy bottle, while also sucking surreptitiously on the bottle herself. The baby had to have the best of care, and Susan saw to it that the therapist got all the necessary baby paraphernalia for her. To make the baby happy was now their common concern. Starvation anxiety and fear of object loss were acutely brought to the fore by a milk delivery strike in the city, and by a newspaper report about children who had died in a hospital, as the result of unknown causes. Susan had failed to notice in the newspaper report that adults—including some mothers—had died also.

She now turned to the therapist for an explanation of her mother's illness. She wished to understand a dream in which the "mother was killed," and expressed some degree of puzzlement about her persistent fear of "being bad." It was easily established that "being bad" and "being sent away" were, in Susan's mind, links in a chain of events. Yet the far more pathogenetic aspect was to be found in the retaliatory, destructive, aggressive impulse that was part of this sequence of events. Susan had regressed in the transference, only fleetingly and surreptitiously, to the archaic mother; she now replaced the regression by identification. Identifying with the therapist, she experimented tentatively with her femininity: she asked the therapist to help her sew a skirt.

The sexual conflict reappeared in the sessions, once again under the impact of early puberty. Now the therapist had become a partner in bringing order and insight into Susan's conflicted sexual identity and anatomical confusion. The practice of anal masturbation and the cloacal theory were brought to light. Susan started to write a sexual dictionary; in doing so she displayed her utter confusion, as well as her wish for clarification. When the typical regression of early adolescence took place, it had a different quality from the regressive manifestations of the earlier stage in treatment. At that time, the regressive manifestations had been simply the assertion of never-abandoned infantile positions.

The difference between the two types of regression lies in the fact that, in one instance, no essential progression to advanced drive and ego positions had been attained while, in the other, a retreat was effected from an advanced position to a more primitive one. If we use this distinction and refer to the regression as either descriptive or dynamic, then we can say that Susan's regression at the age of 13 was phase-specific and, therefore, dynamic in nature. The essential precondition for genuine regression is the attainment of an advanced position from which to regress. Descriptive regression would, then, be identical with the reassertion of drive positions that never had yielded to developmental transformations.

Susan's case convincingly demonstrated the linkage between drive arrest and its deleterious effect on ego functions. By the time the dynamic and obligatory regression of preadolescence can finally occur, the ego must have advanced to a more age-adequate level; it must have emancipated itself, to a considerable extent, from its dependence on the drives and simultaneously gained in strength through increasing differentiation of functions. Among these it is the self-observing ego that occupies a high ranking place of importance at this time, because it assures that regressed ego aspects or components do not lose touch with the advanced ego state from which adolescent regression has issued. Adolescent—in this case preadolescent—regression is normally transient and therefore not pathognomic; its appearance in Susan's therapy was, developmentally speaking, a welcome sign.

Schematically and metaphorically, one might say that each victorious return of the adolescent ego from a regressive foray that has ended in the slaying of one or the other of the chimeras of the past, enlarges the ego's competence. This gain in the power of mastery over infantile dangers encourages, in turn, a new regressive thrust, this time to *more* primitive, *more* dangerous and, genetically, *deeper* layers of the past. We observe this concept on the clinical plane in Susan's advances in symptom resolution; it was achieved in steps and stages, proceeding in a seesaw movement: each partial resolution resulted in a developmental advance that made possible, in turn, a deeper therapeutic approach to the essential pathology.

Treatment within a developmental period is, necessarily, subject to a fluctuation of "success and failure." It would be an error, born of impatience and shortsightedness, if treatment were to be terminated at the time when the symptomatic status of the patient presents a more favorable picture. This train of thought brings us to a consideration of the "working-through" process and its decisive role in therapy. We shall now turn our attention to this subject in a separate discussion.

CHAPTER 9

A DEVELOPMENTAL CONCEPT OF "WORKING THROUGH"

It is a unique aspect of psychotherapy that its duration is not determined only by the time it takes the therapist to understand the patient's illness. If it were indeed so, this would expedite matters and Susan would not have had to remain in treatment for almost five years. The nature of her illness was understood by the therapist quite early in treatment: child and family history, the symptom picture, Susan's behavior in the sessions, her comments, dreams, fantasies—all these had been assembled, without difficulty, by the end of the first year. The

100

result was a good grasp of the illness, in terms of its genetic, dynamic and structural aspects. In addition, the three psychic institutions—id, ego and superego—had revealed, by that time, their respective role in the child's disturbance. Yet such wisdom—rich as it was—did not help of itself to expedite the child's recovery. The reason for this is obvious.

Any thought, confrontation, explanation or interpretation that is imparted to the patient must be complemented, in the patient, by a commensurate ability to accept and integrate the therapist's presentation. We ascribe this ability to the ego. Consequently, the therapist imparts to the patient only so much of his knowledge and insight as the patient is at the time capable of putting to use, integratively and adaptively. Implicit in this technical rule is the assumption that the patient's conscious desire to get well remains opposed, for an indefinite length of time, by powerful influences that lie outside his volitional control. Susan's expectations, fears and fantasies in relation to treatment revealed a host of influences that were keeping the pathological condition relatively intact. They could not all be interpreted as resistance, as we shall see.

The therapeutic alliance is the protector and promoter of the therapeutic process. It operates independently of the influence of those forces that are disinclined to participate in the therapeutic work. It is the therapeutic alliance, in fact, that gradually renders these forces ego-dystonic. This very process strengthens the observing ego, and brings the observable ego into sharper focus. Self-observation and introspection are thus promoted. Therapy makes the most extensive use of both of these; in fact, its very existence depends on them. The child's insight into the origin and purpose of his defenses; the focusing on certain behavioral items for shared observation; the child's spontaneous recall and associations—all these standard features of child therapy serve to lower the defensive barrier and to acquaint the child with the roots of his discomforts. Partial gains in symptom resolution follow in the wake of such productive therapeutic movement, only to be, paradoxically, followed by standstills—indeed, by reversals.

The clinician is familiar with the fact that, even after ego resistances and defenses have been dealt with adequately, there still remains an "adhesiveness" to those instinctual positions or modes of drive discharge that were once thought to reflect a quality of the instincts themselves. We have come to regard this kind of resistance—since it lies outside the conflictual complex and therefore outside the realm of the ego—as non-defensive. The strength of non-defensive resistances varies greatly from case to case and we could define the "working through" process as the systematic effort to draw non-defensive or id resistances into the conflictual orbit.

Whenever a resolution is effected of the conflict between drive and ego, there still remain derivatives of the drive that have escaped the reach of the observing ego. These pockets or hiding places in the personality, where the original pathology still survives, need to be rooted out in order to effect cure. This is the task of "working through"; its aim is to secure each partial therapeutic gain.

Greenacre has suggested that there exist cases in which infantile fantasies of a typical nature have received a "special strength, form, and pressure for repetition through having been confirmed by external events."* In Susan's case, this external event is represented by the "exile year." Such an event—which is not, in and of itself, the original trauma that needs to be unearthed in therapy—nevertheless appears to be the subject of the working through process, because it embodies the organ-

---

* Greenacre, P. Re-evaluation of the Process of Working Through. *International Journal of Psycho-Analysis,* Vol. XXXVII, 1956, (p. 440).

izing principle of the emotional illness. Greenacre refers to the fact that generic childhood experiences and conflicts receive a specific and pathogenetic valence when they become organized around some event that serves as a verification of the many antecedent piecemeal experiences and their associated fantasies, assembling them into a quasi-traumatic new whole-experience. It is not solely the reconstruction of the earliest infantile experiences or fantasies that will effect curative change; the working through of the quasi-traumatic event that has organized the preoedipal antecedents is equally necessary. This working through of the organizing event constitutes the major focus in child psychotherapy, by contrast with child analysis.

Any form of child therapy proceeds within the orbit of an ongoing developmental process. This prompts me to offer a developmental view of working through, and to relate it to those resistances that defy defense interpretation in the treatment of children. For the sake of brevity, I shall refer to these resistances as "developmental resistances." Since they lie outside and beyond conflict, they have to be drawn into it during treatment. They appear to be bound up inevitably with developmental sequences in personality formation. In such cases we can see how each stage of development bears the stamp of the original pathogenetic history. This we observe via drive modalities and ego manifestations, both of which help therapy further along its course.

Yet we cannot help recognizing that the totality of the pathological complex is never available for investigation at any given time. Only partial issues can be dealt with; or, more correctly, whole issues can be dealt with only partially. The pathogenetic experience and its conflictual sequelae become available to investigation, at any point during therapy, only so far as they are relevant to, or in consonance with the drive and ego organization that has been reached in treatment at that precise moment.

Therapy aims at effecting a forward movement of the instinctual drives through the loosening of fixations. Such gains accrue in the integration and consolidation of the ego. The newly occupied forward positions of drive and ego bring the therapeutic work to a temporary halt, or impasse, which is often looked at erroneously as a defensive holding position. Since it does not yield to defense analysis, it is usually called "resistance." The thought offers itself that this kind of resistance constitutes an id resistance; what we observe, however, discounts this view. After some time has elapsed, during which ego consolidation has taken its often slow course, we note with surprise that there is a spontaneous return to the pathogenetic complex, and the therapeutic work is set in motion once again. The ego maturation that was attained during the therapeutic fermata not only facilitates the therapeutic work but pushes it ahead.

This resumption of the therapeutic momentum directs our attention to a significant difference between this and the preceding stages in therapy. Therapy now reaches, via symbolic expressions or derivative manifestations, more primitive drive positions than it had ever reached before. This is not due simply to the child's greater familiarity with therapy, or to the growing trust in the therapist. While these factors undoubtedly exert a positive influence on the deepening of therapy, there are developmental factors at work that warrant our attention.

In reconstituting the normal sequence of development through therapy, we observe a repeated appearance and re-appearance of the pathogenetic trauma. It presents itself repeatedly, yet with a different emphasis each time, because it makes its appearance in the specific drive and ego modality that belongs to the developmental phase the child has reached or is re-experiencing at any given stage in treatment.

In terms of this formulation, "working through" is the

reflection of a developmental recapitulation of the pathogenetic core, as it is carried forward along the developmental sequences. Consequently, the pathogenetic core
appears, disappears and then reappears, at all levels of
psychosexual development. It is an implicit function of
therapy to correct the incomplete or arrested sequences
of psychosexual progression and, concomitantly, to promote ego differentiation. The developmental level at
which the pathological process can be tapped, at any
given point in therapy, is dependent on and collateral to
the stage of ego development; it is not simply and wholly
dependent on the presence or absence of ego resistances,
defensive operations or transference reactions.

Anna Freud* has commented on the fact that working through requires not only the ego faculties of assimi-
lation and integration, but also the availability of an
observing and an observed ego. This view stresses the
interrelatedness of the forward movement of the instinctual drives, on the one hand, and of ego differentiation
on the other. The working through process is identical
with this dynamic correspondence.

I shall now return to the case of Susan and relate
the thesis set forth above to the course of her treatment.
The reader is familiar, by this time, with all the relevant
clinical data. What is introduced now is a new dimension, under which the material presented earlier is to be
viewed. This new dimension is the developmental con-
ceptualization of the working-through process.

The traumatic event ("exile year") that served as the
organizing experience for the total range of preoedipal
injuries to development, has already been recounted in
detail. Susan's first revelation in treatment was the role
that anal fixation played in her emotional life. Orgies of
messing and smelling filled many hours. Eating of feces,

* Freud, A., *Normality and Pathology in Childhood.*
International Universities Press, 1965, (pp. 27 and 221).

symbolically represented both by finger paint and by in-
juring the therapist with fecal matter through touching
her, revealed the extent to which oral and anal-sadistic
impulses were still in full force. The role of magic was
conspicuous. This regressive revival came to a stop when
Susan rather suddenly decided to work and to stop playing any longer. She meant it and she did it. A period of
descriptive, if not dynamic, resistance followed.

The question arises whether this change heralded a
turning away from infantile positions for good,
or reflected a reinstatement of the defensive organization
that had so far kept the symptom complex intact and
immutable. The practical implication for therapy lies in
these alternatives: either looking at this change as a progression in development that should be left unchallenged,
or seeing in it a resistance to treatment that has to be
challenged, in order to be overcome.

At this point, we had to admit that defense interpretations remained ineffectual. It seemed therefore, that
the girl's manifest resistance reflected a need for integrative processes to do their work or, in other words, for
ego consolidation and differentiation. A "developmental
resistance" was at work. This kind of resistance is in the
service of the therapeutic work; as a stage of ego integration, it must be regarded as being prerequisite to a
return to the pathogenetic theme. As we were able to
observe in therapy, the resistance followed in the wake
of a confrontation with the intensity and specific quality
of her anal-sadistic impulse.

It was only after a further degree of ego consolidation
had been attained, that Susan was able to reach a deeper
level of her deviant development, without experiencing
excessive anxiety. The so-called halt in this girl's treatment was accompanied by a change in the symptom
picture, but not indeed in the illness. When this first
plateau in therapy was reached, the nightmares disap-

peared and the learning problem temporarily receded into the background; on the other hand, the enuretic condition and the lying worsened. We concluded that ego growth must be given time to consolidate before drive fixations and developmental deficits can be approached anew. Usually, the young patient gives the signal when this point is reached; then child and therapist join forces once again in bringing progressive development into flux by loosening it further from its pathogenetic moorings.

Each time a return to infantile states and their exploration was brought to a halt, a phase of ego growth, of consolidation and adaptive efforts asserted itself. I need only mention how the repetition and investigation of phallic envy gave way to an assertion of girlishness; how the investigation of anal (cloacal) masturbation was replaced by a turn to organized activity, while the exploration of genital (phallic) masturbation was followed by broadened social awareness; how, in place of the regressive pull to the preoedipal mother, encompassing her passive strivings, what emerged was "bossiness" and a show of euphoric independence; how the stage of bisexual identity gave way to an identification with, or imitation of, the oedipal father; how the investigation of the year in exile and the catastrophic loss of the mother provided the search for the penis with a compulsive and restitutive quality.

Once we had arrived at the "organizing experience," it then became possible to interrelate the various isolated pathogenetic trends in the child's early life, thus facilitating an eventual developmental advance of the entire personality. This synthesis, which is typical of the end phase of therapy, encompasses the totality of the pathogenetic trends, ideally without leaving any enclaves, where some of them can linger on. Through the repeated return to the pathogenetic theme, an ever larger range of unintegrated drive components is drawn into the conflictual complex. This oscillating process of working through is characteristic of therapy whenever it proceeds within an ongoing development.

This means that, whenever a new level of integration is reached in treatment, the remnants of the original pathogenetic nuclei remain, for the time being, inaccessible; they do not yield to defense analysis, but will reappear after a halting wait. They present themselves, at that time, in the modality of the developmental phase that has since been reached or that has now moved into the foreground. In this way, the residues of conflict and fixation become subject to ever wider awareness and to investigation at the various levels of development and psychic functioning. This is what constitutes the process of working through.

Whenever treatment is completed within an ongoing development, there always remains the possibility that pathogenetic remnants will survive, to assert themselves at the time when maturation introduces a new and novel developmental stress. A developmental concept of "working through" might thus explain the empirical fact that, if therapy is terminated in childhood or initial adolescence, it often has to be resumed in late adolescence or early adulthood. It seems to lie in the nature of development that the long-range outcome of therapy is not predictable during the stage of immaturity. We are familiar, of course, with child therapy cases in which a favorable outcome at the time of termination has weathered later emotional stress. We assume that, in such cases, the alignment of psychosexual development with physical maturation and social integration has, in turn, extended ego autonomy to the point at which new maturational conditions of stress can no longer make contact with the remnants of trauma, except in an adaptive form (Blos, 1968).

Not until development has ceased and the mutual

influences of inner and outer conditions have been unalterably stabilized can one say with certitude that the pathogenetic condition has lost its valence or up-drift or, in other words, has ceased to exist. It is the unattainability of this condition in human life that attests to the relativity of the therapeutic achievement. However, an approximation to our therapeutic goal is best secured by reliance on the "working through" process.

CHAPTER 10

A STRUCTURAL AND DEVELOPMENTAL ASSESSMENT: SUSAN, AGE 13.

Termination will now be considered in greater detail. When a therapist decides to terminate, he follows certain guidelines. We posit that the basis for a valid decision as to continuation or termination of therapy can be established only by a structural and developmental assessment of the case. We shall apply this requirement to Susan's treatment, and define the status of her personality integration and functioning when she reached the age of 13.

From a structural point of view, the balance between ego and id had shifted in favor of the ego. It was indisputable that ego functions had gained in stability, reliability, and autonomy. The drive for achievement was no longer wholly, but only marginally, endowed with aggressive, retaliatory urges; more important, it had ceased to serve, by displacement, as proof of genital completeness, of being a "girl-boy." Success could now be enjoyed without guilt.

The emotional disengagement from primary love objects had facilitated the formation of new object relations. Susan began to scan the environment for identificatory models among peers and adults alike; she entered into social situations in which her need for emotional mutuality could be articulated. Susan acquired friends.

The role that achievement played in her total personality functioning had changed. In looking at her aspirations to perfectionism before treatment and during the periods of resistance, it had become obvious that achievement of any kind—whether this be cleanliness, obedience or unselfishness—constituted a reaction formation and was therefore defensive in nature. Her virtuousness was but a compulsive atonement for instinctual transgressions, among which masturbation and aggressive fantasies played the major roles. A vicious circle was formed by instinct gratification, guilt, body damage anxiety, renunciation, and restitution fantasy. This course was followed with the precision of cause and effect. Thus, psychic energy remained bound in a defensive system from which Susan could not escape. An abnormal development was in progress that would certainly, by the termination of adolescence, acquire the fixity of a deviant personality organization, unless therapy intervened.

The superego's influence on Susan's deviant development lies directly at the surface of the clinical picture. In order to trace the origin and fathom the depth of this influence, we have to relate it to its two-fold sources, one of which lies in the preoedipal, the other in the oedipal stage of object relations. The earlier of the two, the archaic superego, derived its severity and primitivity from projection of infantile aggression in its various forms. As a result of the early suppression of oral and anal drives, and further of the establishment of premature ego control over the pregenital instincts, Susan's aggressive and retaliatory urges acquired inordinate proportions. Since precocious ego accomplishments were necessary for drive control, such as would elicit and secure the mother's positive attention and emotional presence, this sham maturity became the child's protector and guarantor of her mother's love.

The repetition of this infantile adaptation in the transference made it possible to bring Susan into contact with the strength of her aggressive drive, and with the aim and object of her aggression. Thus, the archaic superego grew to be less severe and less monstrous. The disappearance of her nightmares, her fear of the dark, her abandonment panic—this was, in large measure, attributable to the relative decline of the archaic superego. Of course, it was the child's progression in both ego and psychosexual development that diminished the influence of the archaic superego.

This advance to a stable organization of the oedipal superego was, however, slow in coming. Its arrival was heralded when guilt feelings ceased to be externalized in the form of catastrophic danger situations—such as being destroyed, devoured and abandoned by a persecutory environment that in essence represented the malevolent, archaic mother. Oedipal guilt is, by contrast, the result of intersystemic conflicts that seek internal resolutions, defensive or adaptive. In addition, Susan's developmental progression to a higher level of integration became manifest when identification began to replace object possession, and when achievement became the means for self-esteem regulation and social participation.*

The change in body image deserves our attention at this point. It was possible to follow its transformation, from the cloacal body ego to the phallic-clitoral body ego, and finally to a comprehension and acceptance of the female genital and of the total body, in turn, as feminine, attractive and complete. This progression was not a spurious one, because it was paralleled by ego progression, in terms of a more mature sense and grasp of reality. This ego advance in comprehension—namely, in "the capacity to distinguish between ideas and perceptions"*—became manifest in Susan's learning, in her understanding of causality and logic and in her ability to plan and to organize.

As can be deduced from this metapsychological description, the changes in personality functioning that were observable at the age of 13 were comprehensible in terms of structural changes, the only changes that assure permanency. Furthermore, from this kind of change we can infer that mobile psychic energy had become available for adaptive measures. In short, we can say that Susan was now in a propitious state of readiness to encounter the conflicts and stresses that adolescence proper and late adolescence held in store for her.

This structural assessment will now be complemented by a developmental one. A developmental assessment requires a normative model to make possible comparison or evaluation. In what follows I shall present, in condensed form, the model of the preadolescent and early adolescent girl, because these are the adolescent phases

* For a discussion of the dyadic (preoedipal) and the triadic (oedipal) stages of object relations, see "Ben," Chapter 16.

* Hartmann, H., "Notes on the Reality Principle" (1956), in Hartmann, H., *Essays on Ego Psychology,* International Universities Press, New York, 1964. (p. 256).

of development against which Susan's present status at 13 has to gauged (Blos, 1962).

A. *Female Preadolescence*

The consolidation of the latency period permits the phase-specific characteristics of preadolescence to appear. These must not be confused with a mere intensification of infantile drive and ego positions. The prepubertal increase in drive pressure leads the young adolescent girl, first and foremost, into the regressive turn to pregenitality. In addition, a regressive pull in object relations exerts itself, converging on the preoedipal mother or, to be exact, on the archaic mother of infancy. The expression of pregenital interests and activities remains restricted, in great measure, to the company of girls, producing giggles and secrets that are typical for this age. The regressive pull to the preoedipal mother and to passive nurturing is normally resisted and overcompensated by means of action and play acting.

The turn to heterosexuality, in reality or fantasy, is the chief defensive maneuver that closes the door to regressive object relations; consequently, it lacks the qualities of femininity, as well as of genuine heterosexual orientation. The girl at this age plays at being a "little woman"; far from being feminine, she is the aggressor in the game of love. Colloquially, this is the stage of "puppy love." The conflict of female preadolescence resides in the regressive pull that threatens to engulf the girl in infantile positions, and the task of preadolescence resides in the successful resistance against such regression. During this phase of psychic restructuring, the girl's relationship to the mother shows the hallmark of infantile ambivalence, rather than of oedipal rivalry; in fact, an overlapping of the two is the rule.

B. *Female Early Adolescence*

The phase of preadolescence glides, imperceptibly, into that of early adolescence. This latter phase is characterized by the bisexual position of the girl; she is now the proverbial "tomboy," who is, however, not always in demonstrable evidence but can suddenly be replaced by narcissistic self-containment. Both these positions would render this period rather conflict-free, were it not for a maturational forward push that relentlessly summons the integration of social roles and of body changes (menarche) into a coherent, stable body image and its social articulation. The conflict of early adolescence revolves around bisexuality, and the major task of this phase resides in its resolution in favor of a female self-image. This process is aided by the mobilization of narcissistic defenses that can, at this stage, assume flagrant proportions. Forerunners of romantic love are to be observed, as well as all sorts of beautifications, in an attempt to speed up artificially the maturational schedule. The defensive reversal of these trends, as in asceticism, only highlights their conflictual nature.

It follows, from what has been said about the two initial phases of female adolescence, that normally there are in evidence a host of accommodations to puberty that fit into some of the general categories of psychopathology. To the extent that these accommodations operate in the service of progressive development—namely, if they promote the process of psychic restructuring—then they are rendered phase-specific—that is, they lie within the scope of normal development and are not indicators of psychopathology. It must not, however, be overlooked that phase-specific accommodations always represent points of developmental crisis with a high degree of risk, as evidenced by the relatively frequent outbreak of emotional illness (neurosis, delinquency, psychosis) at the critical junctures of the adolescent process.

If we now turn our attention to Susan, and view her personality at the age of 13, the following picture emerges. Regressive manifestations have declined in favor of a defensive holding position, with constant forays into progressive and adaptive development. She has renounced (repressed) and outgrown the need to regress to the realm of pregenitality that had assumed such large proportions during therapy. Tentatively, she is now turning to the tender emotions of romantic love. This love is not yet, however, attached to any object; she is floundering in a fantasy world that she shares with her girl friend, in exchange for the other's fanciful make-believe tales. The play-acting with her girl friend, in which they both played lovers, each in turn being boy or girl, belongs to the realm of experimentation in fantasy; it is not indicative of those fluid ego states that are characteristic of the schizoid personality.

Susan's body had become endowed with narcissistic libido; a sense of body intactness, as well as of self love, has emerged. There are few remnants that hark back to the state of despair when she was sure that her body and her mind were "wrongly put together." She now experiments with her feminine charm and realizes, to her delight, the power that she exerts over boys. It was the decline of her retaliatory competition with boys that initiated the resolution of her "boy complex." Of course, the attenuation of her infantile ambivalence toward the mother also played an essential part in this process and was reflected in a more stable sense of self.

Susan now feels that she is a girl like other girls, not a freak or some curious mixture between a boy and a girl. Her sense of self has acquired a new stability, having weathered the psychological perils of an illness (flu) and of her mother's renewed hospitalization during a psychotic episode. The girl was now able to look at her mother's illness without any reactivation of infantile rage, guilt and self-deprecation, and without the recurrence of her former sense of incompleteness or of her fear of irreparable damage being inflicted on her body and mind. Self and object-representations were no longer subject to rapid and facile cathectic shifts; instead, they maintained their boundaries rather well under stress.

The intertwined strands of regressive and progressive movements that are so typical of a 13-year-old girl are charmingly reflected in Susan's description of a game that precedes her falling asleep. This game is made up of several different roles and scenes. The pillow might be the mother with the child cuddling-against her softness; or else the pillow might be Billy, her so-called boy friend, whom she hardly knows and with whom she has never exchanged a word, but whose make-believe closeness fills her with a flow of sweet emotions. A variant of this pre-sleep scene is played out by her hands, which are no longer needed, compulsively, for masturbation during falling-asleep time. One hand is a boy and the other is a girl—or, we might say, Susan is both. She gives directions to either hand for the fondling and caressing of the other.

This scene represents the paradigmatic expression of the bisexual and narcissistic trends that are in ascendancy during the phase of early adolescence. Susan's fantasy life falls well into the general domain of the initial stages of adolescence; it is devoid of the defensive sameness it possessed several years earlier. Her friendship with girls, her interest in girls' clubs and organizations, and in parties that are well planned to avoid over-stimulation between the sexes—all these attest to her growing participatory adequacy. She has acquired a social role that is commensurate with her interpersonal competence and moral standards.

It is to be expected that interest in therapy will decline when the child's life becomes more satisfying and engaging. The fact that Susan's involvement in her social life and school activities is working against her interest in therapy has to be seen in terms of an age-adequate engrossment in these matters, and not simply chalked up to "resistance." Only when a state of indifference or opposition aims at keeping the pathogenetic agents out of therapeutic reach, and thus aborts the process of therapy, can one speak of resistance. When, however, phase-specific regressions constitute the prelude to drive progression and ego expansion, then the changed attitude of indifference toward therapy requires a developmental evaluation. What appears, superficially, as the young patient's flight from therapy, might well be his way of asking the therapist not to tamper with his efforts to manage his growing-up by himself or, as the saying goes, to "move under his own steam." Resistance of this kind is of a different order altogether, and its voice should be listened to.

This differentiation, as here schematized, can be attained only with the greatest of difficulties. It could not be otherwise, because no absolute, but only a relative, assessment of the balance between the two different kinds of resistance lies within our reach. Incomplete as such an evaluation may be, that does not justify ignoring this problem. For one thing, I was convinced that Susan's growing lack of interest in treatment represented a legitimate—i.e., phase-specific—assertion of her progressive development. Once set free, progressive development had to take over, and to carry the growing organism, including its lasting vulnerabilities, propensities and predispositions toward maturity. Such were the considerations that entered into the decision to terminate treatment at the time when Susan had traversed preadolescence and was already groping her way through the phase of early adolescence.

At the time when the decision is made to terminate therapy, the problems of child or adolescent have not ever reached the vanishing point. The important and consequential achievement of therapy lies in the fact that fixations have been loosened; that psychic energy has been freed by symptom resolution; that the ego has acquired adaptive mastery of tension, and that, concomitantly, the conflict-free sphere of the ego has gained in scope. All these therapeutic changes in personality functioning can be summarized by saying that development has been liberated from stagnation and arrest, that it has recaptured the momentum of growth. This provides reasonable assurance that a forward course of development will henceforth be pursued. When the decision is made to terminate the treatment of a child or an adolescent, one is confronted with far more perplexing considerations than one had to face at the time when therapy was first recommended.

Even if an adolescent patient like Susan shows improved functioning, in consonance with her age, and is unquestionably better integrated and more effective in her daily activities, she is nevertheless bound to become enmeshed in the phase-specific tensions and conflicts of the developmental stages that lie ahead. In other words, should the adolescent patient show the typical reactions that belong to a particular stage of development, then, it still remains a most subtle and demanding task to differeniate between the transient symptomatology of a given phase and the continuance of the original pathology that has, seemingly, not yielded to treatment.

For example, the phase-specific conflicts and transient accommodations of preadolescence involve such problems as regression, bisexuality, and narcissism, in conjunction with typical defenses. Their pathognomic valence can best be gauged by tracing the antecedent course of development. This permits the clinician to form an opinion as to the phase-specificity of behavioral changes. On the basis of such an evaluation, a reasonably valid argument can be advanced for either termination or continuation of treatment. In some cases, an interruption of treatment is indicated, with the expectation that the therapeutic work will be completed, more effectively and enduringly, at a later age. Of course, we always' have to ask ourselves how much of altered personality functioning is due to treatment, and how much has to be credited to growth and maturation.

Clinical issues such as these led me, initially, to investigate the adolescent process as a whole, in terms of its phase-specific and sequential patterns. The delineation and description of the five phases of adolescence was the outcome of my analytic work with adolescents. Clinical data, gradually and over many years, yielded the theoretical formulation of the sequential order that comprises the adolescent process (Blos, 1962, p. 124). It has been the object of this study not only to set forth a clinical account of the theory of adolescence, but also to determine the extent to which these developmental criteria can serve as reliable, evaluative reference points and guiding principles in the treatment of adolescent deviancies.

PART II **Ben**

The Initial Stage of Male Adolescence

CHAPTER 11

THE CLINICAL PICTURE

Ben is 12 years old. He is obviously a prepuberty boy with the "pudginess" that is so common at this age. He is a squat boy—short, stocky, and well built. He knows why he is to enter therapy; at least he knows what is on his parents' mind when they asked for help. He knows that his parents and his teachers are dissatisfied with both his conduct and his scholastic achievement. His father and mother have both been pursuing him with scolding, spanking, and all kinds of punishment and threats, in order to change his behavior. Ben has a knack for provoking his parents; his provocations have a compulsive character, and ultimately he forces his parents to punish him. He thereby succeeds in defeating the purpose of all punishment. For some time, Ben and his parents have been enmeshed in a sado-masochistic tug of war, the crude and ferocious nature of which has been exploding into an endless chain of emotional scenes.

The parents think that Ben should be doing better in school since he is a bright boy; being the oldest of the three children, he should not be constantly playing and fighting with his two younger brothers, age 5 and 7. They think that his coming down to their level is a sign of his "immaturity." His social life is restricted to his life at home: he prefers the company of his brothers to that of his peers; he has no friends and is socially isolated. Most of the time he is noticeably dissatisfied with everything and everybody. This pervasive dissatisfaction barely masks an undercurrent of depression and of aggrieved, global resentment. Ben is an unhappy boy with a chip on his shoulder, an angry boy who is being victimized by a malevolent world, a righteously vengeful boy, born to a fate that has darkened all hope of his ever finding a place in the sun.

The difficulties in school loom large in the list of complaints his parents bring forth. He is disruptive in class; he talks out of turn; he clowns in an exhibitionistic manner. He might demonstratively take off his shoes, or kiss a boy in class to "get a laugh," or lift a girl's skirt as a "gag." No form of punishment by teacher or principal has any lasting effect. On the contrary, punishment only seems to make Ben more prone to provoke the teacher and to force her to punish him again. He gets along decidedly better with men teachers than with women teachers. Homework, on those rare occasions when he does it, never presents a problem to him; he executes it well, with ease and speed. At present, however, he is barely passing his grade. While he has never repeated a grade before, the possibility of such a calamity has provoked intense panic and resentment in both parents. Despite the incessant trouble in school, he likes school and never misses a day.

Ben is a ticqueur, with a variety of tics: (1) eye tic (blinking); (2) mouth tic (wetting his lips with the tongue); (3) nose tic (moves his nose "like a rabbit") (4) shoulder tic (jerking of shoulder, bilateral); (5) abdominal tic (pulling and pushing the abdomen in and out, with ribcage involvement). He carries himself in a rather rigid and erect posture. He is a nail biter.

It is easy to involve Ben in conversation. He is verbal and bright, eager to enumerate his complaints at great length and to outline his demands and rights with equal expansiveness. In holding forth he is extremely serious, even solemn; he lends to his words the weight of unquestionable importance, urgency and factualness. A delightful sense of humor, as well as a capacity for amused reflectiveness, was to come to the fore in the third year of treatment. At the present time, however, Ben is totally absorbed by his grievances. He complains endlessly about the arguments and fights between his parents, always proving his points with a detailed recounting of events, witnesses, and who said what. He reiterates in endless variations the arbitrariness of the punishment he receives; he says: "The punishment never fits the crime."

There is no doubt that a kernel of truth is contained in the boy's accusations and grievances. The emotional climate of the home is one of perpetual turmoil and unpredictable moods. The mother has frequent episodes of depression and rages, during which she hurls derogatory, indeed devastating, insults at her husband, who has long since failed to be the provider or the man she expected him to be. Her mental state following such episodes borders on depersonalization. She resents the fact that nobody in her own family has given her a sense of worth. In return, she feels anger and hate toward them, coupled with a sense of physical revulsion. She feels "boxed in," and says: "This is no family, only people living under one roof." She adds: "But I have responsibilities toward my children, and I want to keep the family together."

For about 3½ years Ben was the only child; the mother remembers with pleasure the affectionate, lovable and responsive baby. The only troubled times were related to his eating: the infant tired easily during feeding and fell asleep, only to wake up and cry before his next feeding time. In the middle of the first year the child became active and moved about in the crib; he walked at one year. He said words early, and spoke fluently at 2½. Toilet training was uneventful, we were told; it started at 8 months and was completed at 2½ years. The child had chicken pox and measles, and a hernia was discovered at 5. A specialist was consulted who advised against an operation, because, the mother reported, "the hernia had gone back in" and was causing no further complication. Ben was apparently a bright little boy; at least, this is a characteristic the mother remembers with great clarity. In fact, there was a time when the child instilled in her that exalted and ecstatic feeling for which she had always craved. At that time, Ben showed signs of "extraordinary intelligence." The little boy thus became the mother's "near genius" son, on whom she bestowed those expectations and hopes on which her future life was to have been built.

It is of interest to note that this show of intelligence was most impressive at the age of about 4, when Ben became interested in calendars and eagerly studied them. He was able, the mother reported, to determine precisely on which day of the week any date within the range of 40 years would fall. This mental extravaganza was short-lived and very likely never existed at all. It no doubt reflects the mother's elaboration of the child's curiosity during her pregnancy with her second child. The memory of the mother seems to have been contaminated by a fantasy; her need for a compensatory wish fulfillment was at that time enhanced by a pregnancy that was unwanted, because the mother was convinced that she could love only one child.

The mother's first disappointment in her firstborn came when she was pregnant with her second child. The lovable, gentle, little boy "exploded", as the mother put it: he threw temper tantrums at the slightest provocation with the result that the mother withdrew from him. This, of course, only made things worse. The calendar obsession, for as long as it lasted, restored the mother's love. Intellectual performance and emotional gratification became antagonistic at an early age. From here on, any situation that aroused anxiety made Ben fall back on the time when an unforgivable injustice was done to him, obviously by having admitted a competitor into his unchallenged life with his mother.

At 5, Ben suffered from nightmares. To calm him down, the mother put him to sleep in her bed. In the light of the mutual dependency between mother and child, the second child was indeed an unwelcome interloper for both of them. We might assume that this shared need for exclusive possession of each other compounded a trauma for the firstborn. He tried to please the mother by intellectual feats or, rather, by a shared make-believe; when this containment of his possessive need for the mother broke down, a rage reaction appeared, in the form of temper trantrums. In their nocturnal form, these appeared as nightmares, which finally brought him into physical contact with the mother, by being taken into her bed, and thus re-establishing the bliss of infancy. We shall see in the case material how far these assumptions reflect the true course of events.

During the latency period, when he was attending the primary grades, he was an unaggressive, indeed passive child, quiet and subdued in the classroom, never raising his hand and conforming docilely to regulations. When he entered school at 6, nightmares had ceased to plague him. Masturbation became apparent during these years, when he would compulsively rub himself in the crotch. He did this while fully dressed during the day, irrespective of the social situation, and much to the embarrassment of his parents. This form of masturbation was the only one observed; it was given up when he was about eleven years old.

The second major wave of disappointment in Ben's life came during the phase of preadolescence. He now carried the battle for personal recognition and exclusive privileges from the home front into the school. His resistance to learning became interwoven with a noisy clamor for independence from restraining controls. The spectacular provocation of punishment hinted at superego interdictions and at a masochistic exploitation of suffering and victimization. The tic syndrome pointed to internal conflicts of a neurotic nature, with a tendency to somatization.

The father was well aware of Ben's disturbance; in fact, he asked himself how much he was contributing to his son's unhappy state. Both parents had had a deprived childhood, and both were forced, early in life, into emotional self-sufficiency. This very similar background made both of them seek in their marriage and parenthood the gratifications of receiving and being given, without the obligation of reciprocity. The father makes this parental position quite explicit when he says that he "expects Ben to give me first; then I will give him too." In a very real sense, the child was forced into the role of the parent. The father's failure as steady breadwinner only aggravated his need for demonstrative love and respect from his sons, especially from his oldest, Ben. He wants Ben to kiss him and to sit on his lap.

Defeated as a good provider, as an adequate husband, as a self-respecting male and as a competent father, he periodically withdraws emotionally from the family. When he returns home after work he usually falls asleep.

At present, he works as a salesman of automobile parts. The competitiveness of this business makes him anxious and hesitant: he becomes fearful when he has to stand up against men in the field, pushing for sales, or bargaining shrewdly. At home, where his aggression is no longer controlled by social anxiety, he inflicts random punishment on his three sons. Since Ben's early childhood, he has punished him by using the strap. "I used Ben as a scapegoat," the father says with remorseful helplessness, admitting shameful defeat in the face of overwhelming odds. If Ben is a scapegoat, who else is the object of his aggression but his wife, who no doubt prefers the son to the father? Nevertheless, the father fervently wishes that he could be a better father, because he loves Ben and wants to do his best by him.

When a child is living in a family of borderline parents, or of parents with a character disorder, the etiological components within the clinical picture are difficult to sort out. At first sight, the line of demarcation remains vague between, on the one hand, an intrapsychic pathological process and, on the other hand, a condition that is reactive to a noxious environment. Incongruities in Ben's clinical picture were assigned to a diagnostic ambiguity that is not uncommon in child cases, especially in cases of Ben's type. We deliberately abstained from a definitive assessment and delegated this task to therapy itself.

That is to say, the therapist remains acutely aware of indications, at all levels of inference, that permit a differential answer to the assessive uncertainties left pending at the beginning of treatment. The course of therapy thus becomes identical with a progressively more succinct and refined assessment, which often leads to a revision of the original diagnosis. It should be made clear that the term "diagnosis" here refers to the nosological delineation of a disease entity; the term "assessment", by contrast, refers to an abstracted projection of the total personality as a functioning system. It states the degree of personality intactness, relative to maturational and developmental norms and attainments, as well as to environmental assets and liabilities. The components of psychic structure —ego, id and superego—are described in their interaction, thus revealing the level of psychic functioning in terms of object relations, reality testing, cognition, defenses and defensive organization.

In Ben's case, the diagnosis of a "compulsive symptomatology with depressive trends" says little about the treatability of this condition in this boy. Assessment must furnish the answer to this question, even though it is rarely obtained fully at the outset of treatment, but is reached only as treatment progresses.

An etiological differentiation is always of the utmost importance. It not only gives firm ground to prognostic considerations but significantly influences the conduct of therapy. Correctness and appropriateness of the therapeutic technique, in any given case, influence, even determine the therapeutic productiveness or sterility as well as continuance or disruption of treatment. Ben's distortion of reality, along with his sense of persecution and his masochistic trends, all pointed to a severe ego pathology with a reparative—that is, a restitutive—effort, directed toward changing reality so as to fit his infantile grandiosity. Ben conveyed, quite explicitly, that he felt no need for "changing himself"; he expected, indeed he insisted, that the world around him must change to suit *his* needs. Furthermore, his social isolation and complete family involvement could either, in a positive sense, be assigned to the ego's vigilance vis-à-vis two confused and confusing parental figures or else, viewed negatively, it could be assigned to an ego regression of a quasi-symbiotic emotional parasitism.

A question of the utmost importance posed itself— namely, whether the boy's denial of reality was in the service of the id or the ego. That is to say, did the denial adapt reality perception to his instinctual needs, or did it instead serve to protect the ego against being contaminated by a quasi-psychotic environment? In either instance, dependency needs and a sense of helplessness in the face of a persecutory, malevolent world contributed substantially to the magnitude of the inner and outer, the psychic and physical dangers that were operative in the boy's life.

Several anamnestic and rather isolated data could not at first be worked into a coherent developmental outline; they had to be stored away for future usefulness, whenever their meaning should become clear. There was the early (age 4) obsessive occupation with the calendar, and the intellectual feats of computation, which brings to mind the *idiot savant* or the atypical child. As indicated earlier, there was good reason in this case to doubt the reliability of the informant. The other fact pertains to the mother's statement that when she held the little child on her lap, she felt him melting into her body. This makes us think of childhood schizophrenia; however, no confirmatory correlates existed in the cognitive sphere. Nevertheless, these data must be kept in mind, for whatever they are worth, because during the course of therapy they will be confirmed in their pathognomic significance or else they will be discredited as erroneous.

It was decided to accept Ben for psychotherapy. Whatever the admixtures of neurotic and atypical components in the clinical picture, it was felt that the boy could gain from treatment, since the evidence of internal conflict was irrefutable and ample and the wish for treatment did exist. How justified the initial diagnostic latitude was, could become evident only during treatment, when more had been learned about the sources and nature of his anxiety, about his fantasies, and about his capacity for a therapeutically useful relationship (transference). These crucial features of the case could not possibly have been known from the history of the symptom picture alone. The boy not only wanted treatment, but preferred to have

a woman therapist.* This unusual demand on the part of
a 12-year-old boy was granted, even though its significance was not understood at the time.

Ben entered treatment at the age of 12.1. He was
seen once a week. Treatment was terminated when he
was 15.2. The total number of interviews came to 110
sessions.

* It gives me great pleasure to express my appreciation
to Sylvia Aranow, PSW, for the skill and understanding she
applied to this case. Her grasp of the clinical material and the
tactful handling of difficult situations, made supervision
extraordinarily rewarding. Her thoughtful and meticulous
records of treatment sessions, as well as of the supervisory
conferences with me, were both of invaluable assistance in
carrying out this clinical research.

CHAPTER **12**

BEN COMES FOR TREATMENT

It must be remembered that Ben's psychotherapy is, in this study, the subject of developmental research. A special introduction to Ben's treatment history is therefore called for.

In this introduction, I want to give an account of the therapist's as well as the researcher's ideas as to the phase-specific development of a young adolescent boy. It is against this conceptual backdrop that symptoms, drive and ego development were assessed, and treatment was carried out. Furthermore, I shall pay explicit attention to the technical problems of therapy, by differentiating between those problems that are due to phase-specific conflicts, those that have their origin in deviant development (psychopathology), and those that arise in response to a noxious environment. The same differentiation applies to defenses, to the defensive organization, to conflict resolution or to adaptation. It is to be expected that this scrutiny of pathognomic valences will not only increase the efficacy of treatment but, beyond that, will also help to define more precisely the phases of preadolescence and of early adolescence.

It is essential for the research aspect of this study that the reader be informed about the so to say "preconceived" set of ideas with which treatment is undertaken and the therapeutic situation consolidated. This body of ideas is to be found in the theory of male adolescent development, as I have formulated it over the years (Blos, 1958, 1962, 1965). With this foreknowledge the reader will be able to follow the case material more easily and to comprehend with greater clarity how it unfolds.

Adolescents, especially young adolescents, are either brought for treatment by their parents or referred by such outsiders as teachers and counselors. It is when one of these considers the child's behavior to be abnormal, and realizes the total ineffectiveness of all pedagogical measures that treatment may be suggested. Young adolescents or children rarely ask for treatment themselves. Whatever the reasons and intentions of the adult who brings a child or an adolescent for treatment, the latter approaches treatment with a quite different and highly personal set of ideas as to the aim, meaning and function of such a strange enterprise. These ideas, amorphous and shadowy as they may be, are contained in conscious and unconscious fantasies about the purpose of therapy, as well as about the person of the therapist. We can easily detect in these fantasies certain infantile elements that pertain to the benevolent or malevolent, but always omnipotent, parent of early childhood and furthermore to magical, prelogical thoughts that will materialize in these mysterious talking sessions.

A large sector of the patient's mind is taken up by what I shall call "the expectancy factor," which contains his chaotic agglomeration of ideas and affects as to what might or might not happen in therapy. It includes what is doubted, yet known; questioned, yet believed; wanted, yet rejected; feared, yet wished and hoped for, and it is present in the young patient's mind when we meet him. The expectancy factor is not only operative along regressive lines; a progressive trend is also operative, even if only in small measure, pushing toward maturity and adaptive competence. The ways and means by which the child expects to accomplish this regressive or progressive adequacy differ from case to case. Attention to the manifestations of the expectancy factor at the very beginning of treatment will reward the therapist with an insight into the child's comprehension of the therapeutic situation. Condensed in this comprehension are both the pathological trends that brought the child to treatment and the recuperative potentialities that will make treatment possible.

When Ben was 12 years old, he became aggressively determined to have his age and his maleness respected, with all the distinctive features of privilege and power. He made it known, soon after treatment started, that what he expected was to enlist the therapist's help in changing his environment, in manipulating his parents through suggestions and through the assignment of blame and blackmail. Thereupon they would become the benign protectors of his needs, and would surely grant him material benefits and special privileges. He was willing to "play along," so long as the therapist's influence was directed toward these ends. Therapy was for Ben a means to "getting a better deal" in this worst of all possible worlds. The knowledge of this expectancy factor assisted us in the initial conduct of psychotherapy, as will be shown in what follows.

Ben was in the initial stage of his adolescence (early puberty), and he wanted nothing more desperately than to be "equal to grown-ups." He attempted to achieve this goal by trying to involve the environment in his make-believe. He had substituted for emotional maturation and ego differentiation the demand that the environment recognize and respect his illusory grown-upness. He wanted external, unequivocal assurance that he was a competent and fearless "big boy." In doing so, he side-stepped the need for internal change and tried to assuage his anxiety, guilt and shame by berating the environment for stifling his manhood. As the result of his stubbornly holding fast to this position, Ben's adolescent development had to fail.

Whenever Ben realized his incompetence, he found himself caught between rage and resignation. Determined yet gentle, the therapist kept his painful self-image at the surface of the boy's awareness. It was expected that his toleration of displeasurable affects might thus gradually increase, if it were experienced in relation to himself, instead of solely in relation to others. What this therapeutic endeavor aimed at was the internalization and structuring of conflict. The painful self-image acted as a sustained irritant, the realization of which moved the therapeutic process and its implicit task slowly onto an egosyntonic level. In other words, when Ben recognized his depreciated self-image as a derivative of his helplessness, then he could stop blaming his environment for his own shortcomings. At that point, treatment would have become identical with the effort to overcome his infantile dependence on external self-esteem regulators.

These were the thoughts that dictated the therapist's attitude toward Ben's complaints. This kind of therapeutic intervention was undertaken with increased vigor, after it had been ascertained that his striving toward genuine forward development never faltered so completely that it could not be rekindled. In addition to Ben's genuine eagerness to transcend his state of helplessness, we must never underestimate the assistance that our therapeutic work received from his innate maturational propulsion. Indeed, we often hardly know how much of the child patient's improvement is due to therapy and how much to his autonomous development. *Natura sanat, medicus curat.*

The expectancy factor operates in relation to any new situation with which the child is confronted. Normally, it is kept in the background, and does not unduly blur the perception of new circumstances. In other words, the child's hold on reality, or the stability of his ego functions, prevents irrational and infantile rudiments of thought, such as are recognizable in fantasies, from determining his behavior. The realistic assessment of new circumstances in which the child finds himself, is sustained by social interaction; this is, by its very nature, an evaluative process, which interprets mutually the behavior of the interacting participants. Thus, the adult supports the ego of the maturing child.

The interaction in the therapeutic situation is of a totally different nature. Here we are eager to learn what the infantile thoughts and affects are; we want to bring to light the fantasies that accompany the experiences of everyday life or, more specifically, those that become attached to the therapeutic situation and to the person of the therapist. The latter is not only receptive to, but indeed actively elicitive of the irrational, non-sensical or random thoughts that are passing through the child's mind. It is only natural for a child or adolescent to react to a situation as unfamiliar as psychotherapy, with accustomed patterns of thought, fantasy and behavior. These habitual reaction patterns are also observable in daily life, without, however, disclosing their mental content there and then. When they appear, with clarity and consistency, at the start of therapy, they do not necessarily represent a genuine transference, but are simply the only way the child knows how to act and react anywhere.

Transference, in the broadest sense, refers to the specific, irrational involvement with and affective relationship to the therapist; these revive a significant relationship of the child's past (transference) or present life (transference phenomena).* From the first moment of therapy, Ben expected—as he would do anywhere, but less explicitly—the therapist to agree with him about the intolerable injustices inflicted on him by an unfair world and, therefore, to help bring about a rectification of this condition as well as to join him in his demand for retribution from the perpetrators. This attitude of his was global. Only when the therapist admitted her inability to change the world for him, did it become clear what the essence of his grievances was, and what had rendered him totally unable even to consider that he, himself, could change.

The therapist of the adolescent is confronted with a particular difficulty, which is inherent in adolescent development. In order to make my point I have to take a circuitous route. What seems to lead us astray, however, will sometimes only bring us closer to the problem at hand.

We expect the patient in psychotherapy to disclose his secrets, to surrender his privacy and to verbalize his most treasured thoughts and most precious fantasies. These contain the drive and ego fixations that have forestalled his adequate and harmonious development; and it is the task of therapy to bring those components of emotional development that have been arrested at various infantile levels into the forward current of personality growth. Clinical experience, however, has taught us that infantile disturbances of development, as they are pre-

* See: "Susan," Chapter 8.

served in phase-deviant gratifications, inhibitions and fantasies become, so to speak, scooped up anew by each developmental forward surge. For example, an oral modality will find expression, if a fixation exists, at all subsequent levels of psychosexual development, as each of these is propelled into ascendancy by physical maturation, or simply by age progression.

It is therefore to be expected that drive fixations or regressions will become, in puberty, linked to the genital modality of drive expression or, more accurately, will become attached to the adolescent self-representation. In this way, for example, a fixation on infantile rage or oral greed will evoke in the young adolescent boy who craves independence, a host of aggressive fantasies; these are aimed at the controlling female, the archaic mother of the oral phase. The executive role for these destructive and attacking fantasies of an oral modality is delegated to the genital which, indeed, functions as a non-specific organ for the discharge of all kinds of tension states during the initial stage of adolescence. It is the stage of "phallic sadism," which appears, normally, as a regressive and transitional phenomenon in the young adolescent boy (Blos, 1965).

To return to the particular difficulty encountered in the treatment of the young adolescent boy, it will now appear reasonable to assume that the therapist's intention to penetrate the boy's inner life is perceived by the boy as an attack or a demand for submission. These reactions are significantly influenced in their intensity and duration by the ambivalence and anxiety that are attached to specific fantasies. It is therefore to be expected that the boy will resist passive compliance; in fact, this resistance is proportionate to the strength of the regressive pull toward passive dependence and receptive nurturance.

When the testing of the therapist's intentions, real and imagined, has lost its urgency, then the adolescent will hopefully join the therapist in his endeavor and will take it, almost on faith, that there are other and more gratifying ways of life than the ones he has pursued. We summarize this later attitude under the term "the therapeutic alliance." This concurrence of purpose is of such importance as a safeguard to the treatment process, that we often give priority to its formation, even against the interpretation of infantile material. We do this in order to prevent therapy from becoming a long-drawn-out struggle for superiority, for "who has the last word" or "who must tell whom what he thinks." It takes the last ounce of therapeutic tact to neutralize the alternative of submission versus dominance in the treatment of the young adolescent boy.

One further point of a general nature needs to be made. We always search for the infantile sources of inadequate or deviant development when we are treating a neurotic child. This uncritical and relentless interest and attentiveness can bring about, in and of itself, the amelioration of a symptom or, less conspicuously, but equally often, the change of a symptom. This is due to the fact that symptoms, as compromise formations, have a history and development all their own. Their entire development has to be traced up to the present stage, in order for us to be able to comprehend how the pathogenetic legacy from preceding levels of immaturity has effected an abnormal compromise solution. In Ben's case, this pathogenetic legacy had to be traced up to the phase of early adolescence.

It is typical for this phase that the negative oedipal configuration now moves into the foreground. What once, in early childhood, was a non-giving mother becomes, during the latency period, a malevolent world; during early adolescence, it then becomes an unloving father, who refuses to live up to his son's need for a strong or ideal father who will be his protector against the archaic mother. Regressively, the mother becomes an object of fear when the boy enters the phase of preadolescence.

We can see how the anxiety that is attached to infantile frustration and rage progresses through the developmental phases, acquiring in this process new characteristics (objects, aims, defenses), while basically remaining true to its original, often traumatic, arousal. In order to trace fixations through their transformations, along the line of normative developmental sequences, it has proven helpful in the treatment of adolescents to have in mind a sequential outline of drive and ego development, as it pertains to the adolescent process. Symptoms acquire additional meaning during the course of development, thus revealing their overdetermination.

It is this fact that makes it necessary to return during therapy, repeatedly, to the same problems. Only thus can one hope to loosen the anchorage of these problems to one or another of the various developmental stages. This process, which is called "working through," always encounters evasions and resistances; but unless this work is done, there will remain certain pathogenetic residues that can once again activate a disturbance, at one of the critical developmental junctures that still lie ahead.* Even with the most careful handling of this problem, it remains a clinical fact that any prediction as to normal development in the future amounts to guesses. Yet it must be considered a therapeutic gain, under any circumstances, if the forward movement of emotional development has been effected; or, in other words, if an arrest of emotional development (adolescent fixation) has been forestalled. A positive therapeutic experience, however limited, always remains a personality asset.

* See: "Susan," Chapter 9.

CHAPTER **13**

THE INITIAL PHASE OF TREATMENT

A 12-year-old boy, on starting treatment, will likely be reticent and evasive, even if he is talkative and compliant about answering questions. Ben was talkative, but not in a spontaneous way; rather, he let the therapist take the lead and tell him what she wanted to know. Three elements had to be recognized in this attitude toward the therapeutic situation: one pertained to his wish to be taken care of and to be relieved of his anxiety, through the nurturing protection of the therapist; the other lay in his belief that the caretaking person would surely know what is needed to know about him, and that, as an omnipotent good helper, she would hardly need to be told anything more than what makes him feel bad, in order for her to be able to dispense the appropriate relief. He had, in short, endowed his therapist with magical powers. Fantasies about female power were operative in Ben's desire to have a female therapist. From experience, he knew that the female, the mother, directed the destiny of all four males in the family; to be in the hands of a benevolent woman seemed desirable, safe and advantageous.

Being in the position of a petitioner who is appealing to an authority for the redress of injustices committed against him, Ben related for many months an endless list of grievances that he had suffered in the past and that he now had to suffer. These concerned his mother, his father, his brothers, his teacher and his schoolmates. The refrain to his tales of any controlling action, whether it was taken by parents or by teachers, remained the same: "The punishment doesn't fit the crime." He was frightened of punishment; yet he constantly maneuvered himself into a situation that called for it. Any inferences with regard to his own provocative participation in these minor or major catastrophes were met with a sense of indignation. In fact, they were received as accusations of the most outrageous kind; or, fitting into the general theme, they were regarded as being maliciously designed to justify the punitive actions of his tormentors. Assigning to him any responsibility for the unfortunate events was, in his eyes, simply another form of punishment—namely, one of withholding sympathetic understanding and rejecting his grievances as unimportant. Ben wanted a benevolent partner who saw everything as he did himself, and who by virtue of possessing adult power and authority, would influence his parents to be more lenient and generous, more respectful of his person and tolerant

of his behavior. All he himself could do, under the circumstances, was "curse under his breath" or "kick the
furniture."

Through long-drawn-out sessions, Ben presented himself as a powerless pawn in the hands of powerful people.
Not only their good intentions, but even their willingness
merely to consider his happiness had to be doubted. The
latest newcomer to this assemblage of powerful people
was, of course, the therapist. What good would it do to
talk about things? All that mattered to him was an actual
improvement of his daily life, as measured by material
advantages and demonstrative considerateness. No wonder the "talking sessions" discouraged him—indeed, enraged him—yet never to the point of his leaving the
room. He had become tied to his helper and imaginary
tormentor.

By maintaining the belief that the entire cause for
his trouble was external Ben silenced his own fear that he
was "mentally ill." He had "come across" this topic in a
dictionary, and in "some magazine" he had read about
play therapy and how children indirectly reveal their
feelings about their family. He was not willing, of course,
to play with childish toys; games were more to his liking,
especially chess. What he enjoyed most in that game was
chasing the queen (*never* the king) across the board and
"knocking her up." It was clear that he was familiar with
the sexual meaning of this phrase. Aggressive, retaliatory
feelings toward the therapist took the form of a displaced
sexual attack; it was his way of divesting the threatening
female of her superior powers. In order to grasp the
genetic line and the dynamic quality of this theme, which
was struck rather early in treatment, one had to wait for
its reappearance within various contexts; only then could
it be woven into the interpretive and reconstructive work
of the treatment process.

Another way Ben used to control feelings and fantasies as potential sources of anxiety became evident in his

conception of himself as a "mechanical man." This was purely *metaphorical* speech; it contained no trace of the well-known robot-like self-representation of the psychotic child. In a somewhat sarcastic and ridiculing way, he referred to himself as being made of wheels, wires, springs, etc.—like a clock. Everybody wanted to figure out what made him tick; but "nobody can figure it out" was his triumphant statement. True to his conviction that the subject was not worthy of further discussion, since *he* had nothing to add, all he could say was: "Let's drop it."

The defense mechanisms of denial and displacement had been demonstrated amply during the initial phase of therapy. Identifying defenses, however, represents only a partial gain in our understanding of them. There always remains the problem of tracing their history: the genetic factors leave their respective imprints at the various developmental levels the defenses pass through. A defense is usually elaborated by time, and one or the other of these elaborations will allude to the danger situation that is evoking the defensive action. Our aim is to recognize the prototypical danger situation in historical and psychological depth. The root of denial is never to be located exclusively in the negative hallucinations of earliest infancy. Pain-rendering reality is made non-existent by this mental process. Denial operates on a high level, yet remains close to magical thinking, to an identity of thought and perception. At more advanced stages of development, denial instigates ego regression to the stage of prelogical thought. In fact, it is typical for the preadolescent boy that his thought processes are affected, selectively to be sure, by this regressed form of cognition. The well-known rituals and superstitions of this age belong in this realm of mental functioning.

In Ben's case, magical thinking played an extensive role in his mental life. He believed that, if only he concentrated sufficiently on a wished-for event (such as, for example, winning a pen in a raffle), circumstances would be forced to comply with his thoughts; similarly, *not* thinking about something would keep it from happening. Negative magic was applied in relation to undesirable events, such as sickness and accidents. Most of the time, however, when Ben was treated badly by circumstances he thought of himself as being just "unlucky." The theme of "good luck" and "bad luck" was a red thread, woven into the fabric of all his tales. He is the victim wherever he goes: the teacher yells only at him, the parents deprive only him of his pleasures.

Ben's fear of his teacher assumed proportions of terrifying fright and panic; when he exclaimed: "She will murder me," he meant it literally. He continued to describe himself as extremely nervous in the teacher's presence: he "shivers" when she calls on him. He expects her to "grab me by the shirt," if he does not know the correct answer. Strangulated by panic, he is tongue-tied. "It makes me cry and I can't breathe." Ben's provocation of the murderous (castrating) female has two aims: on the one hand, it affirms his autonomy of action or, in other words, preserves his masculine identity; on the other hand, it gives him proof that the inflicting of punishment does not violate the intactness of his body and mind (castration), and consequently does not represent any real danger. Both aspects of the provocation are therefore security measures. The degree and persistence of inner danger can be gauged by the compulsive character of his provocativeness. The question arises at this point: what are the *specific* and *prototypical* danger situations against which the defenses are erected? The choice of the defenses, as well their behavioral and verbal expression in treatment, offers the clues to an answer.

We recognize Ben's identification with the aggressor, who is "equally murderous"; second, we recognize in the denial the active obliteration of exterior danger. This denial appears in counterphobic form, and is responsible for most of the boy's intractable and provocative behavior. The danger situation, prototypical and traumatic, makes its appearance in male preadolescence with a psychic content that is relevant to this stage of development. Ben's case serves as a good demonstration of this. The intrapsychic danger situation is one of losing hold of his masculine identity, while the constant threat to his masculine identity emanates from an unusually strong regressive pull toward passive dependency and nurturance. The ego's defensive role is clear.

At this point, however, we have to ask a further question—namely, what are the *specific drive components* that are responsible for this boy's counterphobic provocations? In the first place, it is the aggressive, sadistic drive, which finds relief in the tormenting of others; in the second place, it is the masochistic submission that regressively gratifies dependency needs. The sadistic self-assertion appears as egosyntonic, by contrast with the masochistic surrender, which is ego-alien.

There is still another psychic structure, the superego, which requires consideration as a participant in the defensive (ego) and gratificatory (id) processes. Guilt throws a shadow of dysphoria over Ben's sado-masochistic involvement with the outer world. Both guilt and atonement, which are experienced by Ben as victimization and helplessness, are bound to a self-activated chain of events, the function of which is to keep anxiety at a tolerable level. When he bursts out, unexpectedly, and confesses: "Yeah, I'm a bad, bad boy," he is revealing the guilt that follows on his sadistic provocations. We encounter, on the other hand, masochistic gratification in his submitting to self-induced punishment. His state of helplessness, of "bad luck" and of "unfair" treatment are but the signs of a masochistic need that, we must assume, is anchored in traumatic experience. The threat of emotional surrender mobilizes, in turn, the frantic assertion of his masculinity.

The dynamic cycle has now become clear by our

having traced its course through the three psychic structures. A judicious tentativeness, however, is in order because these inferences were derived solely from first impressions. Nevertheless, in order to move ahead in therapy, a working hypothesis is needed, to give direction for the time being. The crude instrument with which we start our explorations must be incessantly refined by elaborating or discarding the hypotheses we have formed. The patient never ceases to give us the material for such refinements. We tried initially to ascertain the dynamic and economic aspects of Ben's personality functioning through their reflection in the three psychic structures. A pathological, self-defeating cycle, if once established, feeds on itself; that is to say, an observable pattern (symptomatology) is repeated, with a monotonous sameness.

At an unexpected but brief disruption of this monotony, Ben remarked: "It's funny. I can't remember what went on at home recently, but I can remember things that went on years ago." What he remembers are the nightmares he had when he was 5, and the fact that "father was not home at the time and mother let me come into her bed." He has difficulty, at present, in falling asleep; he tells of a recent nightmare about his teacher who, in the dream, has a twin sister. He confirms with a broad grin the interpretation that the therapist is the twin sister, and that fears, similar to those he has experienced in school, are making him cautious in therapy. "Let's drop it" was his usual reply to a disquieting subject.

It is apparent from this vignette that his ego is permitting Ben to indulge in infantile wishes, by keeping them at a temporal distance, as "just memories." Conversely, the very same emotional and instinctual needs, when they pertain to the present, are "not remembered." When the therapist presented an interpretive linkage, the patient ignored it; yet he never responded with a global, negative attitude to therapy. The boy wanted *something;*

what was it he wanted? In pursuit of this answer, I shall now present a synopsis of two sessions.

(A) On one occasion during the first six months of treatment, Ben was holding forth, as he did frequently, about the injustices inflicted upon him. While talking, he picked up a "father doll" and fingered it between the legs. While doing this, he related that he had looked into his father's closet and had discovered his Christmas present; he had confessed this to his father, who had duly punished him. Abruptly, he announces that he calls girls certain names he cannot repeat here; "You have to be under 20," he adds. He does not like girls because they are stupid. They are different from boys, because "they have long hair and one extra rib."* He has never cared to find out what the "real difference" is between the sexes, and settles the issue by stating that "one is born female and one male." Yes, he once asked his mother about this, and was told that "a female can have a baby and a man cannot." This negative definition of maleness (hair, rib, baby) reflects the boy's concept of sexuality: the procreative female possesses a superior power; she is to be envied as well as feared. Actually, Ben has no clear conception of the genital differences. He knows that the woman has a vagina and that the man has a penis, but he adds: "Yes, I know I have a penis, but what I don't know is whether a girl has one or not." For the rest of this session he is absorbed in changing the father doll into the mother, by assigning housewifely tasks to it, and in bending the boy doll's legs to do the split.

(B) Once, when Ben has been dwelling on his fear of the teacher, which followed his provocation of her, he suddenly breaks off his train of thought, moves to the blackboard and writes the word "Help." In response to

* This is a revealing falsification of the creation of Eve; it says, in essence: the man's loss is the woman's gain. Of course, this was not interpreted at the time, but was kept "in storage" for possible future use.

questioning, he is at a loss to explain why he wrote this word. Is there really nothing to understand about this cry for help which follows his revelation that he fears "the teacher might kill me"? He responds to this with irritation and smart-alecky evasiveness, brushing aside all talk by saying that he simply gets into "moods," and there is nothing he can do about it. The therapist sympathizes with this deplorable condition, and Ben confirms her estimate by nodding his head. All of a sudden, he changes the subject—a shift in which we detect the disruption of topic but not of theme. The association that follows concerns his father, and how much he misses his company: he would like to be taken by him to a ball game.

Discouraged by this thought he turns, restlessly, to painting, after having warned the therapist that he is "no good." The paintings are of a boy's face and of a clown. Both pictures fill Ben with discouragement: "It's nothing —it's lousy—look at the ear!" In both pictures, it is the ear that arouses his feelings of discouragement. In one picture, the ear is deformed and too big; in the other, he has spilled paint where the ear is supposed to be. Giving up painting, he declares that, after all, his father is really a "nice guy," even if he yells too much. When the end of the session is announced, he jumps up with relief, then stalls and casually drops the remark that ordinarily he buys a candy bar on the way home, but since he is broke today, he has to do without one. When the therapist offers no financial aid, Ben leaves the office without saying a word.

These sessions are typical of many; in their repetitiveness, however, lies a pattern.* The session usually starts with an effort to communicate "something of im-

* The general trend of such sessions is synthesized for the sample session B as follows: (B, 1) Help; (B, 2) The teacher might kill me; anxiety, panic; (B, 3) Just moods; (B, 4) I miss my father; (B, 5) Ball game; (B, 6) The lousy ear; (B, 7) Father is a nice guy; (B, 8) Candy bar.

portance" to the therapist (B, 1). As soon as his remarks have been given meaning by being put together into a comprehensible thought (B, 2), he takes flight by moping or clowning (B, 3). He reacts to interpretations, explanations or explorations as he would to attacks, or to demands that he submit to a woman's superior knowledge (B, 4). Then follows a restitutive fantasy, which usually fades out quickly (B, 5). Another effort to communicate "something of importance" follows; once again, it is abandoned before it is understood (B, 6). Reassurance is once more sought in a wish, a thought (B, 7), a fantasy or a plea for concrete nurturance (B, 8).

Ben's treatment had progressively given evidence of one who is eager to be helped and who feels totally misunderstood. There is no question that those who were responsible for his treatment were beset at first by an uneasy sense of not quite comprehending the case. Some signals, however faint, are always worth listening to, before they are drowned out in the din of standard explanations, the most common of which is "resistance." Ben's failure to live up to therapeutic expectations could not be assigned solely to resistance, to family pathology, to fear of breakdown, etc., because the boy was apparently trying desperately to convey significant pieces of information to the therapist who not only failed to comprehend the message, but had become convinced of that failure.

The trends of therapy, as described above, cover a period of about eight months. While they are not atypical for the initial phase in the treatment of a preadolescent boy, there were, nevertheless, certain features about them that gave rise to therapeutic skepticism. The sameness of complaint and the absence of therapeutic movement, for example, raised the question of treatability. Interpretations, explanations or shared observations as inducive to self-observation—all these had been quite ineffective. The vicious cycle of the symptom complex, as described ear-

lier, asserted itself without letup, and in such undimin-
ished force that the parents in desperation began to
question the usefulness of psychotherapy, and thought
seriously of removing their son from the family and placing him in a residential treatment center.

Fortunately, it was possible to stop the parents from
rushing into any hasty action. The mother, in the mean-
time, had started psychotherapy and, despite her exas-
peration and disappointment, she was able to understand
that placement of her son was no solution, but rather an
evasion of the problem. Declaring the boy untreatable at
this stage would have been tantamount to admitting that
his pathology had eluded our grasp. A decision of such
consequence had to stand squarely on scientific rather
than on pragmatic ground. The fact could not be denied
that Ben was eager to continue treatment, that he was
well related and intelligently participating. He had given
evidence of an internal conflict, which he was guarding
tenaciously against any intrusion. Whatever the direction
in which the material drifted in therapy, it was always
magnetically pulled back to the complaint of how unfairly the world treats him, and how helpless he feels
about altering his lot.

At this juncture, I undertook a careful review of the
material that had been collected during the eight months
of treatment. The new insight I gained, the hunch that
impressed itself upon me and then grew into a working
hypothesis; and finally the data on which the inferences
and the conclusions were based—all this will now be told.

CHAPTER **14**

THE ANALYSIS OF
A STALEMATE IN THERAPY

In my review of Ben's eight months of therapy, it had become quite clear that there was no indication of borderline functioning; the boy had a good hold on reality. In the areas of his compulsive provocation and his persecution complex, of course, there did prevail prelogical and magical thinking. The nuclear pathology exerted its influence on the boy's general attitude toward life, his self-image, his sexual identity, and his projection of himself into the future. All these aspects of mental awareness were marked by a pervasive sense of dissatisfaction and helplessness. The regressive amelioration of this dysphoric, indeed, depressive affect, was only partially accepted by Ben and only with conflict.

The anxiety that is engendered by regressive passivity in a prepuberty boy is intensified by the fact that at that time the genital modality of drive discharge is in ascendancy. This maturational fact brings the still continuing need for the nurturing and protective mother into opposition to the emergence of genital sexuality. The fear of regression to infantile dependence, of submission to the archaic, omnipotent mother in infancy and early childhood is experienced projectively by the preadolescent boy as a fear of the female—or, to be specific, of the castrating woman. In the realm of castration anxiety belong both the imputed or actual impediments to maturation ("the controlling mother") and the effects of parental narcissism, rather than pride, in relation to their son's achievements ("my son, the 'A' student"). The catastrophic fears that were so eloquently verbalized by Ben in relation to the teacher fit precisely into the typical preadolescent, conflictual configuration that I have described in theoretical terms (Blos, 1958, 1962, 1965). Equally confirmatory of my theory of preadolescence was Ben's turn to his father as a protector against the preoedipal, archaic mother. The father at this phase is not yet the competitor in a triadic—namely, oedipal—constellation. Ben feels secure in the company of men; indeed, it is the emotional unavailability of the father that renders the son's appeal a hopeless cry for help.

All this is typical of the preadolescent boy. Nevertheless, the persistence, if not aggravation, of Ben's symptoms—in general, the monotonous sameness of them— gave cause for concern. It was not, at this point, the treatability of the boy that was in doubt, because that question had already been resolved in the affirmative. It was now a question of a more precise and profound grasp of the pathogenesis and of the mode of operation by which the pathological condition had succeeded in keeping itself so intact. We had thought of the sado-masochistic involvement of the ego, and its disastrous effect on the formation of adaptive faculties; but the therapeutic effort directed toward this end had failed. Yet Ben's disturbance was of a neurotic nature; it should therefore have been, at least in some observable fashion, responsive to psychotherapy; the problem was, certainly, not one that needed environmental controls for its correction.

From my therapeutic experience, I had come to suspect that, in instances of such an impasse, there exists a secret in the family or in its history which, in the young patient's mind, has fallen into the shadow of amnesia. This type of amnesia was not the result of the child's use of repression as a defense mechanism; instead, the forgetting was due to a command by the environment, through gesture and example, to forget and to ignore. The repressive force was thus an external one (Blos, 1963). It is the abortive effort to integrate the lost experience into the ego and its memory system that results in typical forms of psychopathology. Among these, the "acting out" syndrome occupies a prominent place.

Another kind of secret, one of an equally pathogenetic valence, relates to a bodily defect that was not, and is not now being attended to, one that was and is in fact deliberately ignored by the parents. The selective inattention of the parent is here complemented by an equally selective inattention on the part of the child. Regardless of the denial that has been enforced by the environment, the bodily anomaly, whatever it may be, is nevertheless reflected in the body image or in the self-representation. Thus, it indirectly exerts an influence on attitude, mood and behavior. It should be noted that both these kinds of secrets are *external;* it is only secondarily that they become an integral part of the child's central psychopathology.

Ben's case material pointed to a condition of undescended testicles. From my clinical studies in cryptorchidism (Blos, 1960), I knew that the omission of this condition from the health history of the child is nothing unusual. I had also learned that this condition, if ignored by the parents, is never spontaneously brought to the therapist's attention by the boy. It can only be imparted from indirect evidence, such as the choice of symbols, body image, gender identity, somatization. It is furthermore reflected in a state of rebellious resignation, which affects behavior in a significant way by assigning magical intentions to it. The genital condition has to be introduced by the therapist in conjunction with the recommendation or request for a medical examination.

A genital anomaly had never been mentioned by Ben's parents. On the basis of indirect evidence in the interview material, the mother was asked whether Ben had undescended testicles; an affirmative answer was obtained. The mother then reported that, when Ben was 5, the doctor had diagnosed a hernia and a condition of undescended testicles. The hernia receded spontaneously, but correction of the cryptorchidism was deferred to a later age. Never again did anybody refer to the genital anomaly.

Experience had also taught me that the omission of the genital defect from the therapeutic work leads to a stalemate, with features similar to those noticed in Ben's case. There is to be observed a chain of constant and repeated onsets of meaningful communication that, seemingly, lend themselves to interpretation or to serve as a stepping-stone to exploration; yet, somehow, all these promising onsets come to nought. It is not until the genital defect is made a matter of mutual knowledge between boy and therapist that those obstacles are removed that have kept the symptom complex intact. Interpretation, ego support, sympathetic participation, permissiveness or generosity—all these endeavors soon come to the end of their efficacy; they are considered by the boy to be useless, if well-meaning efforts. A cryptorchidic boy usually holds on to therapy with an unshakeable pertinacity, in the hope that "everything will be set right."

Ben's unreasonable demandingness for material things and, further, his sense that some injustice has been done to him—both these attitudes, although they may be glibly interpreted as infantile, regressive phenomena, appear, at least in part, in a different light when they are related to a genital defect. The search for physical completeness, so readily labeled as a phenomenon of infantile merger or fusion, here appears as a normal request for restitution, which the boy is bringing to the attention of Mother Nature. In all fairness, he should be given not just some but all the parts, and in their proper places, that belong to a complete male genital. In puberty, this serious defect acquires a particularly distressing connotation, as a result of the fact that it leaves the boy's awareness of maleness in a state of uncertainty, and muffles the affirmative declaration of a male body reality, which is so essential for a maturing boy.

The degree of anxiety that is attached to this uncertain genital state is proportionately greater, the stronger the regressive pull to passivity and submission. This tendency exists, of course, prior to puberty; but it asserts itself more powerfully during the phase of preadolescence. Aggressive self-assertiveness and demandingness now alternate with helpless appeals for physical comforts and supplies of self-esteem. All these strivings are, in the main, directed toward the mother. The sexualization of these antagonistic tendencies leads to a sado-masochistic entanglement with the environment, as has been illustrated in the case of Ben. As always in such cases of young adolescent boys, there exists an intertwining of infantile preconditions, which clash with preadolescent strivings and pubertal body changes.

At this point, I owe the reader an account of the reasoning that led me to the hunch about Ben's having testicular troubles. It should be made clear at the outset that no one facet of the material will, in and of itself, justify such a conclusion. Only the assembling of many facets will add up, like a mosaic, to the recognition of a suggestive image. The decoding process of this genital anomaly had become well known to me through my clinical studies in cryptorchidism among early puberty boys (Blos, 1960).

For the sake of clarity, I have organized the pertinent interview material into four topics; these, by their very choice, will permit a discussion of the psychological and behavioral characteristics of cryptorchidism.

Symptomatic Acts

When Ben arrived for his first interview, his fly was open. In itself, this means nothing in particular, but the observation was kept in mind and the question was asked whether he was unwittingly calling attention to his genital; if so, what particular mental content was to be attached to that fact? Will it repeat itself? It did not; but the genital area remained a body area to which he repeatedly called attention, by tugging at his pants in the crotch and by fingering this area while searching for something to say. It was not clear whether these hand movements were indicators of masturbatory and exhibitionistic trends or were reassuring and protective gestures, similar to those of little boys who hold on to their penis when they are frightened or anxious.

Ben's lying had a compulsive quality and, at the same time, a conscious and manipulative aim. The effort to control others, rather than being controlled by them, was quite obvious. Furthermore, lying had the quality of a "make believe" game, which derived its pleasurable admixture from the fact that it altered reality, at will and with ease, through the magic of the spoken word. Closely allied to these phenomena was Ben's use of denial as a reassurance and a source of narcissistic supplies. This defense had become sexualized, thereby taking on the characteristics of a symptom.

A symptomatic act of a quite different order was to be found in Ben's habit of losing and forgetting. He was forever losing his books, his sneakers, his bus pass, his hat, his cap. The loss of his bus pass was particularly startling because this pass was his most valued possession; it made him feel "superior", "manly" and "important." Was this losing of objects based on guilt feelings? Was it a masochistic act? Or was it, perhaps, an unconscious abrogation of his maleness?

There were to be found, in the material, instances of an inexplicable nature: words or actions rushed in with startling suddenness and disappeared as abruptly, like falling stars, without a trace of their origin or destination. What remained was the therapist's wish to understand the meaning of it all. As one illustration I remind the reader of the word "Help" that Ben wrote on the blackboard. This spontaneous SOS sprang "just from a mood," he explained; but we felt convinced that the cry for help had referred to a specific danger situation. On another occasion, again abruptly, Ben turned to the blackboard in order to work on a long division by adding zero after zero endlessly. These activities were usually followed by conversations that obscured rather than enlightened; similarly, explorations into the meaning of his actions remained futile.

Body Image and Organ Equivalents

The body image is part of the self representation. As such, it has two components: one pertains to the body as it is perceived, the other to the body as it is conceived. The body concept contains irrational connotations, which possess a decisive influence on behavior and moods. Ben says quite clearly: "I know I have a penis; but what I don't know is whether a girl has one or not." It therefore remains a moot question whether a girl is different from or similar to himself. The exploration of the doll's crotch, male and female, followed a retelling of his grievances and of the unfair treatment he receives. Concomitant conversations left no doubt that he did not possess a clear concept of boy and girl, male and female, despite the accurate anatomical knowledge he had obtained from a book his mother had given him.

The fact is that he did not want to know; indefiniteness in sexual differentiation had become the source of his reassurance and his hope. The confusion and vagueness of his sexual identity is reflected in his body image, which, in turn, determines the irrational component we discovered in his reality testing. It has to be kept in mind that the undistorted and stable perception of one's body reality is *ipso facto* complemented by a similar one of the outer world. The smaller the discrepancy between percept and concept of the body reality, the more reliable the reality testing capacity.

Ben's paintings and drawings indicated a decisive dissatisfaction with body parts. There was always something wrong with the ear; it was either missing or too big or just a color blob. The concentration on the ear could well have been a displacement from below to above. What did it signify? Organs appearing as pairs are always used by boys with undescended testicles as substitutions or organ equivalents. The people Ben painted were a ball player and a magician, both restitutive impersonations.

In conjunction with this, the many references to balls (baseball) and the fear that he—especially his eyeballs (another paired organ)—might get hurt while he was playing, moved the suspicion of a "ball problem" into the realm of probability.*

In order to protect his eyes, he wore sunglasses when playing baseball; then he announced a defect of his eyes —namely, color blindness. This deficiency was exaggerated, if it existed at all; nobody in the family had ever heard of it. It was therefore a message entrusted to the therapist, who was expected to decode it. The fact remained that his favorite game, baseball, was made dangerous by all sorts of potential accidents, such as "breaking your leg" or "having your head smashed in." He had never experienced an accident but, he thought, he had once been in a hospital for "sticking a cherry pit up my nose." On second thought, he was less sure whether it had been him or his brother. At any rate, the cherry pit could only be retrieved by going to a hospital.

He remembered the hernia incident as taking place when he was 5 years old, but he was confused about its location, saying it was near his penis. He did not know what a hernia is; all he knew was that it was there once and then that it was not there any more. Body damage fears were pervasive. Ben was keenly aware of his small stature and his overweight. He reasoned that the reason why the boys did not like him was on account of his physical appearance. What was it, the question arose, that is so devastatingly wrong in his physical condition? In a boy of his age one would, of course, first think of the desire and fear to "grow up"; but this familiar theme did not fit Ben's case sufficiently well to render a satisfactory explanation. Ben was dissatisfied with his physical self, and he expected everybody else to be equally

* See: Blos (1960) with reference to "ball playing" and "paired organs."

aware of his bodily state, to take advantage of it or to reject him on account of it.

Restitutive Phenomena

The involuntary abdominal movement attracted our attention from the beginning of treatment. There was nothing Ben could say about its history; in fact, this tic-like symptom did not bother him. Once we had formed the hunch of the presence of cryptorchidism, this strange movement took on the meaning of a restitutive gesture; concomitantly, it confirmed the hunch. The quasi-involuntary movement, we reasoned, had the purpose of pushing the testicle into the scrotal sac. In this sense, it was correcting a defect that was the unceasing source of anxiety. If our supposition should prove correct, then the bodily movement would lose its bizarreness and become instead a purposeful, even if involuntary, act.

Ben attached, by displacement, an enormous importance to certain of his material possessions or mental abilities, yet without deriving from them any lasting satisfaction. On the contrary, he wished for their loss, or unwittingly brought their loss about. Trying to consider these losses in the light of his victimization—namely, as expressions of guilt feelings and atonement sacrifices—made no sense to the boy; he could only point to the events of the day as irrefutable proof of the unfair treatment he was always receiving and of the injustices that were always being inflicted on him. Conversations always came to the same end: nothing ever changes for the better, and there is no hope for him, being born "unlucky."

One object to which he attached enormous importance was his bus pass: to have it securely in his pocket made him feel like a "big man." Then he lost it. Another valued possession was his superior intellect: reminding himself of his smartness made him feel good. At one time, he decided to learn all the street names in the city—an almost impossible task—in order to find his way around better than anybody else. Riding the buses with his bus pass would help him to achieve this goal. In the light of my cryptorchidism studies, I recognized in the spatial exploration of streets as the pathways of ingress and exits—or, generally, in Ben's geographical curiosity—a concern with body topography. Typically, the street project was never followed up. The thought of his being able to perform this feat was enough to restore Ben's sense of mastery. Might we not also recognize a restitutive endeavor in Ben's clowning, his making fun of himself and others, especially of the woman teacher? Can we not paraphrase it by saying: "It is not me but you who is to be laughed at; I am laughed at only because I am clever; when I laugh, it is at your expense; I pull the strings and you jump"?

Associative Links

What a 12-year-old boy is able to say about his inner life is usually limited; this is not the age of introspection, self-observation or psychological curiosity. He can disclose only what is available to his awareness, such as actions and events. Yet he will also state certain themes that are highly personal and private. These themes are usually left dangling; they remain incomplete in relation to the role they play in psychic functioning and, particularly, in relation to the illness or the symptom complex. Any theme, once struck, has to be complemented by references that afford it a special meaning or valence. Toward this end we rely on the child's use of symbols, gestures, play, play acting and paraphrases, and particularly on his associative linkages.

These linkages are presented by way of the seemingly disjointed talk, the jumping from topic to topic, the disruption of one ongoing thought by another, the shift to the expressive mode of action. It is in this indirect way that the therapist obtains the most useful information about the inner life of the patient or about the pathological processes at work. To recognize in the sequence of themes, even though they are heterogenous and without any rational connection, a pertinent, homogeneous and meaningful message—this remains the therapist's special task. To illustrate these remarks, two associative sequences will now be presented.

One day, early in treatment, Ben arrived in a highly nervous state. He could not stop thinking about his teacher, a woman, and the physical harm she might inflict on him by "hitting him over the head." No such hitting incident had ever actually occurred. A reference by the therapist to his endangered brain power was laughed off by him; nevertheless, the fact remains that he *knows* she is going to harm him bodily. He then dropped the teacher theme and picked up a basket he had started to make two weeks earlier. He settled comfortably and contentedly in his chair and began working on it. Gradually, he became selfconscious when he noticed that the therapist was watching him; he blushed and became fidgety. Finally, he gave up his basket work, went to the blackboard and drew a scoreboard for basketball. While drawing it, he told of a boy with whom his mother forbade him to play, because the boy likes to fight. Ignoring the prohibition, Ben played with him anyway, and he was punished for this by his mother, who had found out. How? "A girl snitched." He cannot understand his mother. He then returned to the baseball theme, giving the therapist the puzzle of "how a team can have six runs and no hits," and telling her that it is almost impossible to solve. Could *she*? At this point, he had urgently to go to the bathroom. Upon his return, he declared that he wanted to play checkers, warning the therapist that he was going to beat her, so she'd better watch out. He played very poorly, got trapped, and wanted to give up the game.

Organizing the manifest content of this session into a sequence of discrete themes, makes it read as follows:

       (1) Fear of the castrating woman (teacher).
to: (2) Flight into the girl's role arouses embarrassment (basket work).
to: (3) Turn to baseball, the world of boys.
to: (4) Having a fighter friend is of no avail.
to: (5) Challenging the ingenuity of the therapist (the puzzle).
to: (6) Rise of anxiety: urination.
to: (7) Ready to attack the therapist (checkers).
to: (8) Fear of his own aggression invites surrender and defeat.

Unifying the above themes, produces the following coherent sequence of ideas:

To avoid bodily injury inflicted by the castrating woman (1), I have the option of identifying with the female (2); this is pleasant but unacceptable (3); there is no solution left but to fight back (4), and to identify with the aggressive friend; this is no solution either, because fighting (5) sexualizes the attending anxiety (urination) (6); only aggression can restore the sense of masculine intactness (7); at one point, this always turns into inhibition, seeking safety in defeat (8). In brief, the above sequence documents Ben's ambivalence about his sexual identification and the gratification he obtains from the alternation of fight and defeat; in other words, it highlights the inordinate strength of castration fear and wish, both propelling him relentlessly, in a vicious circle, from attack to resignation.

The second associative sequence puts several themes, with which the reader is already familiar, into the original context of a treatment session.

Early in treatment, Ben arrived 15 minutes late; he is "in a foul mood." "I'm mad" he blurts out. What about? "The weather." If it continues to rain, he will not be able to go to a ball game that is scheduled for about two weeks from today. He then relates how well he does in Sunday school, where he has a male teacher. The real trouble is with his teacher in school: she makes him shiver and he becomes nervous; he cannot answer her because she makes him feel like crying and he cannot breathe. He then jumps to saying that he is color blind; he knows the names of the colors, but is too fearful to say so. He wants to draw and paint, and he draws a baseball player with a large head and no ears, "so he can't hear the umpire," no chin and a long neck. He points to a mistake he has made on the right arm, which holds the glove with the ball in it. He mentions an accident of a professional baseball player who "broke his leg or something." Abruptly, he states that he himself was in the hospital once for "sticking a cherry pit up his nose." He adds, "Maybe it was my brother." He returns to drawing, this time not of a person but of a ball field and a house. He dawdles and loses interest in what he is doing. Suddenly he looks as if he is in distress. Upon inquiry, he complains of a pain in his stomach and asks for permission to go to the bathroom. When he returns, he is feeling better, but he denies that there was ever anything wrong with him physically, or that he had felt any pain or discomfort at all before going to the toilet. He is eager to terminate the session, and he leaves the office a few minutes before his hour ends.

Organizing the manifest content of this session into a sequence of discrete themes reads as follows:

(1) Persecutory affect displaced to weather.

to: (2) Security in presence of male teacher.

to: (3) Helplessness and anxiety in presence of female teacher.

to: (4) Organ defect (color blindness).
to: (5) The defective self image (no ears).
to: (6) Accident and hospital (broken leg, cherry pit in nose).
to: (7) Cherry pit and hospital: confusion between self and brother.
to: (8) Pain in his stomach, bowel movement.
to: (9) There is nothing wrong, there was nothing wrong with my stomach.

Unifying the above themes produces the following coherent sequence of ideas:

The whole world is out to ruin my pleasure (1); the presence of men reassures me (2); women frighten me (3); something is wrong with my body; has permanent harm been done to it? (displacement to eye, ear, chin, arm) (4, 5, 6); how the confusion between self and brother fits into the associative sequence, is not clear (7); the pain is in the stomach (8); pushing the bad pain out (magical gesture) makes me feel good. I am sure nothing bad ever did or ever will happen to me (denial) (9).

Certain data that have been mentioned as being significant added up initially to no more than a hunch. It was in the light of further analysis of interview data that the proposition of cryptorchidism was advanced. Associative sequences, like the ones just reported, lifted hunch and proposition to the level of a conclusion. This conclusion rested on indirect evidence—namely, on the interpretation of associative links and the symbolic representation of the body.

At this point I have to emphasize once again that the explanatory conclusion was not derived solely from the manifest content of Ben's verbal communications. It would be absurd to impute any special significance to the relief obtained by attending to the need for a bowel movement. This act gains psychological significance only if it is placed in a chain of an associated sequence of expression, be it verbal or motoric, graphic or symbolic. Associative links, even though they are not verbalized, attract our attention and, through interpretation, give meaning to the spoken word. When words fail to tell all, it is the voice of silence, the associative link, that speaks.

Most revealing was the association that linked the cherry pit that had been stuck in a duct or canal with the stomach pain and with the relief obtained by actively pushing out something. The boy's denial that the manifest and associative sequence was relevant or meaningful fitted in well with his facile ego regression, in the face of danger, to the stage of prelogical thinking, or to the magic of negative thought. It can be considered a triumph of the ego to replace the regressive trend by the preference for or rejection of certain school subjects; this was to be seen in Ben's outspoken lack of interest in the study of the body (biology), as contrasted with his emphatic interest in the study of the stars. The heavenly bodies, after all, remained at a safe distance and could be counted on forever. The so-called abdominal tic, now understood as a magical gesture to "press out" the testes from the "stomach", became understood by way of the material just cited. From the data analysis, it became almost a certainty that it was anxiety about actual body incompleteness, coupled with a question as to its reparability, that was occupying the boy's mind. It had acquired the position of an "idée fixe," or of a supervalent thought; consequently, everything else became of secondary urgency or of minor importance.

This dynamic constellation looked like a massive resistance; actually, it represented a singleminded insistence on being understood, first and foremost, in terms of the actuality of his major—and justified—concern. This insistence found expression in the boy's unshakeable commitment to therapy, despite his complaint that "it doesn't do me any good." It was not until the physical condition was attended to by a physician that anything else—such as internal conflict, the affects of anxiety and depression, the realm of defense and adaptation—would be able to attract his sustained attention. It was thus no surprise to see Ben's "resistance" diminish markedly and rapidly, after the question of a genital anomaly was introduced by the therapist and a medical examination was arranged. This intervention afforded the boy enormous relief. The testicle problem was suggested by the therapist when Ben asked. "Do some boys grow faster than others; why don't I?" At the time he asked this question, his height was 4′8″ and his age 12.10.

The condition diagnosed by the physician was one of "retractable testicles"; this was not, therefore, true cryptorchidism: no operation or hormonal treatment was indicated. The explanation of the abdominal, seemingly involuntary, movement was confirmed by Ben as, initially, having been a voluntary contraction of the abdominal muscles, in order to push the testes into the scrotal sac. He had practiced this for a long time. Eventually, a habit had developed that served, we might say, as an automatic regulator of anxiety, by making it possible to forgo the involvement of thought and volition. Clinically, these movements had the appearance of a tic.

A word of caution is in order at this point, to prevent the reader from drawing an erroneous conclusion, either skeptical or optimistic, from the preceding discussion. The intervention by the therapist—namely, the confrontation of the boy with his genital defect—did not aim at resolving his neurotic illness but rather at making it accessible to therapy. Cryptorchidism was not considered to be the psychogenetic agent in Ben's emotional disturbance, but the organizing principle around which it had coalesced. It is crucial to recognize the fact that the physical anomaly had deflected onto itself the anxiety that had originated in various sources and developmental stages. A complex symptom structure now became simplified and concretized in terms of a physical condition.

In the light of the fact that the boy was in the pre-pubertal stage, the importance of physical adequacy and normality of the genital can well be understood. Priority had to be given, at this age, to physical normality and intactness, before the vicissitudes of drive and ego development could acquire a state of urgency and thus attract his attention. Access to these vicissitudes was blocked off, in Ben's case, by the physical condition that clamored for "a wrong to be righted." When the genital condition was recognized and named, when furthermore medical attention and judgment was made available, then suddenly the gates opened to that vast psychological hinterland that stretched out behind the physical forefront. In that unknown territory were to be found the pathogenetic sources of the illness. Once the therapeutic stalemate had been overcome, treatment could resume its normal course.

CHAPTER **15**

THE FORMATION OF
SEXUAL IDENTITY

Emergence of sexual identity during early adolescence is a precondition for the progression to the heterosexual position in adolescence proper. Children know whether they are boys or girls, of course; there is no doubt about that in their minds. The environment confirms their gender identity in countless ways that are borne out by the child's own observations. Yet we know, from the fantasies and dreams of children and adults alike, that apart from the factual knowledge there exists a set of ideas and imageries that do not correspond with the facts as the child knows them. Indeed, it is not difficult to ascertain that the two sets of ideas can exist, even consciously, side by side. They do this as easily as a person's rationality will tolerate a superstitious belief: the magical gesture of "knocking on wood" constitutes no denial of one's rational comprehension of the world.

The distinction between gender identity and sexual identity can be made in the simplest terms, by saying that gender identity pertains to the differentiation of maleness and femaleness, while sexual identity pertains to that of masculinity and femininity. Gender identity is rarely questioned consciously, while sexual identity is the subject of widespread uncertainty. An older adolescent girl had this distinction in mind when she said: "If I were true to my sex ('sexual identity') I should be a boy ('gender identity')." The frequent adolescent doubts about homosexual tendencies of a feminine or masculine modality are ample proof of one set of variants by which sexual identity can be defined.

Whenever sexual identity is grossly doubted, in terms of adequacy or normalcy, then we observe that the shadow of this doubt falls on the physical structure, the genital. The whole problem, thus concretized, becomes one of a physical condition; the organ is either too small or deformed, or it is simply different, "not the way it is supposed to be." By displacement, this doubt can find expression in relation to any part or physical characteristic, such as height, proportion, shape, skin texture, etc. Ben never doubted his gender; what he doubted was his masculinity. The condition of a genital anomaly pointed, in his case, to the way in which a pre-existing self-doubt was to become concretized.

It follows from what has been said that sexual identity is the broader and more complex of the two formations. We find within its borders a multitude of idiosyncratic, gratificatory modalities, possessing various and shifting intensities and qualities of opposite sexual valence. These are derived from earlier stages of development—namely, from preferential body zone modalities; from object relations and their interactional patterns; from identifications and, last but not least, from constitutional drive propensities and ego endowment. To further clarify this point, I direct the reader's attention to the fact that, for example, a strongly preferred oral modality is persistently carried forward up to the oedipal level; as a consequence, the triadic constellation becomes endowed with a passive, receptive drive quality. Should these strivings come into conflict with ego interests, they might then be denied drive expression and instead make their appearance in sublimated form, in keeping with the individual's ambition, talent and inclinations. This final step is taken in adolescence, while its antecedents were already recognizable during the latency period and even earlier. This does not alter the fact that the sexual drive becomes decisively modulated during adolescence, under the governorship of genitality. By the end of adolescence, there emerges an enduring sexual self-representation, structured and conceptualized as sexual identity.

Sexual identity does not simply follow from knowledge of one's own gender; it is decisively affected by ideas about the opposite gender. The body difference of gender gives rise in each child to thoughts about the origin of this difference, the changeability of gender and the desirability of one's own gender, as compared with the other. Comparison, evaluation and wish either elicit the illusory possession of body parts that belong, or are imputed to belong, to the opposite gender or else they lead to a disclaimer of body parts that belong to one's own gender.

Even though they are contradicted by perception, these fantasies exert a decisive influence on the self-representation. The motivational valence of the body image, which is based on gender identity variants or on outright body structure fantasies, is equal in strength to the objectively perceived body. Positive or negative fantasies about gender attributes, relative to self and to others, often possess a far more real quality than do the ones that are realistically perceived or consensually validated. The roots of the many complications that accompany sexual identity formation in adolescence can be traced to some aspect of infantile sexual theory that has acquired an enduring effect in a particular child. It should come as no surprise to discover that these infantile distortions make themselves felt with decisive urgency at the time when sexual maturation—namely, puberty—has arrived.

Ben's testicle condition, no doubt, complicated the formation of his sexual identity; secondarily, it also affected his persecution complex or his victimization compulsion. The interview material, up to the impasse, had contained many references to the problem of gender identity, to mutilation anxiety, to castration fear and wish. None of these communications, however revealing they were in their fragmentary form, ever moved beyond an opening statement of the respective problem. Onsets, beginnings and repetitions—in short, hints, bits and pieces—were all the therapist had to work with. Naturally, the nature of the resistance was exhaustively investigated, but to no avail. After the genital anomaly had been lifted by the therapist into the light of mutual recognition, these onsets and beginnings lost their guarded restrictiveness. In other words, it now became posible to extend the exploration of the symptoms into their pathogenetic core.

As soon as one begins to trace the roots of a symptom in psychic organization and life history, an increasingly complex system of intertwined traces makes its appearance. Each of these requires its share of separate and focal attention before the pathological process as a whole is understood and can be affected. This aspect of treatment is called "working through"; it belongs, essentially, to the later stage of treatment. However, in describing a symptom complex through its developmental continuities, it seems advantageous to use as a vantage point the stage of insight that has accrued from the working-through process. The tortuous and winding trail that leads to the top of the mountain can be traced from nowhere more clearly than from the summit. In the following, I shall trace one such trail—namely, sexual identity formation. I am well aware, of course, that this is but one component of several which, in their interaction, brought about a satisfactory outcome of treatment.

Ben knew of his genital condition, of course. In fact, it was his knowledge of it that was responsible for his preoccupation with his own genital and that of others. When first confronted with the genital anomaly, he flatly declared that he had never seen anybody's testicles and did not know anything about his own. He did not object to a medical examination, except by voicing his fear of what the doctor might do. Under the impact of the examination, his tendency to somatization asserted itself. He developed a stomach pain to which both he and the family referred as an appendicitis attack. Upon being confronted with this homemade diagnosis, however, the doctor declared that no operation was needed. The interpretation of anxiety displaced from a "genital" operation to an abdominal one (nothing "bad" had to be "cut out") helped Ben to reveal the fact that he had often examined his testicles and found that "one was lower in the scrotum than the other." He was afraid of a "genital operation" because "you never can tell—at the last minute something could happen." Of course, what he meant was castration (Blos, 1960).

In an effort to master his anxiety, he asked about the operation procedure. He wanted to know details and facts, and these were given to him with the help of verbal explanation and simple, anatomical sketches. But the information he needed in order to cope with his anxiety had to do with quite another area, as became apparent when he asked whether "women have balls and a penis." This prelogical concept merged with his knowledge of the absence of "balls and penis" in the woman. It contained both, the reality of castration and its denial.

At this point, the impact of a circumstantial coincidence has to be mentioned. Just prior to the testicle discussion, as fate would have it, Ben's mother went to the hospital for the removal of a benign lump in one of her breasts. The "cutting out" of a "bad lump" superimposed itself on Ben's testicular condition. The two paired organs (breasts and testes) had to suffer the same fate; this meant for the boy the excision of the "defective" testicle —or, simply, castration. He disclaimed any knowledge of the reason why his mother was in the hospital. In a light vein he added that she probably needed to get "a rest from him"—or, we might add, to displace him by another child, as she had done when he was four years old. At any rate, by resorting to his facetious explanation he was unwittingly conveying his feeling of guilt: it was his bad behavior that had driven away the mother, who had, in consequence, to suffer the destruction of the breast.

Ben's ambivalence toward the breast is plausible, if we look at the breast as the age-old prototype of the giving or withholding environment—or, in terms of emotions, of the contentment of satiation or the rage of frustration. The feeling that "mother is angry with me" is a reversal of "I am angry with my mother." This reversal became apparent when he followed up his denial of the mother's operation and his confession of guilt with the discussion of a voodoo doll. A boy wishing another child to be sick stuck a pin into the doll, which, then, rendered the child sick in the very place where the pin had "hurt" the doll. This sympathetic magic could barely hide the hostile and sadistic affect toward the mother who had left him behind, anxious and feeling guilty.

The fear of the phallic woman appeared repeatedly in

Ben's fantasies. He had only recently experienced a nocturnal emission (age 13), and he was not sure about the nature of the fluid. He thought that in coitus the man urinates into the woman's vagina. Noticing that the fluid on his pajama was different from urine, that it was indeed semen and a proof of the intactness of his testicles, he nevertheless found again an argument for the superiority of the female. "How come," he asked, "a girl of five can have a baby?" He had read an account of this in the newspaper. We are reminded that it was at just about that age that he had lost his mother to a sibling. We should not be surprised to find that it was at this period that there emerged his envy of the mother's procreative power, and his wish to have a baby himself, in identification with her. Whenever he had to "repair a loss," he resorted to an abdication of his masculinity.

Let us return to the session in which Ben spoke of the five-year-old mother. While the thought of intercourse excited him, the thought content shifted, more and more vividly, to aggressive, destructive fantasies. At this point, his mounting excitement became suddenly shrouded in silence, until it burst forth into a vivid description of a "new gun, which would not disintegrate a person but would set fire to a person's clothing, to his body and could even blind the person." Restraining his sadistic fantasies, he then suggested that scientific efforts should be directed toward peaceful goals—such as the invention of an X-ray machine that could tell, immediately after conception, whether the baby would be a boy or a girl. He added: "It would be better for the man (father) to know all about it first." In that way, he thought, a father could get ready for his son and for the clash of wills that was bound to come, because a boy who has been declared to be a boy from the first moment of life is a challenge to the father. Ben terminated this conversation with the cryptic remark: "If the father has a boy, he'll go crazy trying to control him."

The above material was elicited by the impending medical examination. It was Ben's fear of the doctor—or, conversely, the imagined failure of the doctor to control the patient—that revived the boy's competitive struggle with the father. Any restriction or prohibition that was imposed by the father became an emasculating attack. The ambivalence of sexual identity automatically transposed any experience of inequality into these terms. The closer he came to the medical examination, the more sensitive or "touchy" Ben became, both at school and at home. He neglected his homework almost completely, finding it impossible to complete a report on the digestive system—i.e. on the anatomy and function of the controversial body area, the abdomen. For the first time he became reluctant to go to school, as the result of his physical self-consciousness, as well as of the thought that his genital defect must surely be known to teacher and peers. The boys, he said, make fun of him: whenever he walks into a room, they start muttering: "Kill it, kill it, kill it before it multiplies"—("they call me 'It'"). An amalgam of fact and fantasy is apparent in this account; nevertheless, it suffices to make school a dangerous place.

The involuntary contractions of the abdomen became more frequent and noticeable. The therapist shared with Ben what was assumed to be the relation of these movements to the testes complex. Ben had already confirmed this interpretation of the muscular contractions. Apart from confirming the meaning and function of the "abdominal tic," Ben now felt free to offer a detailed account of the experimentation with his testes. He knew how to make them move down by thigh pressure, and he was familiar with the sensation of their changing position. He had worked out a way to control these unruly testes, which moved around as if they had a will of their own. He had found a spot on the side of the lower abdomen where pushing —as one would a button—would make the testis of the respective side move into the scrotum. He had examined the comparative size, consistency and position of the testes and had repeatedly compared them with those of his brother, with whom he secretly got into bed. He had found his brother's testicles "mushy, small and wrinkled," but he always found them in the scrotum; they never moved away from it. He had even demonstrated to his brother how his own testicles could move up and down.

Somatization affected his foot, his eyes and his chest at the time when the visit to the doctor was scheduled. His identification with the mother, who had undergone a breast operation, was pointed out to Ben, and the result was that a postponement of the examination was averted. His despair about what would happen to him after the doctor saw him had by now reached extreme and dangerous proportions. He burst out crying, expressed the wish that a car would run over him or, on another occasion, that his parents would kill him. These emergency situations were met by direct interpretations, which brought him into touch with his unconscious thoughts and fantasies. The two emotional extremes that were apparent in this crisis were those of sadistic-aggressive dominance and masochistic, passive surrender. In its simplest terms, the "either-or" proposition was one of "killing or being killed." Male identity, while it was desired, was also feared; once established, it would release a reservoir of uncontrollable aggression. This Ben expressed by saying once: "If I used all my strength, I might kill someone."

During the session preceding the day of the medical examination, Ben recalled a dream from the time when he was three years old. The dream had been so real that up to this day he cannot decide whether it was a dream or really happened. He remembers that he was lying in his crib and he remembers waking up in the night and all of a sudden seeing a mechanical man, a robot, coming into his room. "Get this," he continues excitedly. "I took my blanket and covered my feet and put my hands underneath. Why did I do that? Why just my hands and feet? Why not my head?" He still remembers this dream with an uncanny sense of realness.* This is a typical nightmarish dream, in which the child's castration fear (legs and hands), and his projected aggression (robot) are dramatically expressed.

With the memory of this dream, Ben reached into the dim past of his life, just before seeing the doctor for the genital examination. He unearthed in the robot dream the early terror of body-part loss that was gripping him at this very moment with equal force. He had, indeed, made good use of the two and a half months between the introduction of his testicle condition and the appointment with the doctor. The decision to allow a reasonable time interval proved most fruitful. The boy could be prepared for the doctor's examination through the exploration of fantasies, fears, and historical antecedents that were, directly and indirectly, at the root of his symptom complex. The medical examination revived a body damage anxiety that was now focused on the genital; the defensive organization in relation to it had been built up at an early age, before the testicle problem had played any significant role.

Before the examination took place, the doctor had been informed about Ben's abdominal tic and about his apprehensions and misgivings concerning the genital examination. The doctor had good reason for assuring the patient with these words: "Everything is in the best of order, because the testicles are in the scrotal sac." The condition was one of "retractable testes in a rapidly maturing boy"; it was therefore a condition that would

---

* Another boy of the same age reported a similar fright he experienced nightly from early childhood till his adolescence. He carefully kept his limbs under the blanket, making sure they would not protrude over the edge of the mattress. When asked whether they would be grasped by the monster under the bed (which he knew did not exist), he answered: "No, not grabbed, cut off."

normalize itself in the near future. Ben was delighted. He reported to the therapist, with a smile and a condescending attitude of "I told you so," that the doctor had told him he was "normal." Everything had turned out as he had expected. He had known all along that this would be the case, and he added: "I knew that it ('abnormality', 'operation') could not happen, because I wished it and my wish came true." His overstatement, as well as his recourse to magical thinking, gave reason to suspect that he was warding off an anxiety that had been aroused by the doctor's findings. The lack of conviction in his voice was quite noticeable, even though—or rather just because —it was concealed. At any rate, it injected a note of dysphoria into this joyous occasion. The cause for it soon became apparent.

The doctor's opinion ("you are normal") was, as we have seen, based on good medical reasoning; to Ben, however, it made no sense. He knew well that his brother's testes did not move up and down, while his own still did. To him, this was not normal. Following the examination, Ben became preoccupied with making his testes go up and down; he experimented with this while standing, sitting and lying down. In attempting to puzzle out the contradiction between the medical dictum and his own observation, Ben was giving credence to his perception, and thus revealing a reality-bound ego of considerable strength. Finally, he presented his dilemma to the therapist who unstintingly gave credit to the acuity of his observation and his reasoning. The therapist explained, drawing a simple anatomical diagram, the difference between "undescended" and "retractable" testicles.* Now the words of the doctor began to make sense; indeed, their

---

* Drawing has the advantage that the graphic demonstration of anatomy develops alongside the verbal explanation. The use of an anatomical chart is confusing, at first; it can be introduced later, to endow with scientific validity the simple sketches drawn earlier.

correctness was borne out by the events within that same year.

The final comprehension of his genital condition set Ben off on a train of exhilarating speculations. This experience, he muses, is something to tell his children and grandchildren about; an operation would have been even more sensational. His experience is really something *unique;* perhaps he will some day become a teacher and tell all his students about it, or maybe a doctor specializing in this field. We recognize in all this his wish to announce to the world that he is a whole man. He finally says that he will probably become a salesman like his father, or perhaps a ball player. Subsequently, he did became a ball enthusiast of major proportion, playing baseball, softball, any kind of ball. He said: "I could play ball every day, all day long." In the year that followed, he became an excellent ball player, esteemed by his team. A sense of competence emerged after his body intactness was restored. It is of special interest to note that, concurrently, an absorbing interest (team sport) developed that was personally meaningful and socially integrated.

The emotional disengagement from infantile love and hate objects proceeds while the adolescent is gaining in evaluative distance from them. The overvaluation of the parent is the result of infantile dependence on external narcissistic supplies. The realistic evaluation of the parents, however, forces the adolescent to discover new sources of narcissistic supplies within the self and in his interaction with the rest of the environment. This developmental advance represents, essentially, what I have conceptualized as "adolescent individuation" (Blos, 1967). The reason why I allude to this process at this point, is to show the far-reaching consequences of a therapeutic intervention that, in and by itself, may seem to be hardly worth mentioning. It reveals its vast ramifications only if it is viewed within the context of a theory of adolescent development.

After an explanation about retractable testicles was given to Ben, he admitted hesitatingly to his experimentation with his testicles, preceding and following the examination and, furthermore, to his confusion as to what was really happening. This cognitive blind spot was dispelled, once he could understand and clearly visualize his genital anomaly. This clarity of comprehension exerted a beneficial effect on his thinking or, in general terms, on his comprehension of the world around him. One could detect a rise in the level of his cognitive autonomy and, therefore, an advance in the reliability and certainty of thought. Anticipating later developments in treatment, it must be mentioned in this context, however, that the extrication of his thinking from automatic, unconscious references to body damage, was decisive for a realistic, instead of an infantile, evaluation of his parents. Re-evaluation of the parents with an attendant disillusionment in them is a normal and essential aspect of the adolescent process.

Once Ben's sexual identity had been freed from the fear of permanent damage, it passed through those stages of sexual identity formation that a boy normally traverses during his preadolescence. Ben's previous fear of the woman was now to be investigated. Her imputed castrating intentions had been due to the strength of the regressive pull to the archaic mother or, in other words, to fixation points at the preoedipal level. The mother's protection was both wished for and feared. Ben's life history tells us that this pattern was consolidated after the second child was born, at a time when Ben was four years old. The trauma of this event resulted in a regression to earlier, preoedipal levels—which may be responsible for the pertinacity of prelogical or magical thinking that the case material reflects.

In this connection, I shall now report an unusual variation of the typical infantile sexual theory, especially because it is told by a boy. Ben's discovery that the female had no penis (he had never been altogether sure about this) led him to believe that he had a penis because "it is sewed on" (his words). We are justified in assuming that, in his mind, the female genital is the only and original one, shared by male and female alike. The "sewed on" theory is in line with the boy's distrustful, apprehensive, insecure and pessimistic attitude toward life; he had no sense of permanency nor certainty, but rather one of impending disaster. On the ego level, these beliefs and attitudes affected ego functioning by depressing its vigor, its executive autonomy, or simply its efficacy.

As in early childhood, so now in preadolescence only demonstrative provocation of the mother could assure an emotional response from her. Provocation, executed under the stress of contact need, gave rise in turn to anxiety, as a result of the violence of the mother's response. What followed in the end was the child's surrender and submission. At puberty, however, this cycle became unacceptable; as a result of the emasculating connotation it carried at this stage of physical growth, it became conflictual. Whenever the mother requested that Ben do the shopping, clean the house, or wash the dishes, etc. the boy feared that these activties would have a feminizing— i.e. castrating—influence on him: doing feminine chores might turn him into a girl. The perseverance of magical thinking, as well as his fear of his feminine propensities, made Ben adamant in his opposition to requests of this nature. In school, for instance, it was sufficient that a request be made by a woman teacher for it to be countermanded by him out of hand as unfair and insulting. It is of interest to note that the complaints about women teachers that had abounded in the sessions during the first eight months disappeared from the material after the physical examination.

Now, an equal flood of complaints emerged, this time about his peers. All the boys, he reported, were after him: yelling, punching, bruising him, and even cursing his mother. All 17 boys in his class would climb on top of him; "I am," he raged, "at the bottom of the pile. It's a fox hunt, dogs and horses go after the little fox. No, I can't take it; it can't go on," he shouted. The worst of it was that Ben could not fight. He slowly let on to the fact that, whenever he wished to assert himself, an inhibition of aggressive action would take hold of him. It afforded a gratification of his passive wishes, which were unconsciously putting him into the role of the woman in the sexual combat, as he understood the parental relations. This inhibition of the aggressive drive was enforced by two factors; one pertained to the quantity of aggression and the fear of losing control, the other to masochistic gratification, obtained from being physically abused by his peers.

Summarizing these developments within a theoretical framework, we can say that Ben's preadolescent castration fear of the woman (the archaic mother) was exacerbated by a persistent regressive pull and by the inhibition of his infantile rage. A resolution could come only after the affirmation of his genital intactness. This event, coupled with pubertal maturation (emissions) and growth (gaining height), propelled drive and ego development toward competitive interaction within his peer group. His complaint was simply this: they do not love me; the only way they will give me their attention is by beating me up. The fact that he himself actively brought this about was totally incomprehensible to him.

Of course, this complaint echoes Ben's early grievance in relation to the second child. Sibling envy and anxiety, which were due to his enormous retaliatory aggression, were displaced onto the classroom, where teacher and peers took the roles of mother and brothers. This summary of fact and theory indicates the direction that therapy had to follow. Ben's masochistic, homosexual drive development had to be prevented from hardening into a fixation at the phase of early adolescence. Therapeutic attention thus became alerted for signals pertaining to this theme.

Ben had mentioned that he used to examine the testicles of his brother (the one who was nearest to him in age) at night, when he went into the brother's bed. Sleeping together had not only served the purpose of examination, but afforded him erotic gratification as well. He liked to "cuddle up close" to his brother because "on a cold night it feels nice and warm sleeping that way." Since sleeping together was strictly forbidden by the parents, the brothers started the night by going to sleep in separate beds. The shared bed stood against the wall of the parents' bedroom, and the boys could hear what went on in the adjoining room. "Of course, we have to be very quiet, and not talk or bang against the wall."

Uppermost in Ben's mind was his desire to make his brother love him. He was jealous of the youngest brother, who received "kisses and hugs" from the middle child, and he wanted to break up the alliance between the two. A peculiar relationship developed in which: (1) Ben identified with his brother—e.g. "Did I have this dream or did my brother?" or "Was it me or my brother who had the cherry pit up his nose?" (2) Ben envied his brother, who had an intact genital—e.g. "He has so many dreams and I have so few." (3) Ben desired his brother's physical love—e.g. "hugs and kisses," "cuddling together." In these three ways of relating to his brother we recognize Ben's effort to deal with the trauma of abandonment (at age 4); beyond that, however, we also recognize in the homosexual involvement the stage of drive development that is typical for the boy during early adolescence.

It was the lamination of these trends that threatened to bring the boy's progressive development to a standstill. The need to cuddle at pubescence repeated the cuddling in mother's bed, when he was little and afraid to sleep by himself. We had reason to expect that Ben's "love life" with his brother would throw light on his psychosexual development, because the derivatives of his sexual orientation could not fail to extend their influence on object relations, generally (parents, peers, teachers), and on ego functions, in particular.

Soon after Ben started to discuss his relationship with his brother, they both changed their position in bed by "lying back to back." All erotic sensations (buttock contact) were denied by "playing word games" in bed. We assume that guilt feelings had been aroused by the discussion of their sexual play, which Ben then disavowed by changing position and keeping his hands off his brother's body. It was suggested to Ben that, conceivably, cuddling pleasure can also be derived from "lying back to back." Following this suggestion Ben told of a sexual game he had recently played with boys of his own age.

Soon after the clarification of the testicle problem, Ben had ventured into sex games with a few boys. We might ask: where did he, the outcast of the peer group, succeed in finding any boys to play these games with? His previous declaration about having no friends had been, in part, a denial of the secret associations he had actually been entertaining with them. He and his friends had played "spin the bottle": the loser had to take off his clothes, piece by piece, until he was naked. This naked loser then had to crawl on his hands and knees through the legs of the other boys who stood astride him, paddling his behind as he moved along. Ben was paddled more than once. Another game, played outdoors, was called "cans up"; in this game, a boy had to hit the turned-up buttocks of a row of boys with a ball.

It was during these games, Ben said, "I learned about sex and especially about the penis," meaning its erectibility. Mutual masturbation was encouraged by his boy friends, but Ben was afraid of being "felt up." He revealed that he did not experience the "great feeling" of sexual excitement that the other boys derived from being touched. He became aware instead of a genital anesthesia, while recognizing a preference for being slapped on the buttocks. We recall here the frequent beatings his father had administered to this body part, the erotogenicity of which made itself felt again at puberty. This pointed to the urgent need to draw the relationship to his father into the focus of treatment—a subject that will be pursued in a subsequent chapter, devoted exclusively to it.

The effect of his new insight made itself apparent in several ways. A wave of repression set in: he gave up sleeping with his brother, and developed contempt for him and his girlish ways of kissing and hugging. "He is like a girl," Ben exclaimed in disgust. Concomitant with this change, the defensive repudiation of his guilt feelings lessened, and his victimization compulsion lost some of its power. He announced one day that "Nobody is ganging up on me." Last, but not least, heterosexual fantasies appeared. Initially, they were flight phenomena, with a tenuous heterosexual quality. "My daydreams," Ben reported, "are not about the teacher any more, but about a girl who is stripped and then turned into someone else." Into whom? "Someone like myself." He, then, created his own girl in a daydream—a girl nobody knew.

The daydream started when a boy was "going after me on a bus." He continued the daydream by describing a scene in which he strips the girl, "just a little, by taking off her blouse." Suddenly, he arrests time, with the help of a stop watch that makes the whole world stop, so that everything remains motionless. (This idea was taken from a TV program.) Then he changes the scene. The boy who bothered him on the bus is now sitting in Ben's seat, with his hand on the girl's blouse, in broad daylight, riding on a bus. He will certainly be punished when he is caught for "stripping a girl" and then Ben will be relieved of his persecutor.

This daydream not only reveals the persecutory defense system but, in equal measure, it lays bare Ben's shifting sexual identity. The interlocking of the two represents the foundation on which a perverse drive organization flourishes. The daydream is transparent: Ben's active wish to strip a girl is halted by making the other boy continue the stripping; thus, he is relieved of sexual molestation. By providing the "persecutor" with sexual gratification, he removes his own person from the attacker's grasp. Yet, he himself also participates, by proxy.

It is worth noting that the boy who stimulated this sexual fantasy is one whose physical prowess Ben envies: his height, his strength, his hitting power—none of which Ben can match. This envy forces him into the passive role, which only augments his persecutory anxiety. In connection with this daydream, Ben remembers his habit of "looking under girls' skirts" (see: "The Clinical Picture"), while the boys in the neighborhood were "picking" on him. With some amazement, he makes the observation that the boys have generally stopped using him as a scapegoat. Dream and fantasy material had helped to "make sense out of the confusion"; in turn, the need to repeat the conflict in action ("acting out") had become markedly reduced.

Ben was now at the height of the phase of early adolescence. The characteristics of this phase made their appearance in exaggerated form, thus carrying forward the earlier deviancies of psychosexual development. A pathogenetic core has to be dealt with anew at each phase of adolescent development. It thus came as no surprise to see Ben enter the stage of narcissistic object choice, or to observe his transient identification with boys who possessed the envied and admired—usually physical—attributes such as strength, height, courage, skill, daring, ruthlessness and fighting power. Being their victim, he became a part of them. While these narcissistic phenomena, including the homosexual aspect, belong to the phase of early adolescence and are no indication of a homosexual drive organization, the degree of Ben's passive trends was such that they could only be regarded as pathological. There is no doubt that, without therapy, the fixation on the phase of early adolescence would have brought about a consolidation of the sexual drive in the form of a perversion. It was this that had to be forestalled.

Despite the displeasure engendered in him by the recounting of his fantasies and episodes, Ben continued to bring them to the attention of the therapist. Many contained only thinly disguised homosexual wishes. When Ben, with indignation and disgust, rejected his brother's "girlish" or simply "crazy" behavior, he was on his way toward giving up the infantile relationship with him. What followed was a displacement of these same trends to school and neighborhood; but by this time he had come to realize (during the last year of therapy) that what he had been fighting in the environment was a part of himself. In the same measure as the sense of persecution and the need for victimization faded away, Ben was able to resort to aggression when needed—as, for instance, in self-defense. Proud as punch, he told of his first victorious fight with a boy and of the crowd cheering him when he hit well. While telling of this event, Ben swung his legs over the side of the chair and draped his arm nonchalantly over the back. This was a turning point in his life.

The insight he had acquired into his passive wishes was demonstrated when he compared the "love play" of his two brothers to a relationship he had once had with a boy. The way his brothers kissed each other, then fought and then lovingly looked at each other, reminded him of himself and his friend: "We would fight and then make up, fight and make up." Ben had gained psychological distance with regard to such cravings—which is proof of the fact that the observing part of his ego had emerged. Signal anxiety, which had once ushered in a regression to prelogical or magical thinking, now aroused his curiosity and puzzlement. It is this state of mind that is conducive to therapeutic work.

Defensive identification was now replaced by adaptive identification, which is typical for a boy at this age; this was to be seen, for example, in the tight association with "the bunch" on the ball field. He expressed contempt for the "sissy kind of boy who hangs around girls all the time, who only goes into shallow water and complains it is too cold." What he now shared with the boys was teamwork perfection, along with a roster of common heroes as their tribal fathers. Ben was accepted by the boys on the ball field. He said: "I guess I am one of them—they always pick me first—it really makes me feel good—it shows I'm improving." He had acquired a greater freedom in the use of his body (pivoting, running), which enhanced his athletic prowess and skill. By this time, being in his 14th year, he had grown taller and thinner, and his testicles were now anchored safely in the scrotum.

Ben's sexual identity formation had gradually moved toward a masculine countenance of a tenuous nature. There were many reversals. Whenever his passive, masochistic urges broke through, we could see the victimization tendency reasserting itself; it had to be worked through again and again, within the context of a new event, either actual or imagined. His flight into victimization had protected him against the menacing uncontrollability of his aggression. No doubt, his flight into masculinity also served a defensive function. As a result of these shifts, back and forth, between adaptive and defensive maneuvers, the feminine tendencies that threatened to overwhelm him, had lost, over the years of treatment, their irresistible power over him.

A final word about the boy's identification with the mother must be added here. The decline of the positive oedipus complex brings in its wake the typical fate of all abandoned object relations. Renunciation of exclusive possession of the mother, in competition with the oedipal father, is achieved by way of the identification with him. But there is more to consider in the decline of the oedipus complex than just this. As always, the renunciation of an object-directed wish is accomplished through identification with the object. Normally, the boy identifies with many of the mother's personality characteristics, such as her attitudes, traits, ideas and goals, etc. It is only when the identification encompasses, first of all, the sexual identity of the mother, that we can speak of a pathological resolution of the oedipal stage. Then, the identification with the renounced oedipal object has failed to become integrated within the biological context of gender identity. It hardly needs mentioning that, under such circumstances, the boy's relationship to his father is bound to appear in an abnormal form during adolescence.

It is of interest to note, retrospectively, that the testicle problem was indeed of a secondary order in the etiology of Ben's deviant development. While this condition served as an organizing principle during prepuberty, it did not constitute the pathological core of his illness. It had attracted our attention by its many elaborations, and because it stood, like a major roadblock, in the way of treatment. In time, however, we came to realize that this specific problem was superimposed on the pathogenetic core and, in fact, concealed it. In this respect, it resembles the plateresque architecture of 16th century Spain, where our attention is consumed by the façade of the buildings and its spectacular stone ornamentations, although these have no connection with the structure of the building they so richly adorn.

It would not be possible, at this point, to render a convincing picture of the structural changes that marked Ben's passage through the phases of preadolescence and early adolescence, nor would it be possible to portray the advances in adaptive accommodations and social integration that he achieved during this period, without tracing two lines of development that run parallel to sexual identity formation. Both pertain to Ben's relationship to his father and mother. It is common knowledge that these relationships undergo profound changes during adolescence. In the two chapters that follow, we shall study those changes that belong to and are typical for the young adolescent boy.

CHAPTER **16**

FROM THE ARCHAIC TO
THE OEDIPAL MOTHER

By now the reader must be impatient to have Ben's illness brought into closer focus by having the family relationships drawn into the clinical picture. The pathogenetic influence of family interaction on the formation of neurotic illness is known, and we are equally conversant with the decisive role of parents in establishing prototypical patterns in the child's feeling, thought and action. These not only appear in the sphere of social adaptation and attitudinal styles; they also influence characteristically all mental operations, including those of perception and cognition. Last but not least, they affect the awareness of the mental and physical self. All these various aspects influence the growing personality and are intimately related to family experiences; naturally, they played their part in Ben's life.

The extent to which Ben had displaced his family pathology onto the social environment, and the extent to which this replication handicapped him socially, have become clear in the discussion so far. While this displacement is typical for the young adolescent, in Ben's case it was carried out without the necessary transformation of highly personal connotations into acceptable and established social roles. Consequently, he was a social misfit. The social failure had become intelligible during therapy, as we have seen. But we still have to account for the origins of the masochistic drive orientation, as well as for the equally persistent fear of the female.

Deviant drive development is always reflected in ego characteristics; in fact, they exert a mutual influence on each other, as we have seen in regard to Ben's variable learning capacity, which depended, more or less, on whether the teacher was male or female. Men reinforced his reality-bound ego, while women made him regress to prelogical thinking. The anxiety he felt in the presence of women automatically effected ego regression, such as is manifested in magical thinking. Further, ego regression was often complemented by erotized bodily interaction (being "a scapegoat" or "beaten up"), which had become most prominent in relation to his peers. It is not difficult to recognize in these replications the prototypical members of the primary family unit: mother, father and siblings.

In Ben's case, the role of relatives or neighbors in his early life had been rather negligible. Whenever the figures of an extended family play an important role in the child's early life, they become a part—that is to say, a split-off part—of the parental figures. Each person, then, becomes associated with specific need gratifications or represents the personification of internalized safeties or dangers, generally thought of as good or bad, benign or quite evil. The primary objects are once again concretized in adolescence, at which time they rise to prominence, either directly or by displacement. This regressive aspect of adolescence is counteracted by the loosening of primary object ties, which effects the final emotional detachment from the objects of infancy and early childhood (Blos, 1967).

The reactivation of infantile object ties appears, at the initial stage of adolescence, in a configuration that is reminiscent of the oedipal phase. It has been my experience that it appears at this stage in the disguise of an oedipal involvement. This pseudo-oedipal configuration works against the regression to preoedipal object relations. It is, therefore, a defensive formation, which I have called the oedipal defense of the initial stage of adolescence (Blos, 1965). The therapist who ignores this formulation would be inclined to look at Ben's "fear of the woman" as due to anxiety, aroused by the heterosexual drive. It would follow from this that the drive belongs to the classical oedipal triangle; anxiety and defense would be interpreted accordingly.

Experience has taught me, however, that the pursuit of this line of reasoning leads further away from, rather than closer to, the conflict we are trying to resolve. The instinctual danger at this stage derives from the regressive pull to the preoedipal mother and the pregenital involvement that this regression entails. As long as we emphasize, by interpretation, the boy's competition with his father, and his wish to have equal or, indeed, exclusive claim on the oedipal mother, then we are actually assisting the boy in his defensive effort to neutralize the regressive pull to preoedipal object relations. We are helping him to consolidate the oedipal defense when we offer our partnership in his effort to obscure the sources of anxiety that lie, after all, in an earlier stage of development.

Before I continue, it seems in order to define the specific meaning and relevancy of the terms used in the heading of this chapter: "archaic" and "oedipal" mother. As is the case with many of the terms used in this study, their definition calls for the setting forth of a developmental sequence that, at a critical point during its course, coalesces into a terminological shorthand, or into a technical term. Even though the patience of the reader may be momentarily taxed by this "going back to beginnings," it remains the only way to bring precision and clarity into an otherwise vague use of words.

The infant's total dependency for its survival is, first of all, one of physical needs and the need for regular attention to them. A reciprocity of needs develops, between mother and infant. The physical well-being of the infant elicits in the mother a sense of competence and satisfaction that is soon echoed by the baby's smile and vocalization. The mother gradually becomes an identifiable object, the provider of physical and emotional nurturance, and the source of a state of well-being. She proves to be the tension regulator and, as such, an intrinsic part of the infant's homeostatic apparatus. This state of primary identification eventually gives away to a recognition of "I" and "You"—a differentiation that ultimately leads to the internalization of regulatory functions.

This advance in development is identical with the formation of the ego, or rather with its structuralization. Secondary identification advances structure formation decisively, through the process of internalization. By the time the symbiotic stage of early childhood has passed, in the third year of life, the dyadic relationship—namely, the essentially one-to-one relatedness of the child to his mother—has lost its exclusive dominance. The relationship to the father who is a source of comfort and safety to the small child is, however, cast in the maternal mold.

He continues to exist for the child in this mold up to the point at which he appears distinct from the mother, with the gradual emergence of a new—now triadic—relationship, which we identify as the oedipal constellation.

Tracing the lines of early object relations has the purpose of pointing out how the character of these relations changes in connection with the persons in the child's earliest environment. This is of importance to note, because the object relations of these heterogeneous stages survive in the child's psychic life, even after their legitimate time has passed, and they are re-animated at the appropriate phase of adolescent development. The pre-oedipal mother of the dyadic period is identical with the archaic mother, while the oedipal mother belongs to the triadic period, which includes the father as a distinct and unique person—a man who possesses powers, for better or for worse, that the mother cannot wield. Some of these powers are desired, some are envied, some are feared— just as was the case with regard to the realm of the archaic mother during the dyadic period. Like any new object relationship, that of the triadic constellation enhances the child's grasp of reality, because the turning outward of object libido diminishes, and eventually reduces to a minimum, the primitive projective-introjective comprehension of the outside world.

The archaic mother is not a separate and self-contained individual for the child. We must remember that the stages of awareness in early life reflect the simple dichotomy between satiation and tension—the former consisting of *taking in,* the latter *of ejecting.* The mother is comprehended by way of a similar dichotomy. On the one hand, the archaic mother is the source of all goodness; on the other hand, she is the source of all evil. Since early child care necessarily involves frustration, pain and tension, there survives from this period a feared and hated part-object relationship, which we identify as the malevolent archaic mother. In accordance with the dichotomy principle of earliest object relations, there also survives, equally global and separate, the memory of the mother as the source of satiation, bliss, safety and goodness, which we identify as the benevolent archaic mother. Both components of the early mother are preserved in object representations, and for a long time they resist reconciliation by compromise or fusion. They exemplify ambivalence in its original uncompromising polarity.

The archaic mother is regressively re-animated during the phase of preadolescence at which pubertal maturation intensifies drive tension. This condition, in turn, necessitates new tension regulators (object relations, defenses, adaptation, etc.), and the original tension regulator, the archaic mother, becomes at this critical point a source of control and safety. It must be remembered that, at the advanced stage of preadolescence, the archaic mother exists as an internalized relationship—namely, as an object representation that had been kept in partial repression until adolescence.

The archaic mother is associated in the child's mind with body control of the sphincters. The training period brings body functions—both their restraint and their release—into a complex system of autonomous operation. Therein we can detect the interaction of influences derived from instinctual needs, object dependency, ego and superego interests and attitudes. While the mother's pride, pleasure and praise was once a reward worth the price of renouncing immediate gratifications, at the pubertal stage of maturation this solution only precipitates conflicts. It is the synchronicity of pubertal maturation and of preadolescent regression to pregenitality that draws the preoedipal mother into the emotional life of the young adolescent boy. Obviously, the regression to the archaic mother, good or evil, is feared by the maturing boy, who resists passive submission and receptive nurturance. In spite of this, the regressive pull wins out, even if only briefly and transiently, and it is no surprise that the controlling, threatening, frustrating archaic mother moves into the foreground of awareness during male preadolescence.

This being the period of sexual maturation and, consequently, of intensified object directed drives, it is obvious that the archaic mother will be drawn into this new drive constellation. Her controlling role is cast, in consonance with sexual maturation, in terms of castration. This is the typical danger situation of male preadolescence. It is responsible for the avoidance of the female during this particular phase; instead, we witness the exclusive group formations of boys, and their positive turn to their fathers. The fact that the boy remains within the safe confines of the same sex can hardly conceal his active turning away from the opposite sex. We observe his guarded emotional distance from, or outright animosity to, or even his crude and cruel rejection of the mother and of all females in general.

This active yet defensive affirmation of having transcended early object relations is normally disrupted by regressive movements, which aim at the reestablishment of a preoedipal receptivity and anaclitic dependency. In the wake of drive regression, the ego is pulled back to primitive and abandoned stages. Magical or prelogical thinking, for example, once again proliferates, after its spectacular decline during the latency period, at the time when cognitive processes of a logical order first become clearly delineated from the early animistic conception of the world. In the preadolescent boy, what we see is a highly developed rationality and power of observation, side by side with prelogical thinking and magical beliefs. The two forms of thought, contradictory as they are, possess at least potentially equal motivational valences. It is this double standard in the thought process that accounts for much of the contradictory behavior of adolescence.

Drive regression and regression in object relations are

comprehended here in their interpendendence; nevertheless, another dimension has to be added, which I shall
call the "maturational imperative" of adolescence. That is
why these move in directions that are diametrically opposed to each other. The regressive stage of preadolescence is characterized by the dominance of dependency
needs and passive wishes. Such infantile positions, however, are anathema to the prepubertal boy, whose sexual
maturation would, indeed, be negated by regression to
receptive nurturance and passive submission to the
woman. No wonder that the regressive pull to object dependency mobilizes "on its way" the aggressive instinct,
for the purpose of defense and of progressive adolescent
adaptation. The aggressive drive appears first in infantile
forms—namely, as the sadistic components that had
played a major part at every stage of infantile drive
development.

It is a common experience in therapy that it is only
gradually that the determinants of pathological behavior
and thought, as condensed in the symptom complex, become elucidated. The recognition and understanding of
those connections that exist between the final abnormal
condition and its natural history are conveyed to the child
through interpretations and explanations. Each such step
opens up a new road to other sources that have also
contributed their share to the manifest disturbance, thus
revealing the intricate nature and complex structure of
the disturbance as a self-perpetuating system. Some of
the contributing factors, however, remain for a long time
stubbornly protected by defenses. Indeed, the abandonment of therapy often constitutes an unassailable defense
against physical removal—in which case, the therapeutic
situation itself has become a danger situation of such
magnitude that only flight is a match for it. The therapeutic alliance is always the surest protection against
such a catastrophic abandonment of the slow and grop-

ing moves toward recapturing the vital momentum of
development that had been lost.

It became obvious early in Ben's treatment that he
harbored an intense fear of the female, that he felt himself indeed to be persecuted, even mortally threatened by
her. This ever-present danger instilled in him a fatalistic
and helpless attitude toward life, since he was finding
himself victimized by evil forces that were bent on his
destruction. While he felt that everybody was against
him, he remained totally unaware of his own aggressive
and provocative intentions and actions toward others.
Their nature could be deduced only from his severe guilt
feelings and his constant offers of reparation. The fear
of the female was a repetitive theme, dramatically displayed in school in relation to his women teachers. He
was thrown into a mortal panic when the teacher asked
him a question and he was not sure he could answer it
correctly. The thought then dominated him that "the
teacher will kill me." He described a painful sensation in
the chest that accompanied this thought. The anxiety he
experienced in school was displaced from the home and
constituted a replication of his relationship to the mother.

Ben's death wishes against his tormentors came to
light only late in treatment, when he admitted to the
frequent thought: "I wish my mother or my father, or
both, would die." Death wishes were aroused by the slightest frustration or mortification he suffered. The thought
of having no parents, on the other hand, filled him with
terror because, he insisted, he still needed them "if only
to get my allowance and my meals." Infantile ambivalence dominated his object relations to a degree that neither his parents nor his teachers—nor, for that matter,
his peers—could tolerate. Thus he was deprived in large
measure of positive interaction with persons inside and
outside the family. It is from these sources that children
normally draw the sustenance for their emotional growth.

Not until Ben was able to tap the resources of the social, extra-familial environment, did treatment achieve one of its essential goals.

When the therapist became acquainted with Ben's fantasy life, his behavior and conscious thought yielded their secret meaning. The victimization complex is a case in point. At first, it appeared that a masochistic drive constellation, basically a feminine identification, was at the root of it. However, as it turned out, this symptom was a composite of several component parts. I shall enumerate them here briefly without discussing their interrelatedness, genetically, dynamically and economically.

(1) *Magical thinking* served to control the outside world. Destructive wishes could be undone by his receiving punishment and in that way the worst could be prevented from ever happening—namely, the realization of the death wish. This provocation of punishment was the magical counterpart to his evil thoughts. Superego influences, manifested in his guilt feelings, however, were proof of higher levels of psychic functioning within the victimization complex.

(2) Ben's states of *helplessness*—such as being sick, bad, uncontrollable, destructive—always aroused his mother's affective response: usually, it made her wildly angry and irrational, but it did establish a contact that Ben easily lost during her states of emotional distance and unrelatedness. This pattern of interaction had been established early in Ben's life, when the alternation of feeding and vomiting became a routine aspect of mother-child interaction. It is noteworthy that the mother never felt the need to hold the baby during feeding.

(3) Both parents reported that the child's feeding time was usually the time of marital quarrels and noisy arguments. Later, meal times became quarrel times. Ben remembered the wild arguments that took place at such occasions. These memories belonged to his latency years. The events in Ben's later life that elicited provocative

behavior were occasions of frustration, belittling and unfairness. His being forever at odds with his parents put
them constantly to the test—who would yield to his
wishes? who would frustrate him?—thus setting one
against the other. He never gave up hope that his father
would assert his dominance over the mother and thereby
demonstrate his allegiance to his son.

(4) From early life on, Ben had been an involuntary
listener to noisy scenes at night that took place frequently
in the parents' bedroom. These culminated in physical
combat between the parents, with the mother crying and
beating the father. Ben's sexual theory that the man
urinates into the woman or on the woman allows us to
infer that this primal scene stimulation coincided with
the period of his still unstable urinary sphincter control.
The combat in the parental bedroom, with the mother
beating the father, favored an identification with the father on the grounds that they were both being subjected
to restraints and the control of wetting.

The erotization of punishment thus had its early
source in identification with the beaten father. Small
wonder that Ben, as a preadolescent boy, wished that his
father would assert himself vis-à-vis his wife, and thus
become his ally in the fight against the castrating archaic
mother. In this connection, it should be mentioned that
Ben felt proud, happy, less anxious and devoid of any
persecutory ideas, whenever the father was successful in
anything, either within the family or in business. In
maintaining this state of confidence and competence, Ben
idealized his father—which led him to falsify or ignore
reality to a dangerous degree. This denial can be summarized in his conviction that "My father is great, but
my mother does not give him a chance." In the identification with the father, he suffered the same defeat as the
latter, making himself too the victim of the powerful
female—the malevolent, castrating, archaic mother.

This outline of the contributory trends that culminated

in Ben's symptom of victimization and basic helplessness allows us to postulate a sequential order in symptom formation. The deepest layer is to be found in a contact disturbance during the oral phase. While a sequential order can be imputed, on developmental as well as historical grounds, it should not be concluded that in therapy a thematic order of these various trends can be followed. All four determinants are at one and the same time actors on the stage of therapy, some at times more eloquent than others; all are continuously interacting until their passions are exhausted—at which juncture a new protagonist, such as Fortinbras in *Hamlet*, takes over the realm.

The small child's indefatigable push to reach some gratification of his contact hunger most probably received a positive enforcement all through infancy and childhood from the father's need for physical closeness to his infant son. At any rate, Ben's search for, and his capacity for a relationship, even if it was highly ambivalent, not only became a lasting source of wonderment to those who studied him, but had to be considered a drive quality that made treatment possible. This is hindsight, of course; no assurance of a source of strength was apparent at the initial assessment of the case. It must, however, be emphasized that Ben's positive responsiveness to the therapeutic situation, and to the purpose of treatment itself, was carefully cultivated by the therapist—as, for example, through the choice of interpretation at any given stage in treatment. Careful screening was employed in choosing the level of any interpretation and in keeping all interventions commensurate with the ego's capacity to integrate them.

Ben's reliance on magical thinking could be subjected to critical questioning (reality testing) only after the fear of the archaic, castrating mother had diminished, and a trust in and dependency on the therapist had been firmly established. He wished her, of course, to be the benevolent archaic mother who would remove all pain and trouble. The therapist had to frustrate these wishes, while at the same time trying to shunt the positive feelings onto the task of therapy, or onto the joint enterprise of overcoming the catastrophic growth impediment. At no time did Ben feel persecuted by the therapist, even though he did accuse her of many a fault and imperfection. These accusations, however, were related to the current stream of his affective involvement with her, and yielded to interpretation and insight.

It cannot be stressed enough that Ben's persecution complex was entirely restricted to, or rather remained in the realm of human malevolent objects; there had never been a trace of infantile fears in relation to malevolent animals or such awful happenings as exploding bombs, rushing waters, etc. The fact that his fears were not of the primitive nature that attributes to the inanimate object world a variety of malevolent intentions, offered at least a partial solution to the question of why he had not developed a psychosis or a phobia. Ben used therapy to establish a relationship of trust that would help him to transcend his basic ambivalence, which had permeated all his object relations and had with equal force affected his sense of self.

Ben's disturbance was one of object involvement, of ambivalence, of fear of abandonment and castration.* Correspondingly, the ego was arrested at the stage of prelogical, magical thinking, which derives its specific quality from the fact that certain particular affects, sensations and perceptions are attributed to the environment. In Ben's case, this was restricted to human objects. It is obvious that, under these conditions, the evaluation of the outer and inner world remains faulty and objectivity of judgment is grossly impaired. Ben demonstrated

---

* In what follows I am pursuing some of the ideas that Charles Odier has developed in: *Anxiety and Magic Thinking*, International Universities Press, New York, 1956.

that there cannot be any awareness of affect or of thought as such, so long as both are largely attributed to the outside world. "Objectification and consciousness are mutually exclusive . . . [this] is an important part of Piaget's teaching" (Op.cit.,p.113). Considerations such as these pinpointed, so to speak, the pathogenetic foci in relation to which treatment strategy was to be oriented. The overwhelming mass of interview material forces the therapist, constantly, to make choices; for that reason, he cannot proceed in treatment without a principle of selection. We refer to this principle as his "working hypothesis." Precisely because it is indispensable for treatment, it must remain open to continuous self-correction, through the constant testing of its relevancy.

According to our thesis, Ben's persecution complex was related to the fear of the malevolent archaic mother; this condition was, in turn, responsible for his ego fixation on prelogical or magical thinking. The therapist, as the good object, had to use the position granted her by Ben to help him advance his object relation to a post-ambivalent level. This, we reasoned, would liberate his thinking from its fixation point of prelogical thinking, and favorably affect his reality testing and his sense of self. We came to think that, in terms of drive development, Ben was fixated on the preoedipal level of object relations and, in terms of ego development, on the level of prelogical thinking. The actualization of his ego fixation was conditional—that is, it was restricted to those situations in which Ben's anxiety rose above the level of tolerance.

The drive fixation appeared, in exacerbated form, in preadolescence; in fact, it kept development from advancing beyond that phase. The ego fixation had rendered the latency period largely abortive. Consequently, the psychic organization of the post-latency boy was not commensurate with the emotional challenge of puberty and adolescence. Conflictual turbulence in adolescence is

unavoidable, just as regression—ego and id regression—
are inherent in the normal adolescent process. In Ben's
case, however, regression revealed the tenacity of ego and
drive fixations, and thereby pointed to an arrest of development on the preoedipal level. It became the task of
therapy to overcome both these developmental lags.

What Ben feared most was *"being ignored"* by his
mother. There was no punishment more severe than the
withdrawal of her attention. In helpless rage, he would
exclaim: "My mother does not love me," or "They (the
parents) can't do that to me; I *need* them." For comfort,
he turned to his little brother, or else he idealized his
father or a male teacher. Women became malevolent objects that had to be appeased. Punishment, the surest
path to appeasement, was therefore provoked—especially
during times of anxious separateness. Being in trouble or
being sick also had restorative benefits that he had
learned to exploit from early childhood on.

Love, attention or closeness had remained on the dyadic level of object relations; only one partner was chosen
at a time, to the exclusion of all others—whether this be
mother, father, brothers, or later the therapist. Disappointment in one of them would initiate a change of
partner, with the pattern remaining the same. This very
sameness demonstrated Ben's inability to use different
individuals in the environment for the gratification of his
different needs. In Ben's case, one person at a time had
to provide, globally, everything he needed. Ben summarized this dyadic relationship pattern by saying: "If I
haven't got my brother Paul, I have my brother David; if
I haven't got them, I have my parents; if I haven't got
my father, I have my mother; but when she is mad at
me, I feel like getting rid of her, too."

Ben's restricted and conditional use of relationships
was reflected in his restricted and conditional—that is,
idiosyncratic—use of words. He manipulated both of
these to suit his needs. It was, in fact, via symptom for-

mation in the cognitive sphere that drive fixations became accessible to the observing ego. The defensive use of ego functions (thought, language) became manifest as transient obsessional symptoms. As one example, I turn to the second year of treatment, when his parents were talking about separation. Ben alluded to this fact, but he did not ever use the word: "separation." When the therapist did use that word, Ben reacted with a massive denial, saying pugnaciously: "How can I feel scared, how am I even supposed to know how I feel, if I don't know anything about it?" Upon being reminded of his parents' fights and their threats, he smiled and admitted to knowing everything quite well. "But," he concluded, "as long as I don't use the word 'separation,' I feel sure nothing will change."

With the therapist's support, however, Ben came to acknowledge the futility of his magic. In a burst of courage, he asked: "What is wrong? what is going on?" He wanted to know. He did not have to wait for an answer, because he made use of his own observation: his parents were now sleeping in different rooms. Then he pondered on this question: "Who kicked whom out of the bedroom? In the movies, it is the woman who kicks out the man; was it the other way around with my parents?" Who is the woman? who is the "*boss*"? His primitive conviction was once again buoyed up, that the mother is omnipotent and the father has to submit to her superiority. Eventually, Ben recognized alternatives in the struggle: is it the malevolent archaic mother who controls the man, or is it the oedipal father who knows no fear? By that time the word "separation" had lost its magical power.

The renunciation of Ben's primitive tension control was followed by a depression, a fear of abandonment, that lingered on unduly long, and was overcome only after the dyadic position of infancy had been transcended. The ability to make this forward step depends on ego progression and, especially, on a clear delineation between fantasy and perception. When Ben was able to use the word "separation" like any other word, for the purpose of communicating a fact, the emergence of this ability signaled the expansion of secondary ego autonomy, as represented in the mature use of language. Progress to this position, however, was neither smooth nor direct. It became impeded repeatedly by the formation of transient obsessional symptoms. For example, Ben became preoccupied with words, such as the names of two schools; he had to choose one of these schools when he entered high school. His preoccupation with the names of these two schools was, in effect, a displacement of the choice he would have to make in case his parents separated: where was he to go? to his father or to his mother?

The resolution of many similarly transient symptoms lent stability to certain defective ego functions, and promoted Ben's cognitive mastery of emotionally disequilibrizing situations, real or imagined. His abandonment anxiety forced him to remain for too long at the prelogical stage of ego development, thereby forestalling ego differentiation. As a result, certain adaptive ego functions corresponding to his age were grossly deviant. How did these distortions appear in the transference? For a long time Ben clung to his prelogical "omnipotence" in the face of the therapist's reality testing. After the dissolution of the persecution complex—or, in other words, after the decline of his dependency on the archaic mother—the magical defenses could be interpreted and related to events, affects, thoughts, fears and fantasies.

In the transference, he imputed destructive intentions to the therapist at any point at which a comment or interpretation made him anxious. At such moments she turned into the archaic, castrating mother. One such reaction is best mentioned verbatim: "You remind me of a wrestler on TV who chops and chops away at and steps on, and chops on, one little foot." Transference phenomena of this nature were utilized in dealing with infantile drive and ego fixations. Only through internalization of the conflict could the preadolescent battle against regression to the preoedipal mother be waged. This, of course, could occur only after "infantile realism" (Piaget) had been abandoned. Then, and only then, was Ben able to see life in the perspective of past, present and future.

He began to realize with amazement that his parents had existed and had taken shape as people, long before he was born. This helped him to see his parents as separate individuals, who lived, felt, and behaved in other ways than solely in reaction to him. He said: "My father was wild long before I was here." Toward the end of treatment, when some of his parents' actions and pronouncements were called "crazy" by the therapist, Ben benignly suggested using the word "immature"; that, at least, implied some hope for change. By this time, Ben's magical thinking had become restricted to that legitimate mental activity that we designate as wishful thinking, fantasy and daydream.

When magic had ceased to contaminate his thought and action, however, there followed at first a sense of discouragement and downheartedness. This could be seen at the time when Ben's mother took a full-time job. To begin with, he felt deserted and ignored. In his customary fashion, he paid no attention to the family's financial plight which, as the result of the father's limited earning power, had forced the mother to seek employment. All he could say was: "My mother wants money more than she wants me. If she loved me, she would stay home." He concluded: "I like to stay home alone, I have me, myself and I for company. I can eat what I want." Alone at home after school, he experimented with food. He made himself sandwiches with mayonnaise, ketchup, mustard, jelly, baked beans, lettuce, coleslaw, hamburger, salami, onions and swiss cheese, one on top of the other. These food orgies did not last long. The absence of the mother did not initiate a permanent regression, nor did it undo the gains he had made in emotional independence. The solitary food indulgence was soon replaced by a renewed interest in school work, by outdoor activities and finally, when he was 15 years old, by his getting a job himself.

Oedipal strivings, whenever they arose, were assailed by his fears of losing his mother as a need-gratifying and protective object. The progression to the phallic phase was impeded, in Ben's case, by the fear of abandonment. Whenever this fear reached a critical level, it was reduced by the renunciation of phallic strivings. It took a long time before the regressive surrender to passivity acquired an ego alien character. He felt that renunciation was being forced upon him by the archaic mother. This imposition of helplessness, taken in conjunction with the loss of his magical powers over her, constituted but another source of preoedipal castration anxiety.

Ben's psychosexual development had moved forward when he entered the oedipal or triadic constellation, in which, initially, the father became the libidinal object and the mother the adversary and rival. When the parents indicated their intention to separate, Ben would cook for his father; he did everything he could to hold the family together. In school, he carried boys' love letters to girls, calling himself the "middleman." While he felt degraded by this position he was, nevertheless, a curious and willing *"postillon d'amour."* He played at intrigues by changing the letters or by making up love letters that would embarrass the partners. Vicariously, he took part in the "love life" of his peers. No, no, he did not want a girl friend for himself. In fact, he would never, never "do it for a million dollars." Upon being questioned about "it," he blushed and said: "No, no, I would never get near a girl, I don't like girls."

An aversion of this nature is typical for the preadolescent boy. What rendered Ben's psychosexual development atypical was his stubborn tendency to identify with the preoedipal mother and to renounce phallic strivings under the slightest opposition or challenge. The boy made every effort, during the preadolescent phase, to replace the archaic mother with a powerful and resplendent oedipal father. In this he gradually succeeded. However, this aspect of Ben's object relations will not be pursued here any further, because the chapter that follows will deal exclusively with the son-father relationship.

I have described the therapeutic effort, which was aimed at loosening the preoedipal, dyadic fixation (phase of preadolescence); but I have only hinted at the formation of the negative oedipal constellation, in which the father becomes the triadic love object (phase of early adolescence). We shall now turn to the development in object relations that reflects the typical oedipal constellation (phase of adolescence proper). This developmental study will come to an end with Ben standing on the threshhold of adolescence proper, after having recaptured the forward thrust of progressive development. At this point, the reader must be reminded that the demarcation of phases is an artifact, constructed for the convenience of establishing milestones along the path of development. What we actually observe are overlappings, movements forward and backward, advances and retreats. Over a period of time, however, developmental directions and attainments do become clearly visible.

I shall now illustrate, by way of dream and fantasy material, the progression from the preoedipal to the oedipal level of object relations. In the second year of treatment, Ben reported fantasies and daydreams that threw light on the stage of psychosexual development he had reached. When he wakes up at night—at about 2:00 A.M., he says—he makes believe that he is punching his teacher, a woman, in the face. The teacher responds to his punches by saying "give me some more"—that is, she encourages his aggression. He then imagines her crossing the street and being hit by a kiddie car in which a baby is sleeping. Such fantasies of a sadistic nature suddenly blend with erotic imagery, in which he "strips girls by taking off their blouses." Just as this happens, the picture changes and he cannot see their faces. He is curious who the girls are; sometimes the face turns into a monkey's face. The stripping fantasy undergoes many variations; some have already been reported in Chapter 5.

These fantasies are quite typical for the young adolescent boy, in that an undifferentiated sexual excitement is elicited by crude aggression, in fighting, punching, stripping. The attack on the woman teacher was aroused by Ben's jealousy of his younger brothers—an attack that reached its climax in his forcible, if only visual and furtive, seizure of the breast. Fantasies such as these contain all the elements of sexual excitation, but without the proper fusion of aggressive and libidinal impulses. In fact, the female is treated like a dangerous object; she has to be subdued and divested of her phallic—i.e., castrating—potency and might. After the preadolescent boy has overcome both his fear of and his regressive pull to the archaic mother, he experiences a revival of the triadic stage of object relation, the oedipal constellation. The woman still remains the source of apprehension and fear, but now her evil power is weakened by the boy's positive relationship to the father as his ally and partner. The archaic mother becomes dispensable when a new source of narcissistic supply and of object-directed gratification is available—namely, when the father has been elected as love object. This often short-lived, rudimentary and transitional stage has momentous consequences, because it is only with its dissolution that the boy is able to reach masculine identification and a definitive structure of his ego ideal (see Chapter 17).

I shall now turn to a forward step in Ben's psychosexual development. The first tentative signs of his approach to the oedipal level deserve our attention as significant indicators of progressive development. Dream material will be used to illustrate this forward movement.

In a dream, Ben was the founder of a Rock 'n' Roll group, similar to the Beatles. He was famous and—in his own words—"all the girls were running after me, but not because they liked me, but because they were angry with me for taking all the popularity away from the Beatles, whom they loved. They caught me and they spit in my face." Without a pause, he tells a dream from "the age of three." This is the robot dream, reported in Chapter 14 which remained Ben's reference image to body damage anxiety. The robot, as we have seen, is the fear-instilling father of the primal scene. Let us now return to the Beatles dream, in which Ben surpasses the unsurpassable Beatles, only to discover that his superiority is in turn avenged by "the girls," whose idols he has shattered. Ben's effort to equal the father's greatness, real or imagined, is thus avenged either by the "mechanical man" (father), or by the vengeful girls (mother), who reject his masculine self-assertion. The two dreams, taken together, show young Hercules at the crossroads, uncertain as to which danger to brave. The triadic constellation appears in this dream sequence with clarity. We might add that the dream conveys a gleeful sense of victory about having surpassed a hitherto peerless idol.

While Ben's behavior, epitomized and paralleled by his dream, still reflected the old theme of being unfairly treated, an awareness was already beginning to dawn in his mind that the wish for self-assertion and the need for punishment are closely related. Both became apparent in his behavior, and now, when the oedipal character of his actions had become flagrantly obvious, he could not escape the recognition of his wishes and fears. He began to wear his father's underwear and pajamas—first secretly and then defiantly. Paying little attention to his parents' prohibitions, he also tried to wear his father's new pullover. While he was walking around the house in his pajamas, his fly stood open, and unwittingly he exhibited himself to his mother. Upon being confronted with his exhibitionism, he became highly indignant. Although his self-consciousness did inhibit the exhibitionism, it was not able to do away with the urge that brought it into being.

He now developed a tic-like symptom, which consisted in a rapid and minute projection and retraction of the tongue between the lips, a token "sticking-out-your-tongue." Coincidentally, his school work deteriorated again, and his provocations—or, conversely, his need for punishment—mounted. He accused his mother of wanting only his intellect—namely, good grades in school. His reluctance to obtain good grades became identical, therefore, with the renunciation of his phallic strivings. He wanted the mother to recognize his physical maturation and his rivalrous wishes to occupy the father's role, or at least to be considered his equal. Ben rejected the mother's demand for good grades, because he experienced it as a submission to her will; instead of good grades, what he showed her was his penis.

In treatment, Ben expressed his dissatisfaction with his woman therapist. Whenever his actions or dreams were translated into insight, he wanted to leave treatment. One day he left his session in a huff, before his time was up. When he arrived the next time, he went to the washroom before coming to the office; and then finally appeared there for his interview, combed and "all slicked up." On another occasion, he brought a little stool that he had made in "shop" at school for the therapist to admire. Obviously, Ben was profoundly involved in the oedipal experience he was able to revive after he had transcended the regression to the archaic mother. He had acquired, albeit belatedly, one of the dynamic and structural preconditions for the normal course of the adolescent process.

It must be noted at this point that the adolescent revival of the oedipal constellation necessitated, in Ben's case, a simultaneous revision and correction of the incomplete and abnormal oedipal phase of his childhood. In many ways, he was now behaving like a little boy who is wearing his father's hat: he carried bundles for his mother and assisted her in heavy jobs around the house, these being a man's prerogative and duty. While assuming this manly posture, he resented the fact that his father did not provide him with a more admirable model; in his words, he wished that his father were "a man and not a punk."

The revived oedipal constellation had an influence on ego functions and psychic structure. To begin with, the capacity for self-observation increased: the outside observer, judge and evaluator became internalized. By virtue of this internalization, the ego increased its independence of the environment. The broadening scope of ego functions reduced the influence of the archaic superego. That is to say, the terrorizing fears ("She will murder me") of the primitive superego subsided, and guilt feelings, typical of the oedipal superego, were strengthened. Right and wrong acquired an abstract quality, and became removed from Ben's previous animistic comprehension of the world. This shift parallels the decline of the archaic superego and the ascendancy of the ego's evaluative function. We can ascribe this advance to a firmer demarcation between object- and self-representations, and to the ego's rejection of and resistance to magical thinking. This cognitive advance is concomitant with psychic differentiation—namely, structure formation. Thus, two essential conditions for adaptation came into existence—the capacity for delay, made possible by "trial action in thought", and the capacity for predictive reasoning.

A more realistic appraisal of his parents made Ben turn to supplementary sources of gratification; at the same time, it removed his learning and thinking from affective involvement with the parents. When he graduated from the eighth grade at 14, he did so after passing all his subjects and receiving an A for effort. With his increasing participation in the usual outdoor activities of his peers—or, conversely, with the emotional disengagement from his parents—Ben's mouth tic and his exhibitionism disappeared. Jokingly, he remarked: "The way my mother and I get along—well, all I can say is that I'll get a divorce before I ever get married." This statement was followed in the next interview by his saying: "You know I like both my parents about the same." He left it there and turned to thinking about the ball game with his friends and about plans for a summer job.

The real test of Ben's progress came at the end of treatment, when he was told by his therapist that she was expecting a baby. Termination time depended on her pregnancy. Ben's immediate reply was: "I'll be his godfather"; then he added the complaint: "Couldn't the baby have waited?" Of course, preoedipal, oedipal and sibling problems were once again revived; nevertheless, he finally assumed a protective and reassuring role vis-à-vis the future mother: "Don't you worry," he said, "I can stand on my own two feet." As if to soften his aggressive reaction, which had been due to jealousy and frustration, he rendered the critical experience tolerable by giving expression to his positive feelings; he said: "I think I like you."

Instead of continuing to demand undivided love, he resolved instead to go on with the therapist's good work, to carry it away with him as a trust and a possession. Faced with her loss, he identified with the therapist's function, rather than with her physical existence as a woman and a mother. When parting time came, he felt gratitude and sadness; but he did not let any of it get the better of him. Instead, he said: "I've got a different way of looking at things; and I am going to be an old veteran at it, too." For the last interview he appeared "all dressed up," looking his very best. Smilingly, he commented that he deserved something on an occasion such as this. What could that be? A plaque at the back of his chair: "Here sat . . . ."

The developmental progression we have followed in Ben's therapy illustrates typical stages of the adolescent process. We have ample evidence for assuming that corrections and revisions of incomplete or arrested infantile development occur spontaneously, within limits, during the adolescent period. In fact, it is this corrective aspect of adolescence that renders this period vastly complex. To present a comprehensive psychological description remains a difficult task, because progressive and regressive lines of development are taking their course at the same time. The reason why the corrective process could be studied in Ben's case and the complexities of development could be followed in detail was that treatment allowed the microscopic inspection of those psychic restructurings that, under ordinary circumstances, lie beyond the power of our vision.

CHAPTER **17**

THE FATHER IMAGE,
THE REAL FATHER,
AND THE EGO IDEAL

The preceding material has led us to abandon the
expectation that a revival of the oedipal constellation
would follow immediately, in the wake of pubertal—i.e.,
sexual—maturation. Prestages have been described to
this culminating stage, by which adolescence proper is
characterized. Our conclusion has been that the positive
oedipal constellation of the boy is able to emerge only
after the tie to the preoedipal mother has been resolved,

and after the negative oedipal constellation has been transcended.

The negative oedipal constellation, in the case of the boy, is characterized by his passive love for the father. This sort of material is most often dealt with in therapy quite marginally and, at that, erroneously, in terms of oedipal competition or its renunciation. The father theme appeared early in this case as the countervailing theme to Ben's persecutory anxiety of the female. In other words, the irrational fear of the woman was being minimized by an equally irrational idealization of the father. Thus, the great father became the source of assurance and safety.

In order to bring order and light into these changes of adolescent relationships, I shall present them in a sequence of steps that is determined by the logic of developmental progression. The first step, during the phase of preadolescence, pertains to the preoedipal relationship to the mother; the second step, during the phase of early adolescence, to the negative oedipus complex. I shall try to trace these steps in every case. Where there exists an apparent absence of sequential—i.e. phase to phase—progression, one has the right to suspect a massive defense or a developmental arrest. We know, from clinical experience, that the adolescent boy's positive emotional attachment to the father is far more difficult to reach in treatment than his relationship to the oedipal mother. We shall now investigate the development and nature of Ben's relationship to his father, and the conflicts it contained.

While fear of the female is typical of the preadolescent boy, in Ben's case this fear assumed enormous proportions. As is typical in such a crisis, Ben turned to his father for comfort and assurance. The assurance of a man's inviolability and self-confidence had to be exemplified by the father; this much, at least, Ben expected from him. The recognition of the father's weaknesses—his submissiveness and lack of assertion—resulted in two reactions: one was denial; the other, idealization. Taken together, these reactions assured Ben security in the father's greatness and love. On the one hand, Ben imputed to his father qualities of competence and fearlessness that the father not only lacked, but were in fact contradicted by daily observation; on the other hand, the boy complained endlessly about his father's emotional unavailability, his lack of interest in his son or, simply, his failure to love. Ben wished to be close to his father—to enjoy his protective masculinity, as well as his generosity in the form of going together to ball games, to restaurants, to shopping trips; furthermore, he wished his father to bestow on him, the eldest son, special privileges in the home, such as late bedtime, TV priority, and dispensation from household chores that are more fitting for a girl than for a boy. These characteristics of Ben's relationship to his father can be illustrated abundantly from the interview material. The over-idealization of the father serves as a defense against the archaic mother who represents to the prepuberty boy an emasculating and infantilizing threat.

Out of this preadolescent father relationship, in which the father is rather a "pal" and friend than an oedipal competitor, there slowly takes shape a relationship of a different order. In the phase of early adolescence, the boy enters the negative oedipal constellation by first settling on a narcissistic object choice. This move is not defensive in nature; it brings to life the still existent remnants of the boy's passive oedipal love for the father. While this relationship is in direct continuation of the dyadic dependency of the preoedipal period, having since then become part of a triadic constellation, it now assigns to the mother the role of rival and competitor. The young adolescent boy likes to do things with his father, leaving the mother out of them. It is only if this relationship persists beyond its timing that we can attribute to it a defensive aim, to be followed by a deviant (homosexual)

sexual development. Normally, the negative oedipal position of early adolescence is given up and replaced by a definitive structuralization of the ego ideal (Blos, 1962). These theoretical considerations lent direction to the consecutive steps therapy had to take in Ben's case.

First, the defensive overidealization of the father had to be brought into an associative linkage with the fear of the archaic mother. This could be attempted only if the therapeutic alliance—namely, the trust in the dependability of the therapist—was firm enough to provide a so-called "interim" protection against anxiety; then and only then, could the defensive idealization of the father be given up. Concomitantly with the therapeutic work, the affectionate attachment to the father came to the fore. Its resolution follows, in the normal course of psychosexual development, before the boy is able to enter the phase of adolescence proper (positive oedipus complex).

Competition and rivalry with peers were the first manifestations of this forward development. Interest in girls, as well as oedipal transference phenomena, offered the final proof that Ben had transcended his passive attachment to the father. The disillusionment in the father was perhaps the hardest blow for Ben to bear. Only after he had shown signs of an internal restitution, by his wanting to become what he had wished his father to be, could one be certain that the ego ideal had indeed replaced a regressive, narcissistic and passive object relationship.

I have spelled out this theoretical outline of the "father theme" in Ben's case in order to equip the reader with a knowledge of the phase-specific drive and ego positions, before I present the case material that will give substance to these abstract formulations. The overidealization of the father took its cue from the derogatory remarks with which the mother belittled and degraded him. Even though, Ben muses, "my father yells and gets mad," as a person, "he is really a nice guy." This is followed by examples from the past, when "he took me rollerskating as a reward for being good." Ben likes to go with his father to his office. He describes it as an exciting place with a big desk he loves to sit at. He wants to convey the impression that his father is an important man in business who—Ben says with pride—"makes a good living"; he once "made two hundred dollars in one day."

Ben not only exaggerates, but he also falls back repeatedly on defensive idealization. This assumes a more and more generalized form, bearing less and less resemblance to the facts. For a while, he is an outright fanatic on this touchy subject. He prefers the therapist to talk to his father, rather than to his mother. The degree to which Ben identified with the father is exemplified by his saying that he will become a "salesman like my father; marry and have three boys, naming them after my brothers and myself." These identifications were short-lived and, indeed, reactive in nature.

The disdain, scorn and revulsion that Ben's mother heaped on her husband, made the son rush frantically to his defense and vindication. The mother's wish that her son bear no resemblance to his father ("do you want to be like your father?") was answered by Ben with increased idealization and, indeed, with a transient and demonstrative identification with his father. The defensive nature of both was interpreted many times by viewing recurrent behavior or fantasies in the light of the precipitating events and the attendant affects.

The father had noticed how Ben's schoolwork fluctuated in accordance with his own ups and downs in business. He says: "Whenever I do well on my job, Ben does better in school. When I go high, Ben flies. The boy seems to follow me in many ways. He is very proud of my work." It has to be mentioned, in this connection, that Ben's father, being an extremely unsuccessful salesman and consequently a marginal provider at best, had made the most of his son's idealization of him; he had, in fact, become dependent on this source of self-esteem. He not only wanted Ben to succeed in order to feel less incompetent and depressed himself, but he also went after the boy, at the slightest provocation, to extort from him a show of respect, deference and obedience.

It would be rewarding, in this connection, to trace the influence of the father's relationship to his own father, but I shall only mention the fact that Ben was cast in a parental role; thus, the father reversed his generational position, in his desire to receive from his son those emotional supplies that only a father can give his offspring. The father's remark that "first Ben must give me, then I will give him," or "Ben has to respect me first, then I will respect him," revealed the absurdity of the demands that father and son were making on each other. In order to normalize this relationship, the father had to seek therapy for himself. This he did, following it through for almost the entire time his son was in treatment. The father recognized in his son those shortcomings that resembled his own and treated them with brutal fury. In order to live with his own shameful deficiencies, he needed a son who had none; his son had become his potential ideal self, and it was on this basis that there had grown a strong bond of ambivalent affection between them.

While the father resented the demands his son made on him, he wished, nonetheless, that Ben would "go on nagging him" until he would, half-grudgingly, half-pleased, fulfill his son's wishes. Although the father desired to give pleasure to his son, he felt embarrassed to do so. As a result of this bind, the two of them remained cantankerous and contentious most of the time. The father, intuitively, realized that he had always used his son as "a scapegoat, hitting and punishing him without any reason." Alternating with the sadistic interaction, there were frequent demonstrations of affection, such as kissing, embracing, saying endearing words and exchanging confidences. Obviously, the liberation or the emotional independence from the father became complicated by the habitual ways òf mutual drive gratification that had been firmly established in both of them by the time Ben arrived at prepuberty. The sadomasochistic relationship assumed a special intensity during early adolescence; indeed, it became Ben's major task in this phase to relinquish this erotic bond.

There is no doubt that the transition from the negative ("passive") to the positive ("active") oedipal position is so gradual, and is beset with such frequent oscillations between the two positions, that one cannot arrive with certainty at a clearcut line of demarcation. For a while at least, it all remains a matter of nuances and prevalences. The initial—i.e. preadolescent—defensive use by Ben of his relationship to the father, changed when it became competitive and combative, rather than imitating and idealizing. Concomitantly, the need for punishment, or for masochistic surrender, receded markedly. This stage could be reached, however, only after certain steps had been taken in psychic restructuring.

Let me briefly summarize. Ben had elevated the father through defensive overidealization to a position that was designed to assure a flow of narcissistic supplies. He experienced this influx as a rise in self-esteem and a sense of inviolability. He had constructed a father representation or father image that served both as anxiety regulator and as protector against the female, the archaic, castrating mother. In Ben's case, this had assumed exaggerated proportions. Ben depended and continued to depend on the father's perfection and might, and his actual imperfection and weakness therefore became the cause for endless complaints and recriminations. Ben had created an ideal image of his father; if the father failed to live up to it, this could only be due to one fact—namely, that the father did not love him.

Unable to cope with his own sense of deficiency (testes), with his castration anxiety and narcissistic deflation, Ben turned to his father for restorative help. This could be derived only from demonstrative love, privileges and gifts. Having externalized the source of security, Ben was driven to battle with his father, in an effort to force him to fit the ideal image. He needed the father as the guardian and stabilizer of the narcissistic balance or, subjectively, of his sense of wellbeing. The yearning for a good—i.e. "great"—father reflects the child's preoedipal dependency on an external source, the mother, for a sense of wellbeing. This regressive component contributed a special quality of oral greed to Ben's relationship to his father.

The disillusionment in the father was cautiously promoted in the therapy, but it was resisted for a long time. Then the therapeutic alliance and the innate developmental momentum brought about the following changes: (1) the abandonment of the defensive overidealization of the father; (2) renunciation of the external source of anxiety control; (3) toleration of the disillusionment in the father; and (4) progression from the narcissistic object choice, the father, to the stage of masculine identity. The expected outcome of these ego and drive transformations was the establishment of an internal agency, the function of which lies in the neutralization of the narcissistic object libido that had until then been bound up in the negative oedipal position. This agency is conceptualized as the ego ideal; I have described it genetically as the heir of the negative oedipus complex (Blos, 1962).

The ego ideal has a long history and, from its inception early in life, has been throughout a narcissistic formation. My contention is that it consolidates into a definitive organization with the decline of the phase of early male adolescence, and with the resolution of the negative ("passive") oedipus complex (Blos, 1962, 1965). The homosexual object choice of early adolescence is based on narcissistic needs. It has to be abandoned and transformed into a depersonalized ideal, into a way of life that is self-evident in its purpose and validity. The existence and pursuit of the ego ideal remains a permanent source of narcissistic supplies; it is the regulator of the narcissistic balance and experienced subjectively as self-esteem. The extent to which the ego ideal takes over, at adolescence, some of the superego functions will not be discussed in the present context (see: Blos. 1962).

The changing nature of the relationship between son and father has been outlined so far in terms of its timing and its characteristic stages. We have followed the progression from the defensively contrived father image to the realistic appraisal of the father and, finally, to the competitive struggle with the oedipal rival. In order not to burden and blur the description of these developmental steps with too much case material, the delicate and modulating details of these steps have not received the attention they deserve. The emphasis so far has been on changes in object relations—that is, on drive development —with unequal attention being extended to ego alterations. This seemingly lopsided emphasis in therapy rests on the assumption that drive progression always exercises a favorable effect on the synthesizing and adaptive capacity of the ego; in other words, it exerts a positive influence on ego differentiation. This aspect of the total developmental process must now be filled in, and the discussion that follows is undertaken with this purpose in mind.

Falsification of reality is an indicator of inadequate ego functioning. If perception and cognition are slanted by wishes and affects, then judgment and behavior become changeable and unreliable. Ben's complaints about his father illustrate this irrationality of thought. He once said, accusingly: "My father has not taught me how to box"—ignoring the fact that his father knew nothing at all about boxing. According to Ben's reasoning, it was the father's fault that his son could not fight, that he was fearful of being beaten up, or of "killing someone in anger." Feeling weak, unmanly and a coward, he turned to his father for reassurance: above all, he wanted to be "treated with respect." If only his father were to assign him a place of importance and grant him the right to discipline his brothers, then his father would be doing what a good father should. It was a long and tortuous path from Ben's repeated complaint: "My father does not respect me, or my actions" to the realization "I cannot respect my father for *his* actions."

Whenever Ben had a desire that he thought a good father should fulfill, but *his* father did not, then he felt unloved, and told the therapist "My father doesn't like me," or "He doesn't care for me." Sibling jealousy always contributed its share to these complaints. Jealousy once reached a critical point when he and his brothers were taken by their father to a ball game. Here, Ben became obsessed by the thought of "how dangerous it is to be at a game." Why? One could fall rather easily from the bleachers, and there would be nothing to break the fall. He left the game with a headache.

One shortcoming of the father that eventually caused a crack in the monolithic idol was his lack of education. He did not know many of the things that Ben had learned. Initially, this realization gave rise to a grudge against the father, who had disappointed his son, willfully and out of spite. "The boys would laugh at me if they knew about my father." It became particularly clear in the area of education how Ben moved from a narcissistic disappointment ("I want a father who is well educated") to the oedipal rivalry and fear ("I want to surpass him in knowledge"). During the first stage, Ben did well in school when he felt proud of his father's actually meager accomplishments in business. During the second stage, Ben could do well only after learning had ceased to be a function of the erotic attachment to the father. Only after this ego activity became desexualized was it able to acquire the rank of an autonomous ego function.

In the preceding chapter, I described Ben's learning inhibition in relation to his mother's demand that he be a bright boy and an excellent student. Resistance to the mother's demand resulted in a decline of his school performance. After learning became removed from the fear of submission to the archaic mother, Ben's studies improved. This improvement, however, was neither stable nor reliable. In fact, learning became once again involved in the conflictual relationship to the father. This shift and repetition illustrates the affinity of certain ego functions to conflict management, and shows how the same function—in this case, learning—becomes inhibited in different emotional contexts and with different defensive aims.

The realistic appraisal of the father had an effect on Ben's attitude toward his father's educational shortcomings. First, he was concerned not to hurt his father's feelings by knowing more than he did; then he thought that the son's success would make the father proud and happy. The oedipal rivalry was dealt with in therapy, largely in terms of educational competence, competition and achievement. For a short time, Ben liked to wrestle with his father, knowing well that his father was a strong man. He said of his father: "I am no competition for him; but he is for me." He then demonstrated, using two pencils, how they wrestle. Ben's anxious fantasies of ambivalence, which were aroused by such "horseplay," are best conveyed in his own words: "I am afraid to trip my father (when wrestling) because he is so big; he might break something—like the bed, perhaps. The bigger they are, the harder they fall." The elements of aggression, competition, idealization and disillusionment were expressed in rapid succession; they had to be sorted out in relation to wish, defense and recognition.

Ben's disillusionment in his father was most painful for the boy to bear. However, theoretical considerations in relation to ego autonomy and object dependency were responsible for assigning to this problem a focal significance. Ben observed his father with close attention, and he talked about these observations in his sessions. Here, they were evaluated and many came to be recognized as permanent qualities of his father, rather than as transient and changeable characteristics. He had noticed the father's jealous watchfulness at the dinner table when the mother was serving the food. He had further noticed how afraid his father was of his wife. "My father tried to run away from my mother, he was so afraid of her; but she caught up with him and she hit him on his back." This incident suddenly became timeless because it seemed also to have happened when he was a little boy, awakening during the night and hearing his parents fight and his father curse. Slowly, he came to realize the weakness of his father, who is always making promises, in order to hide his incompetence; he says "yes" and "no" without being able to follow through with either.

At the midpoint of treatment, his parents contemplated separation; denial, once more, appeared. "You know," he said, "I always thought it is the man who is kicked out of the bedroom; at least, that's the way it is in the movies. But," he added triumphantly, "in my home it is my mother who is kicked out of the bedroom." When his defensive reversal of the fact was interpreted, he acknowledged it by saying: "My father is a punk." The recognition of the truth was followed by a depressed mood that lasted for days. During the course of it, he remembered from the past a crying spell on the part of his mother, and how the age-old parental discord had always made him feel unhappy and frightened. Temporarily, he fell back on dependency and demandingness in relation to his father.

He discovered with astonishment that both his father and himself were behaving as if they were "accused." "I see," Ben said, "that my father feels accused by my mother because he is not a good father and husband. That's why she wants to separate." By way of identification, Ben shared with his father the anxiety of abandonment. "I need my parents for food, clothes and money; they can't ignore me, because I need them." A sharper delineation was gradually drawn between the parents' conflicts and his own conflicts in relation to them. With the progression toward separateness, it became apparent that oedipal strivings were being elicited by the impending separation of his parents; at the same time they were warded off by repression. Phallic, oedipal strivings became manifest in Ben's exhibitionism and the mouth tic, both of which were described in the preceding chapter.

Ben had become more and more able to tolerate his disillusionment in his father; eventually, he could discuss him in realistic terms without depressive reactions. Musingly, he sized up his father by saying: "My father is strong in hitting; he has a temper. It only looks as if he makes decisions; if my mother ever contradicts him, she has her way." He recognized the father's weakness, at the same time that he had become aware of his own aggressive and critical thoughts and feelings. Headaches often blocked the expression of these feelings. When he had a good time with his friends, he felt guilty because "if I had babysat, my parents could have gone out." His independence and the pursuit of his own pleasure in the company of his peers contained affects of spite, malice and revenge. These affects could be looked at as bridges leading to the oedipal struggle of adolescence proper.

Progression in psychosexual development is never without setbacks. In part, these were due, in Ben's case, to the constant parental turmoil. His anger against his parents mounted to proportions that frightened him.

"When I lose control I throw things or beat up my brothers." In a determined effort to control himself, he decided to retreat to the hallway of the apartment, where he pushed against the wall "until all the anger dribbles out of my fingers." Mounting aggression constantly brought this boy up against the alternatives of "doing crazy things" or falling back upon dependence and receptivity. Ben related many incidents of this kind, with the realization that *he* was the culprit. He said: "Yes, I've got a problem. I provoke my parents and I can't help it." It must be noted that Ben possessed a remarkable abiilty to return to the therapeutic commitment, whenever he found the road toward progressive development blocked.

The disillusionment in the father gradually obliterated the overidealized father image. Then the ego ideal took over the function that had been assigned to the ideal father of early adolescence. The process that transformed the idealized object, the father, into an internal agency, the ego ideal, was tortuous and gradual; it took a long time and abounded in standstills and setbacks. The stage that was particularly marked by delays and evasions, preceded that of open competition with the father, the oedipal rival. At that point, Ben wished to surpass his father's accomplishments. The fact that he possessed the same body build as his father affirmed a physical sameness. However, not until this resemblance was freed from the taint of degradation with which the mother had always viewed the husband, could the boy derive proud self-assurance from this similarity. It certainly displeased the mother when Ben expressed the wish to follow in the father's vocational footsteps; she had expected greater things from her son.

The pertinacity with which the mother undermined the respectability of Ben's father as a man, a provider, a husband and a father, left no other avenue open to the boy but to establish a secret alliance with him. The anxiety and guilt aroused by this solution was considerable and contributed its share to his need for punishment. He knew that he was a "middleman," used by both sides. His realization that "I am caught" became the signal for his determined fight against it. He viewed both his parents critically, saying: "I don't like the way my father acts; but I don't like the way my mother treats him, either. I feel sorry for him." The identification, as well as the commiseration with the henpecked father diminished, concomitantly with the disillusionment in the "great man," the oedipal idol. The result was a more realistic appraisal of the father as neither all good nor all bad. Passive submission to his father, following the parental model, became progressively ego-dystonic. With the arrival of the first tide of the adolescent oedipal rivalry, the old family pattern of blackmail and deprecation was put to use again. New wine in old bottles: the son rose against the father by turning informer. In order to get into his mother's graces, he told her things she did not know about the father's inconsistencies and evasions. He presented himself to her now as if saying: "I am better than my father."

Ben's relationship to his father changed radically. While ranting and raving about his "rotten father," who sets a bad example for his children, he cut himself short, saying: "But I don't have to follow his example." Swear words come to his mind—"dirty words," such as "fuck you" when he is angry with his father. He no longer feels sorry for him; instead, he now starts to formulate his own standards, goals and values in opposition to him. He announces: "I am not scared of him any more"; this statement, of course, was mere whistling in the dark. Ben had identified with that aspect of his father's personality that had always most frightened him (identification with the aggressor). He broke out into an uncontrollable temper, when provoked by him—yelling, throwing things, banging and hitting. He challenged the therapist: "Tell me, what's wrong with a plain red-blooded yell?"

These relapses into defensive identification always led back to Ben's ambivalent relationship to his father; they were plainly precipitated by oedipal anxiety. Setbacks like these afforded a progressively deeper understanding of Ben's difficult disengagement from the idealized father image. The "working through" process—that is, the repeated return to the same theme, in varying contexts and under varying precipitating life situations—represents that aspect of therapy that tests, so to speak, the treatability of the conflictual theme at the various levels of development. Remnants or residues of the pathogenetic core cannot always be adequately dealt with at a given level of development. This makes it necessary for the treatment of a certain complex to be resumed at a later stage in therapy, in relation to renewed failures, occurring at a more advanced stage of development, when the original pathogenetic trend reappears.

With the progressively realistic appraisal of his parents, Ben's behavior took on a different quality. In effect, he was saying: "Even if my parents are crazy, I don't have to be crazy, too." The emotional distance to his parents was reflected in the relative stabilization of his ego functions—in other words, in their independence from emotional shifts. Evidence of this was ample; it was particularly striking in school where his work had improved, his behavior had become satisfactory, his homework was done more regularly and his notebook showed greater order and neatness. Ben hoped that he might be transferred to an honor class. He had cast off the thought patterns of his parents, after he had spotted in those patterns a flagrant disregard of logic and fact. He had to realize that some of the parental thinking was "rather peculiar," "looked crazy," and "didn't make much sense." After adjudicating their thinking, he announced, with elation: "But I can think for myself."

Such forward strides in individuation were followed by a dysphoric mood, which was understood in terms of guilt (progressive component) and of abandonment feelings (regressive component). Guilt feelings, derived from oedipal aspirations and ambitions, constitute the typical conflictual situation of adolescence proper. The realistic appraisal of the parents never fails to become enmeshed in contradictory strivings. The wish for independence augments the feeling of loss and of security as derived from the infantile parent image. The price of independence is the tolerance of loneliness, as well as the acceptance of personal limitations and of the temporality of life (Blos, 1967). I have briefly referred to the ensuing moods as dysphoric states; these include states of discouragement, helplessness, despair, incompetent rage, weakness and worthlessness. The roots of these states, in cases such as Ben's, are to be found in a pervasive ambivalence of infantile object relations.

The adolescent who comes to a more realistic appraisal of his parents discovers, not only their negative characteristics but also their positive ones. This is, of course, the essence of a realistic appraisal. Accordingly, Ben recognized valuable qualities in his imperfect parents and willingly conceded to them the privileges of authority, where their competence was intact. He became appreciative, in contradistinction to his mother, of his father's unrelenting, even if unsuccessful, efforts in his job. Many recognitions of this kind added up to an ability to leave behind the global, projective—i.e. infantile— father image and to advance, in his personal interactions, to a differentiated awareness and appraisal of the object. Instead of depending on the idealized father, Ben had effected a separation from him; this transformed the narcissistic object tie to his father into an internal, desexualized agency, the ego ideal (Blos, 1965).

Ben no longer needed a father who was well educated and a source of pride to his son; he now tried to set his own goals. Freedom of choices presented itself, once the fear of surpassing his father had declined. The option of a "good education" had been removed from the oedipal conflict; moreover, the arena of competition had shifted to his life with his peers. An emergent social life with boys and girls had now replaced the previous total involvement with his parents and brothers. The strides he had made in this respect have been recounted earlier. Of course, the relationship with his father remained pugnacious and rebellious, but it was less marked by regressive trends. The father's characterological peculiarities, as well as Ben's adolescent self-assertion and self-confirmation, were both equally responsible for the continued turmoil. This condition in itself was not considered pathognomic.

When therapy was terminated, Ben had arrived at the stage of adolescence proper; he felt that he had "learned to do it on my own." Ben was then 15 years old; he had not grown as tall as he had hoped, but he had started to shave. In planning for the summer ahead, his choice was a job as a delivery boy; the summer before, he had refused to stoop so low, but wanted to be an "assistant manager in a department store" or else to have no job at all. Seeing the father more realistically had enabled Ben to see himself without defensive aggrandizement and thus to plan and act within his capabilities, and in accordance with the opportunities that the world around him actually had in store for him.

CHAPTER **18**

THE RECIPROCAL IMPASSE OF THE PARENTS AND THEIR ADOLESCENT CHILD

It is widely known that critical developmental stages in the child elicit in the parent certain reactions that, while universal, take on a psychic content and affective quality, both of which can be traced in the parental life histories. The vicissitudes of the parents' drive and ego development are reflected in their interaction with their child—especially at critical developmental stages, of which puberty is unquestionably a major one. Having and raising a child plays naturally into the universal fantasies of rebirth, of reliving one's life and of achieving immortality. The delicate balance that keeps these fantasies from becoming part of reality and an integral aspect of the child's environment is controlled by two factors. Both parents—perhaps one more than the other—serve as a reciprocal check and thus keep their respective fantasies from unduly intruding into their child-rearing practices and into the relationship they entertain with their offspring. Complementarily, by the time the child reaches puberty, he has built up a barrier against the contaminating influence of parental fantasies in relation to him. This barrier had been strengthened by drawing on the corrective influences of a continually widening social environment. In addition, the child's growing faculty of critical appraisal has deprived the parents of their unchallenged supremacy and prestige.

This ideal picture is of course less than true to life, because adolescence cannot take its normal course without regression (Blos, 1967). Adolescent regression rarely occurs as an intrapsychic process alone; generally, it involves the immediate and wider environment in an interactional turbulence. That is to say, the parent of the infantile period becomes once again drawn into the present life of the maturing child and thus becomes entangled in the respective regressive positions. Parental involvement covers a wide spectrum. It extends from ignoring the sexual maturation of the pubertal child to eagerly soliciting his genital activity; from tenaciously eliciting the pubertal child's affection and compliance to withdrawing from him as an intolerable source of disappointment and frustration.

When I speak here of the "adolescent child," I do so in order to emphasize the parent-child relationship. "Adolescent child" refers only secondarily to his maturational status; the primary reference is to the child's generational position. Obviously, this is not altered by age; each parent is a child of parents. Therefore, the puberty of the child brings well-contained vulnerabilities of the parents own childhood and adolescence into an unexpected actuality. That is the reason why August Aichhorn used to say that "Children are brought up by their grandparents" (personal communication). At best, the combination of two parents with different vulnerabilities serves as a system of checks and balances in a new family. Be that as it may, the anxieties experienced by parents during their child's puberty are normally outweighed by the pleasures of anticipation. This makes it bearable no longer to be the parent of a sexually immature and dependent child; through this experience, the parent readies himself for approaching or entering middle age.

The present epoch has cast—chiefly by way of the advertising media—a cloud of doom on aging, with the result that the parent needs the child more urgently and for much longer than before, in order to remain young. This parental need extends well into the child's adolescence. The polarizing effect of this adult trend can be recognized in the "generation gap," so passionately maintained by present-day youth. Adults who fear to grow old become suspect to youth on the grounds that they are denying or ignoring their own maturation. It has become common knowledge by now that youth does not trust anybody "over thirty." A non-conforming hippie has commented that this attitude is "a real put-on"; indeed, it is the converse to the Victorian dictum that children should "be seen and not heard" (Blos, 1969, 1970).

One could describe adolescence in terms of parental tasks and conflicts that are complementary to those that are by now well-defined, in terms of the adolescent child. We are ill prepared to do this in a systematic way, because parents have not been sufficiently studied as integral participants in the adolescent process of their child. We know a good deal more about their role in the development of the younger child, at a time when the parent-child unit appears in greater clarity. In the study of adolescence, and particularly in the treatment of adolescents, it is the rule rather than the exception for the parent to be excluded. This practice of course emphasizes the adolescent task of emotional disengagement from the parent, and of the internalization of conflicts as a precondition for therapeutic work with adolescents. At any rate, one is struck by the fact that the pubescent child arouses in the parent a highly idiosyncratic mode of parental involvement. This becomes recognizable in affective and cognitive peculiarities that were more successfully contained at the time when their child was younger.

It would be erroneous to view these developmental complications as due solely to the idiosyncratic parental involvement in the adolescent process. While the projection of the parents' fantasies and anxieties is often flagrant and may have a devastating impact on the adolescent child, it is the child's receptivity and facilitation of the parental involvement that deserves our attention. The adolescent's failure to detach himself sufficiently from his infantile love and hate objects precipitates a catastrophic impediment to progressive development. The adolescent's belief that it is the parents' changed image of him that will set him free to grow up only highlights his persistent dependence on outside nurturance and definition, which we might call "exogenous identity formation." It is an indication that autoplastic adaptation to the state of puberty is not yet sufficiently within his reach.

Ultimately this condition proves to be one of drive fixation and of retarded ego differentiation. Both have narrowed the scope of secondary ego autonomy, because ego functions have never become sufficiently remote from the instinctual drives. With the arrival of pubertal drive intensification and of genital ascendancy, the deficit in neutralized drive energy reaches a critical balance. Up to this point, the balance has been maintained with the help of the auxiliary parental ego. It is not until the adolescent process gets under way that the child's impaired or arrested ego development becomes apparent. The points at which the child's infantile needs intersect with the corresponding parental trends compound the condition in which a developmental impasse consolidates. The degree to which the superego is developed and integrated into psychic structure is a valid indicator of the internalization of the environment and the ability to recognize the existence of conflict. Progressive development during adolescence is predicated on these two faculties—namely, the internalization and the tolerance of conflict.

Let us now review Ben's case with that last statement in mind. What appeared to be guilt feelings early in treatment proved to be instead manifestations of fear: fear of abandonment, fear of frustration, fear of body damage or castration. In order to be able to avert these dangers, Ben needed instantaneous intervention by his mother. It would be almost too simplistic to say that the mother needed her son for the attenuation of very similar affective states; yet the fact remains that the sense of deprivation and of being cheated by life was equally strong in both. Family life remained for the mother a constant search for restitution—in fact, for oneness with her child—so as to make up for the deprivations she had suffered early in life, from which she had never recovered. Her father had deserted when she was about four years old; her mother had been sickly and self-absorbed to such a degree that one might suspect a psychotic condition, which prevented her from taking care of the family with any regularity. We know only that the children were placed, temporarily, in foster homes, "whenever we became too much for my mother."

Ben's mother needed her own family as a restitutive experience, in which she competed with the children—expecting, indeed demanding, that they understand her needs and grant her equal rights. When she was under stress, a state of sibling rivalry replaced that of maternal care. It is of special interest in this connection to note that the mother wanted only one child—namely, Ben— because, as she said, "I could not love another one." She needed a global one-to-one relationship. To divide her love among several children would only make her confuse their identities. The mother afforded Ben unerring recognition of his individuality, but only to a limited degree, during his infancy and early childhood. A stable sense of self failed to become consolidated during the early formative years. No wonder the mother expected from therapy that her son would be remade to meet her needs. She cooperated with therapy on these terms, but she could never grant the therapist a sustained autonomy of intervention. To illustrate: she instructed Ben to tell his therapist not to give him a birthday gift, after the mother had punished him by withholding her own gift. Such competitive intrusions into the boy's therapy could only be contained by providing the mother with a therapeutic relationship that was exclusively her own.

Of course, we must never forget the insufficient mothering she herself had received, and the highly ambivalent, dependent relationship to her own mother that she still entertained as a married woman. Mother and daughter blamed each other for being too demanding and selfish, for not giving anything, or giving only what is useless to the receiver. The daughter hungered for approval and recognition, in order to overcome a profound sense of worthlessness and hopelessness; and the burden of making her feel whole and good fell on her eldest son, Ben. She exaggerated the child's intellectual stamina, and made demands on him that the child was unable to meet. In the desperate pursuit of fulfillment in her child, she was only perpetuating her own sense of frustration and failure. Thus, unwittingly, she was creating the image of a degraded self in her son, whom she castigated for his evil intentions and his wickedness, proof of which lay in his continued failure to live up to her needs.

This vicious cycle, firmly patterned in early childhood, became symptomatic of a deviant development with the onset of puberty. At that stage, the boy became embattled with his mother. Correctly, he sensed that she was using his achievements and his growth for the maintenance of her narcissistic needs. It is literally correct to say that the child held in his hands his mother's life-line to the stabilization of her functioning. No wonder he spoke, in relation to women, of "killing or being killed." The mother reciprocated in equally concrete terms. One day, when Ben was angry with his mother, she stopped washing the windows on account of her fear that he would push her out. "How could she think that?", Ben exclaimed to the therapist, in utter consternation. This episode occurred at the time when he was already daring to look critically at his parents and starting to establish an age-appropriate, emotional distance to them. Ben resisted more and more his own wish and his mother's expectation that he rescue her from the despair of a disappointing life. This led to another impasse—a common one, indeed, but one that is deserving of our attention.

As I have shown, the emotional availability of the father is an essential condition for the preadolescent boy. It gives him positive assistance in the task of this phase— namely, coming to terms with the regressive pull to the archaic mother. At this juncture of dawning manhood, few mothers can be entirely devoid of the hope that the imperfections of her husband, no less his outright faults, will not be repeated in her son. This wishful thought becomes noxious only when the son is expected to compensate for the father's shortcomings as they are experienced by the mother. The proverbial exclamation "You are just like your father" reads, when decoded by the young boy, "Don't be like your father or I will have no use for you." The mother's degradation of the oedipal father, coupled with her threats to Ben against his turning out to be like him, exacerbated the phase-specific danger of preadolescence.

A secondary impasse ensues from such a crisis. The son is assured of his mother's loving nurturance—whenever he submits to her needs and makes himself subservient to her way of thinking. Again, puberty introduces a new element into this pattern. The boy's identification with the mother suddenly alarms her, because she sees in it a homosexual proclivity that has to be "nipped in the bud." When the 13-year-old boy looked into the cooking pots to see what is being served for dinner, the mother would order him out of the kitchen with contempt and disgust, because she felt the boy was displaying an exclusively female interest. The same scene repeated itself when Ben looked through his mother's cookbook or read a cosmetic catalogue that had just arrived in the mail. Each time, the mother's fear of homosexuality led to an outburst that Ben regarded only as his mother's "funny reaction" to his doings. While such scenes confused Ben, he nevertheless realized that his mother looked at his behavior as "girlish," and that it was to her the sign of a sexual abnormality. Obviously, a deviant psychosexual development could not be ruled out. Before deciding this question, however, one has to take into account the fact that so-called feminine interests are frequently a transient phenomenon during the initial stage of male adolescence. Ironically, the mother in her attempts to forestall a psychosexual deviancy is actually forcing her son into a feminine identification.

I need only remind the reader at this point how intrinsically Ben's prelogical thinking is related to the identificatory impasse. No doubt, Ben's puberty reactively intensified his mother's affective disturbance, thereby augmenting her recourse to prelogical thinking. Her system of reality control fortified her maternal position of the archaic, omnipotent level. The father, of course, could not possibly be a match for these powers nor could he successfully expose or counteract their fantastic nature. Ben's parents could not act as reciprocal checks and balances, helping to cancel out each other's most flagrantly noxious influence on the emotional development of their child. They therefore compounded, rather than neutralized, the growth-disturbing influences on their son. Paradoxically, Ben had borrowed his mother's magical mode of anxiety control in an effort to ward off her emotional hold on him. By way of this circular response, she had contaminated his ego with her own regressed comprehension of reality and her projective control of anxiety.

We shall now turn our attention to Ben's father, and point out the particular mold into which he tried to cast his son, in order to find fulfillment of his own needs. What stands out in bold relief is the father's expectation of being able to elevate his own self-esteem through the accomplishments of his son, and secondly of establishing a father-son closeness for which he himself had been yearning all his life. The generational similarities are striking. The father recalls with grief that his own father was withdrawn and emotionally unavailable to him. He expected to repair this deprivation through the closeness to his own son, from whom he hoped to receive affection, trust and admiration. No wonder he was hurt when Ben felt too old, at the age of 13, to exchange goodnight kisses with his father. Further, the father wished his son would at least have confidence in him, and tell him his feelings and thoughts. He envied the therapist for being the recipient of his son's confidences.

The father expected "reparation" from his son—which put the child into the paternal position. Characteristically, father and son bickered about who is giving whom first—whether this be a gift, attention, respect, consideration, etc. The father never ceased to equate his child's obedience with being loved by him. He might, therefore, become a disciplinarian and an authoritative tyrant solely out of the urgent need to be loved by his son. This erotization of discipline rendered the father's requests or rulings unacceptable to his son, even if they were—as happened occasionally—quite reasonable. Since a resolution of the emotional implications was out of the question, physical fighting ensued, rampant with beatings and recriminations.

The father remembers how the weakness of his own father enraged him to the point of his fearing that he might "kill him." One of these complaints was repeated, literally, by Ben; it concerns the father's failure in protecting the son against the mother. The father had always feared his mother, a domineering woman, whom he had pleased and appeased all his life. He had surrendered his phallic strivings and was now left with an all-consuming fear of women. We can see how Ben's identification with the father was wrought with dangers, because it exacerbated his preadolescent fear of the archaic mother. The over-idealization of the father was the only way out of this dilemma.

The father looked for the expurgation of his own degrading past and present through his son's excelling in whatever he himself had failed in. For instance, he expected Ben to follow through with everything he started, while the father himself habitually drops every task before it is completed. Any shortcoming in Ben that reflected a characteristic of the father received his severest reprimand, often totally out of keeping with the incident. In this respect, the father's self-condemnation coincided with the mother's warning to the son: don't be like your father.

Ben told of his father's expressed wish that he should nag him, make him do things because without such prodding and urging, his father found it difficult to make or pursue any plan, such as going to a ball game or going fishing together. The nagging had to come, of course, at a time when the father was receptive to it.

The expression of the parents' infantile needs in relation to their children confused Ben who referred to it quite correctly, by saying that "My parents come down to my level," or "I am a punching ball for my parents." He sensed that many of their affective responses were unrelated to him as an individual; they were addressed to some image that he was expected to match. In this projective configuration, the boy could never clearly discover the proper constituent parts of himself, or have them confirmed by consensual validation. He felt confused and persecuted. The "facilitating environment," to use Winnicott's term, was inconsistent and contradictory; it did not provide those age-adequate stimuli and reactions that promote growth. In fact, Ben's family life acted like a noxious environment with regard to the child's development. Only a close investigation of the family dynamics could lead to differentiating between the internalized conflicts, with their neurotic sequelae, and that aspect of the disturbance that was reactive to the noxious environment.

Ben could not be expected to overcome the catastrophic impediment in his development, as long as it remained buttressed by both his own gratificatory gain from his illness and that of the parents as well. The treatment of the parents constituted, therefore, an essential part of the boy's treatment. While the inclusion of the parents in a total treatment plan is not always necessary, there was no doubt that, in this instance, the excessive infantile family interaction or, conversely, the extreme lack of internalization, were unmistakable indications for an inclusive treatment plan. The ideal aim of the treatment strategy was for Ben, his mother and his father to come to terms, individually and separately, with the immaturities in object relations indicated above. In reality what was pursued was a containment of the noxious interaction system, as well as resistivity to mutually disorganizing influences.

The grossly deviant parent-child interaction in Ben's

family highlights what is observed normally during adolescence, or, more specifically, during the "second individuation process" of adolescence (Blos, 1967). The pubertal child is critically blocked in his effort to disengage himself from infantile object ties, if the parents persevere at the level of a relationship that earlier befitted the sexually immature child. Usually, one of two avenues is pursued by either or both parents; either the parents' own infantile needs lead them to ignore the child's changing physical status, or else the parent makes himself an identificatory partner of his child's adolescence. In the first case, it is the immature child that is preferred; in the second case, the parent relives his own adolescence by proxy. In so doing, he forces his comradeship on the young and thereby solidifies the interdependence of parent and child. Both these parental positions impede the delibidinization of the infantile objects; in fact, they erect a roadblock to progressive development. In the wake of the infantilization of adolescent object relations, we can always observe that certain ego functions are drawn into the calamity of drive arrest. The case of Ben demonstrates this well.

Adolescent disengagement from infantile objects is normally complemented by a parental progression in development. Whenever this parental change is lacking, the adolescent process is rendered critical and unduly burdensome. Should the parental relationship to their immature child remain essentially unalterable, then the adolescent process is catastrophically impeded. The influence of socially and emotionally disadvantaged parents on the personality formation of their child exerts itself at the earliest age. Immature emotionality tends to perpetuate itself through the generations. Normally, we expect that the adolescence of the child will introduce a new stage in parenthood—a stage that is marked by a gradual decrease in the offering to the adolescent child of nurturing participation and physical comfort.

The parental role that previously suited the dependent child has to be abandoned, and parental gratification, once derived from the child's dependency, must find different and new aims. The parents are called upon to tolerate the emotional distancing to their adolescent child and to accept parental limitations. Both these accommodations presage middle age. It remains a human predilection to abandon the familiar only with conflict or anxiety —that is to say, reluctantly. The élan of maturation usually overcomes the inertia of remaining. Normally, the pubescent child is, to a great extent, independent of the conflict or dilemma that his physical maturation evokes in his parents. The latency period should have prepared him well for the adolescent process to take its course. The preparatory achievement that ranks highest, in my opinion, is resistance against any contamination with parental regression. The case of Ben has demonstrated the defectiveness and the restoration of this resistance, as a precondition for progressive development. The extent to which this restoration has been achieved cannot be stated with assurance until the terminal stage of adolescence has been passed through.

The study of Ben has enabled us to observe, in magnified form, what proceeds less noticeably in the normal adolescent. What Ben attained through therapeutic intervention delineates those stages of development that have to be traversed before the phase of Adolescence Proper can be reached—a phase that corresponded with his chronological age and physical status. When this was achieved, his treatment came to a natural end—at least, for the time being. Treatment was the primary purpose of the work with Ben; in addition, however, it provided clinical substance, not only to the theoretical formulation of the initial stage of male adolescence, but equally to the developmental model of the young pubertal boy.

REFERENCES

The relevant literature on adolescence has been noted in my previous publications. There is no need to burden this monograph with a repetition of those same references. Obviously, my indebtedness is large. Since it was the purpose of this study to correlate my theoretical concepts with clinical work, I must direct the reader's attention to those publications in which, over the years, I have built up the body of my developmental and theoretical views about adolescence. This explains why the reference list below is restricted to my own publications.

Its purpose is simply to put together, so to speak, the complete body of theory that is now to be clothed by the many pieces of clinical material that these two case studies will provide. How well- or ill-fitting these accoutrements are, it is for the reader to judge.

1954   Prolonged Adolescence: The Formulation of a Syndrome and its Therapeutic Implications. *Am. J. Orthopsychiatry*, Vol. XXIV.

1957   Preoedipal Factors in the Etiology of Female Delinquency. *The Psychoanalytic Study of the Child*, International Universities Press, New York, Vol. XII.

1958   Preadolescent Drive Organization, *J. Am. Psychoanalytic Association*, VI.

1960   Comments on the Psychological Consequences of Cryptorchism: A Clinical Study. *The Psychoanalytic Study of the Child*, International Universities Press, New York, Vol. XV.

1962   Intensive Psychotherapy in Relation to the Various Phases of Adolescence. *Am. J. Orthopsychiatry*, October, 1962.

1962   *On Adolescence: A Psychoanalytic Interpretation*. The Free Press of Glencoe, New York.

1963   The Concept of Acting Out in Relation to the Adolescent Process, *J. of the Am. Academy of Child Psychiatry*, Vol. 2, No. 1 (Reprinted in: *A Developmental Approach to Problems of Acting Out*, Rexford, Eveoleen N., Editor. International Universities Press, Inc. New York, 1966).

1964   Three Typical Constellations in Female Delinquency; in: *Family Dynamics and Female Delinquency*; Pollak, O., Friedman, A. S. Editors; Science and Behavior Books, Palo Alto, 1969.

1965   The Initial Stage of Male Adolescence. *The Psychoanalytic Study of the Child*. International Universities Press, New York, Vol. XX.

1967   The Second Individuation Process of Adolescence. *The Psychoanalytic Study of the Child*. International Universities Press, New York, Vol. XXII.

1968   Character Formation in Adolescence. *The Psychoanalytic Study of the Child*. International Universities Press, New York, Vol. XXIII.

1969   Youth Unrest: A Symptom. *The American Journal of Psychiatry*, Vol. 125, No. 9.

1970   The Generation Gap: Fact and Fiction.